Fallen Giant

The Amazing Story of Hank Greenberg and the History of AIG

Second Edition

Ronald Shelp
with
Al Ehrbar

WILEY

John Wiley & Sons, Inc.

Published by John Wiley & Sons, Inc., Hoboken, New Jersey.
Published simultaneously in Canada.

For general information on our other products and services or for technical support, please
contact our Customer Care Department within the United States at (800) 762-2974,
outside the United States at (317) 572-3993 or fax (317) 572-4002.

Wiley also publishes its books in a variety of electronic formats. Some content that appears
in print may not be available in electronic books. For more information about Wiley
products, visit our web site at www.wiley.com.

Library of Congress Cataloging-in-Publication Data:
Shelp, Ronald Kent.
   Fallen giant : the amazing story of Hank Greenberg and the history of AIG / Ronald
Shelp with Al Ehrbar.—2nd ed.
      p.   cm.
   Includes bibliographical references and index.
   ISBN: 978-0-470-48002-1 (pbk)
      1. Greenberg, Maurice R.   2. Businesspeople—United States—Biography.
   3. Insurance executives—United States—Biography.   4. Insurance
   companies—United States—History.   5. American International Group, Inc.—
   History.   6. Adler, Rodney.   I. Ehrbar, Al.   II. Title.
HC102.5.G717S54 2009
368.0092—dc22
[B]
                                                                      2009020120

Printed in the United States of America

10 9 8 7 6 5 4 3 2 1

*For my wife, June, and my sons,
Kent and Russell, who also love to write.*

Contents

Acknowledgments

Writing the kind of story I set out to write about AIG and the fascinating characters that shaped its history required cooperation from AIG executives and alumni, some of whom I had not talked to for 20 years. Yet I never doubted they would talk to me—and I was not disappointed. First, we were and are friends and colleagues who have been through our share of AIG wars together. Second, all of us loved the company and enjoyed exchanging tales about our adventures. As a result, I met with or talked to virtually everyone on my list. That made a huge difference in the book I was able to write.

First and foremost, I have to thank Hank Greenberg, CEO of AIG for nearly 40 years, for meeting with me, along with Edward Matthews, AIG CFO. Even though we are friends, I could understand that for legal reasons he might hesitate seeing anyone writing about AIG. But he did not.

I also appreciate the generosity with his time that then New York State Attorney General Eliot Spitzer gave me.

There are executives who prefer to go unidentified, even in the acknowledgments, and I will respect that. I am deeply grateful to my old friend Oakley Johnson, head of AIG's government relations operations in Washington, for his enthusiasm and encouragement and for obtaining some background material about AIG for me.

Others I can identify are John Roberts, chairman of American International Underwriters and vice chairman of AIG; Houghton "Buck" Freemen, president of AIU and an AIG director; and Ernest Stempel, former CEO of AIRCO. All were full of wonderful stories about the history of the company. Artemis Joukowsky, now at Brown University, but previously in charge of operations in Eastern Europe, among other things, met me in Providence and we had a great reunion. I had fun conversations with the late Ken Nottingham, chairman of ALICO and someone I worked with on many AIG problems. Pat Foley, counsel and director of State Relations, was helpful, as was Robert McCourt, advertising director. Finally, I talked to several directors, including Bernard Aidenoff, retired from Sullivan and Cromwell.

Jeff Greenberg, Hank Greenberg's son and formerly a top executive at AIG and subsequently CEO of Marsh McLennan, was generous with his time.

My old friend Clare Tweedy, who grew up in the AIG family, told me wonderful stories about the involvement of her father and mother and about Starr. She directed me to people I did not know.

Robert Youngman, son of Bill Youngman, Starr's original heir apparent, and I spent considerable time together. My younger son and I had a nice lunch with Mike Murphy in Bermuda. This visit with Mike, SICO counsel, brought back memories of the work Mike and I used to do together in Washington. I also had a helpful talk with T.C. Hsu, formerly head of the Starr Foundation, and Marion Breen, Starr's cousin and assistant and a foundation officer.

But I also had help outside the AIG family. Leslie Gelb, president emeritus of the Council on Foreign Relations, gave me insights on Greenberg's involvement with and generosity to the council. Ronald Abramson, partner with Hughes Hubbard and Reed, helped me sort through the many lawsuits the AIG matter has engendered. And Doug Ellis, my longtime financial advisor, worked with me in sorting through the AIG numbers and the growth of the company. My good friend John Higgins provided guidance, insight, marketing advice, and many other things throughout the process. I appreciate the attitude of my former business partner, Dwight Foster, in understanding my neglect of our business and his enthusiasm for my book.

Working closely with Al Ehrbar has been a delight. He constantly gave me good guidance and good ideas.

My executive editor, Debra Englander, and assistant editor, Greg Friedman, helpfully guided me through this elaborate process, as did Michael Lisk, senior production editor. None of this would have occurred without the success of my agent, James Levine, of Levine/ Greenberg Literary Agency, in selling the book.

When I look at the number of people involved, I conclude that the old story about the lonely writer slaving away in his carrel is a bit of a canard. Lots of people help write a book. It is not the product of one person.

Prologue

When Hank Greenberg had to resign as chairman and CEO of American International Group (AIG) after 37 years because of an apparent accounting scandal, those of us who knew and worked closely with him were stunned.

If you read and believed what the headlines were claiming, more than four decades of outstanding success in the global insurance industry were being forgotten. A man who had walked and talked with kings, presidents, and premiers was being turned out of the financial powerhouse that had charmed Wall Street for decades.

As I continued to follow the daily AIG headlines closely, an idea began to emerge and take shape: Why not write a book about the rise of AIG? After all, I had been a trusted insider for many years and was likely to be the only insider who would dare to write about the company's difficulties. I could bring a very different perspective from that of journalists or management observers.

At the time, I was thinking about writing a novel based on a thinly disguised version of AIG—a company founded in China, the first reverse multinational, operations in 130 countries, and zany adventures such as employees imprisoned in Iran and Nigeria. It had all the hallmarks of an adventure story, with legendary characters based on C.V. Starr, the company founder, Hank Greenberg, and others.

But friends said no: Write a nonfiction book about AIG instead. With the company so prominently in the news, readers, and therefore publishers would be interested.

Even though I hadn't worked at AIG for a number of years, I had spent the better part of my career there. No one who had ever worked at AIG would have foreseen the day that Greenberg would be forced to resign. And, of course, could anyone fill Greenberg's shoes? Someone might run the largest insurance company in the world but could he hold his own with heads of state, politicians, and other powerful leaders?

I reported directly to Hank Greenberg for 12 years and enjoyed it. And though I have been gone from AIG for many years, it is amazing the hold that he has over you. A call from Hank Greenberg or a meeting with him almost always puts you on edge. I felt it when he called late in the process of writing this book. Placing a return call was nerve-racking. While I have had some exciting jobs in my career, none was as exciting, stimulating, demanding, wacky, or fulfilling as my job there. It offered intellectual challenges, worldwide travel, international intrigue and diplomacy, and more.

My only regret is that since I joined the company five years after C.V. Starr's death, I never knew or worked with him. He was another unique leader—like Greenberg—who had laid the foundation for the AIG empire.

In writing this book, I hoped to learn what happened at AIG—the place employees call the most exciting organization in the world. Was it Greenberg's hubris that ultimately led to his downfall or was it a combination of complex reasons and people—the "perfect storm," where business meets regulation and political ambition?

I asked Al Ehrbar, former editor of *Fortune*, to work with me on this project. Al's first instinct was to say that AIG's situation was brought on by Greenberg's "hubris." As we spent time on the project, however, Al realized the situation was much more complex. After dozens of interviews with current and former AIG executives and many late nights reviewing documents, a byzantine and multifaceted picture began to emerge.

Throughout this project my mood shifted from anger at Greenberg and disappointment in the Board of Directors to outrage over Spitzer's heavy regulatory hand. I changed my mind many times while writing and the conclusions I drew, as you will see, are more gray than black and white. But in the complicated international world in which we live, a world where AIG grew and prospered dramatically, every shade is gray. But to show how compelling the AIG story is, Al stood by what he said when we first had lunch to discuss working together. "This is the most exciting project I have worked on in years."

I always kept up with developments at AIG, long after leaving the company. From time to time, I had lunch in the fabulous Chinese dining room, and occasionally saw Hank Greenberg and others. Writing this book gave me a chance to return to a company that had always fascinated me. It has indeed been gratifying and worth every exhilarating and frustrating moment that writing a book brings.

For years, outsiders as well as those who work at AIG have had a perverse fascination with Hank Greenberg. They are astonished at the results he has achieved year in and year out. They are appalled and a bit frightened by his temper. They begrudgingly admire his unblemished outspokenness and knowledge on a variety of diverse topics.

And while they may not understand his difficult personality, they do respect his demanding ways. And they wonder whether it takes these kind of personal traits to produce his achievements.

Hank Greenberg followed in the footsteps of another brilliant leader of a different kind but just as demanding in his own way. And over the past 90 years AIG has been fortunate to have a series of "characters" of many nationalities and talents to work in the company. They conceived of a truly international company before anybody was really interested in international. And they and their long-time leaders—Starr and Greenberg—had to constantly stay ahead of the curve and adjust to changing economic trends, regulatory rules, and political situations. They did so remarkably well—again and again.

In the end, though, this time Hank Greenberg failed to adjust to a changing regulatory climate quickly enough. As a result, he had to give up leading his beloved AIG. While that is unfortunate, he still has the satisfaction of knowing that no one is likely to even approach his record.

Introduction

AIG May Be Forced to Declare Bankruptcy Within a Few Days.
This headline on the weekend of September 13–14, 2008, was far more shocking than the provocative headline that sparked me to write this book in 2005. The earlier one said: **Greenberg Forced Out as CEO of AIG.** How—in just the three years since Hank Greenberg left the mammoth company he built—had his successors, Martin Sullivan and Robert Willumstad, run the world's largest insurance company into the ground?

Initially, this book was written to tell the story of how Eliot Spitzer, then New York's attorney general, felled Maurice "Hank" Greenberg, who had held the position of CEO of American International Group (AIG) for 37 years. I intended to explain what Greenberg allegedly did, trace the impact of those actions on AIG and various executives, and suggest that a new regulatory era is upon us. Finally, it would trace the company to its beginnings in Shanghai where it was founded by C.V. Starr and grew into an Asian powerhouse and force around the world.

The post-Greenberg era has proved to be anything but simple for AIG or Greenberg. There have been more curves and twists than could ever have been imagined. For one thing, Hank Greenberg did not slip quietly into retirement. He kept three of the jobs he had held prior to his ouster from AIG–chairman of Starr International (SICO), C.V. Starr & Co., and the Starr Foundation. When he was running AIG, the first two were treated as part and parcel of the company, even though they were legally separate. In fact, today SICO is AIG's biggest shareholder—with about 10 percent of the company's shares. SICO's AIG stock was worth about $20 billion before the collapse. The matter of who really owns SICO's AIG shares is the subject of litigation.

There also are other lawsuits between AIG and Greenberg's companies. For example, after Greenberg left AIG, C.V. Starr & Co., an operating company that wrote more exotic risks in marine, aviation, and other fields for AIG, soon became a fierce competitor of AIG's. It is generally considered that Greenberg won the feud with AIG in an out-of-court settlement over who and what entity would handle the exotic insurance written by C.V. Starr.

For a long time after he left AIG, Greenberg, while striving to restore his reputation, worked behind the scenes and through surrogates. But with suits pending and the onus of being discussed negatively in the press so often, it is tough to do. Perhaps that is why, after remaining silent for so long, over a year ago he finally went public. He has appeared on numerous television shows and given press interviews, not only about the allegations against him, but about his frustration or outright disgust with AIG management, the presidential election, and numerous other matters. This has been even truer as AIG ended up in shambles.

There has been one extraordinary development that surely gave some satisfaction to those many Wall Streeters, like Greenberg, who suffered from Eliot Spitzer's imperious rule. Spitzer was elected governor by the largest margin in New York history in 2006, but within a year had to resign because of his admitted patronizing of prostitutes. Since then, Andrew Cuomo, who succeeded Spitzer as attorney general, has aggressively prosecuted wrongdoing, seemingly in the Spitzer mode, but with a gentler, more deft touch (although he can be just as hard-hitting). Yet Cuomo cannot find a wrong to right as mesmerizing and publicly appealing as Spitzer's involvement with Wall Street. He recently took a several-day deposition from Greenberg over the long-pending case involving the General Reinsurance charges, the one AIG settled long ago for $1.5 billion but Greenberg has never settled. Greenberg had managed to postpone this deposition for over three years, apparently because his lawyers were fearful it could harm him. But although he could have avoided it by paying a large fine, he opted to be deposed as part of his relentless campaign to salvage his reputation.

Meantime, Martin Sullivan, Greenberg's initial successor, was trying to lead AIG's recovery, mainly focusing on the company's considerable regulatory problems. He had started working at AIG in London when he was 18 years old with no college education. Over the next 30 years, he worked his way to the top, becoming Greenberg's chief operating officer. He was described to me by one AIG executive as very likable, charming, and a thousand times easier to work for than Greenberg. (I remember that at the time I did not consider those to be favorable characteristics for leading the company to new heights, or for that matter, just plain leading it.)

But Sullivan is credited with doing a good job in resolving the regulatory mess. He reached agreement with Attorney General Spitzer and other regulators and paid a fine of $1.5 billion. With the help of longtime SEC Chairman Arthur Levitt, AIG put into place an exemplary corporate governance program. The company was praised by government officials such as the attorney general and the superintendent of insurance as having turning the corner from the Greenberg years. Sullivan had constant legal distractions—lawsuits against Greenberg, a countersuit against AIG by Greenberg, shareholder suits, and others. Clearly, he did not have time or he did not find time to focus enough on business.

When Greenberg finally emerged from an uncharacteristic silence, he vigorously criticized AIG for spending what he termed as an exorbitant amount of shareholders' money to settle with state authorities. But given the alternative, which could have been a criminal suit bought by the attorney general's office, Sullivan and the board of directors had little choice. If the past is precedent, the outcome of criminal action likely would have been bankruptcy.

By early 2007, it was clear AIG wasn't the bright spot it had almost always been. For one thing, the core business of AIG—insurance, which Sullivan knew inside out—was not doing as well as it should. But the first real setback came when AIG reported its fourth-quarter earnings for 2007. The losses, almost all from derivative credit swaps, amounted to $5.29 billion. Then, three months later, the first-quarter earnings for 2008 reported a $7.81 billion loss. These were AIG's largest ever quarterly losses. The firm announced it would raise $12.5 billion in capital, and ultimately did raise $20 billion. In releasing the earnings, Martin Sullivan made a mistake a CEO should never make. He basically said to the world that this was the last write-off, that the problems coming from London-based AIG Financial Products were at an end. In December 2007, Sullivan had said that AIG did not expect material losses from its investments linked to subprime mortgages. Later, he summed up his rosy view that all was great: "Excluding these external market issues, the underlying fundamentals of our core businesses remain solid."

AIG's board issued the usual reassurance about Sullivan continuing as CEO, but many inside and outside the company concluded that his days were numbered. Until this point, the only large shareholder who had publicly complained was the biggest shareholder—Hank Greenberg. But in June 2008, three major shareholders wrote a scathing letter to the board demanding a change in the CEO and in the board itself. The next day, the three came calling—Eli Broad, who had sold his company, Sun America, to AIG and was a director for a while (and a much admired collector of modern art); Shelby Davis of Davis Selected Advisors, a firm based on fortunes made in insurance-related investments; and Bill Miller of Legg Mason. They met with Robert Willumstad, nonexecutive board chairman, and Morris Offit, a fairly new and widely respected board member with a financial background.

The two AIG directors got an earful, both about the CEO and about the board. They made no commitments, but in a short time Sullivan was out. Willumstad lobbied to succeed him and won. At long last, he had achieved his lifelong goal of becoming a CEO, but with a company embroiled in intrigue and turmoil of Shakespearian dimensions. Ultimately his CEO experience was very short-lived, as he was ousted three months later. His tenure would prove to be far shorter than that of his predecessors; he was elected June 15 and it was announced he was leaving on September 17.

By the time Willumstad had taken over the helm, there had been two quarters of losses and the stock had declined more than 50 percent during the prior year. He announced that he would study the company closely, travel far and wide, and have a plan to restructure AIG by Labor Day. Shortly thereafter, September 25 became his D-day. But Willumstad was gone from AIG just a few days before he could have presented his plan.

AIG had begun to unravel three weeks earlier, however, when Willumstad learned that Moody's would lower its rating of AIG in mid-September unless the company raised billions of dollars. This news sparked a panic inside AIG headquarters as senior executives and bankers huddled hoping to raise the money to save the company. But once Lehman Brothers began its decline toward bankruptcy, Willumstad realized his time was short. Investment bankers and other potential investors were invited in to look at the books. In no time, their estimates of the financial needs of AIG ballooned from $20 billion to $80 billion or even more.

One early positive response for AIG was New York Governor Patterson's approval of the recommendation of Eric Dinallo, New York insurance superintendent, for AIG to borrow $20 billion from company funds backing the operating insurance companies and move them to the holding company, AIG. At the time, this infusion seemed significant; but as the shortfall AIG faced kept multiplying, it became a pittance of what AIG needed.

The company and those involved worked night and day over the weekend of September 13-14 to come up with the funds, but made no progress. Investors such as Henry Kravis turned them down. On Monday, September 15, the rating agencies lowered AIG's rating, handing it a devastating blow. Estimates for what the company needed went as high as $100 billion. Frequent calls to Federal Reserve officials and the Treasury secretary were not getting attention because of the concurrent crises at Lehman Brothers and Merrill Lynch.

Finally, on Tuesday afternoon, Secretary Henry Paulson took charge, concluding that an $85 billion loan was needed. He and Fed Chairman Ben Bernanke informed the president and briefed congressional leaders. By Tuesday night word had leaked out that the Fed would give AIG an $85 billion loan at an interest rate of about 12 percent and take 80 percent of the company.

As part of the deal, Robert Willumstad had to leave, and Edward M. Liddy, former CEO of Allstate but also an investment expert, having worked with Goldman Sachs and others, would become chairman and CEO.

The most electrifying Wall Street week since the Great Depression finally came to an exhausting conclusion. Hank Greenberg and other shareholders dissatisfied with the takeover of AIG by the government would not give in. They hired former Commerce Secretary Mickey Cantor to lead a fight in Washington to reverse this decision and considered options like buying AIG themselves. They lost and AIG is being broken up, with the decision to give retention bonuses having so ruined the brand that it needs restructuring even more than it did before. But the amazing story of Hank Greenberg an AIG is not over yet.

"Life is too short to be little."—*Benjamin Disraeli*

"You can't be less wicked than your enemies simply because your government's policies are benevolent"
—*John le Carré,*
The Spy Who Came in from the Cold

Chapter 1

How Hank Greenberg Did It

The Four Seasons restaurant on East 52nd Street is an uncommonly rich venue for celebrity spotting. On the first Wednesday in May 2005, midday diners could glance around the room and see Tom Brokaw, Barbara Walters, Colin Powell, and a bevy of other big names, but the person turning the most heads that day wasn't a famous broadcaster or politico. It was Hank Greenberg, the man who built American International Group into the world's largest insurance company. Greenberg had long been a celebrity CEO, at least among the financial cognoscenti, one whose singular accomplishments lifted him above his peers and gave him a stature that overshadowed all but a handful of other corporate chieftains.

Greenberg's celebrity, like that of most business moguls (and insurance executives, in particular), was not the type that turned heads as he walked down the street. Some might know the name, but few knew the face.

Not until 2005, that is, when scandal at AIG put Greenberg's photo in the *New York Times* almost daily, and a line-drawing of him appeared on the front page of the *Wall Street Journal* at least once a week. Suddenly, Hank Greenberg was the highly recognizable malefactor of the moment, accused of cooking the books at AIG to inflate profits and make the balance sheet look stronger than the underlying reality. That afternoon at the Four Seasons—on his 80th birthday, of all days—Greenberg was having a new kind of power lunch. His companions were two attorneys, Robert Morvillo and Kenneth Bialkin, and they weren't talking deals. Morvillo is a criminal lawyer whose new assignment was to keep Greenberg out of jail, something he had failed to do for Martha Stewart, his last celebrity client.

After finishing his broiled fish and fresh vegetables, Greenberg worked the crowd as he made his way from the Grill Room balcony to the exit. He chatted with Brokaw, stopped by the table of Sir Howard Stringer, who had just become CEO of the Sony Corporation, and exchanged a few words with Richard Grasso, the New York Stock Exchange chairman who was forced out when the shocking magnitude of his compensation became public. Greenberg had been on the NYSE compensation committee that approved Grasso's pay package, including a $180 million lump-sum pension payment. As he led his lawyers down the stairs to the doorway and the street, several of Greenberg's friends were pleased to note that his unaccustomed troubles had not taken the slight swagger from his step.

Faced with Greenberg's woes, most mortals would be staggering instead of swaggering. Even in the context of the rampant scandals of recent years, few executives have fallen so far, so fast, and from such a seemingly unassailable aerie. In February 2005, AIG received a subpoena from Eliot Spitzer, New York State's hyperactive attorney general, for documents relating to what he believed was accounting chicanery having to do with a recondite kind of transaction known as finite insurance. Spitzer suspected that Greenberg himself had arranged the specific transaction in question to add a phony $500 million to AIG's reserves for the year 2000. The party on the other side of the deal was none other than Warren Buffett of Berkshire Hathaway. Spitzer was saying that the sage of Omaha had done no wrong, though executives of a Berkshire subsidiary, General Re, may have been culpable. What Spitzer was saying—on Sunday morning network television, no less—was that Greenberg had committed fraud.

Spitzer's snoops also wanted to know whether AIG had improperly kept some Caribbean subsidiaries off its books in order to understate the true leverage in its operations and hide the full magnitude of the risks it had insured, questions that raised the specter of Enron's notorious "off-balance-sheet entities." Spitzer wasn't alone. AIG also found itself under investigation by the New York Insurance Department, the Securities and Exchange Commission, and the U.S. Justice Department, and was at least peripherally involved in investigations by insurance regulators in England, Ireland, and Australia. Among other things, the SEC wanted to know whether Greenberg had tried to manipulate the price of AIG stock. In one case, he reportedly had put pressure on the NYSE specialists who handle AIG's stock to support the price during an acquisition in 2001, and had lobbied Richard Grasso to put his arm on the specialists as well. More recently, Greenberg had ordered an AIG trader to buy 250,000 shares of stock on the day the company disclosed its receipt of the Spitzer subpoena.

Once Spitzer turned his guns on AIG, bad things happened to Hank Greenberg in rapid succession. On March 14 the AIG directors forced him to step down as chief executive, a move that shocked nearly everyone familiar with AIG. Greenberg had personally selected each of these directors, in most cases because they were close business friends or because they could use their prestige and influence to help the company in the United States and around the world, or both. Now they had decided that the best way to help AIG was to strip their friend Hank of his power. Two weeks later, under mounting pressure from Spitzer, the directors insisted that he relinquish the chairmanship as well.

After he was ousted, Greenberg, in a conversation with a senior executive at AIG, talked about a conversation he once had with company founder Starr about the risk of public companies. He wistfully said, "I should have listened. This would not have happened if we were still private."

R emoving the boss has become standard procedure in twenty-first-
century corporate investigations, especially ones mounted by
Spitzer. In this case, Spitzer promised he would not bring criminal
charges against AIG if the company cooperated in his investigation.
Translation: Help me nail the bad guys, your bad guys, and you get off
with a slap on the wrist; otherwise, you're toast. AIG's directors gave
Spitzer what he wanted, and then some. At the end of April the board
released the results of its own investigation of accounting irregularities.
Though the language was vague, the report made clear that bad things
had been done, and that they had been done by Greenberg and Howard
I. Smith, the chief financial officer who also was forced out in March. AIG
didn't name the two, but said all the malfeasance was carried out at "the
direction of former senior managers."

Through all this, AIG treated Greenberg in much the same way
that companies regularly deal with executives suspected of selling trade
secrets or embezzling. The company would not let Greenberg clean out
his office until mid-May, and even then held back papers pertaining to
two other companies Greenberg chaired that are independent of AIG
but closely linked to it. AIG also kept a Van Gogh and some antique
furniture pending a clear determination of ownership.

All standard procedure, except that there is nothing standard about
Hank Greenberg or AIG. When the board forced him out, Maurice
Raymond Greenberg had been running AIG longer than the CEO of
any other major U.S. corporation. (Greenberg appropriated his nick-
name from Hammerin' Hank Greenberg, a Depression-era slugger for
the Detroit Tigers.) He had been No. 1 at AIG for 37 years, ever since
founder Cornelius Vander Starr turned over the then-private company to
him in 1968. The closest to him in tenure among large-company chairmen was Richard Schulze, who founded Best Buy in 1966. Schulze,
however, relinquished the role of chief executive in 2002.

Greenberg also was far older than any of his peers. At 80, he was
long past the age when most people slow down at least a bit. Not
Hank. He was determined to stay on the job as long as his health permitted, and it seemed that nature might allow him to reign at AIG for
quite a while longer. Greenberg is a remarkably young man for his
years. His mind, everyone close to him agrees, is as sharp as ever. His face
looks more like 70 than 80, and his physical condition is said to be

that of a very healthy 60-year-old. He is notoriously impatient and short-tempered, like many older persons, except Hank has always been that way. Moreover, Greenberg comes from long-lived stock. His mother lived to 105 and her mother, by some accounts, worked until she died at 108.

Greenberg is much more than a survivor, of course. In the nearly four decades that he ruled AIG, he transformed a modest company in the insurance business into not just the largest insurer in the world, but also the No. 9 company (ranked by revenues) on the Fortune 500. AIG's $850 billion of assets at the end of 2005 made it the fourth largest company of all kinds in the United States when measured on that basis. Back in 1968, AIG was best known for being an insurance agency, selling the policies of other insurers to customers in Asia, Latin America, and Europe. It also operated its own life insurance companies in Japan, Hong Kong, the Philippines, and around Asia and owned the majority of several domestic companies, but all of that didn't stack up much next to the giant insurers in Hartford, New York, and Boston. By the turn of the new century, AIG had totally eclipsed Equitable, John Hancock, Aetna, Travelers, Continental, and all the other companies that had towered over it 30 years before. In the process, Greenberg provided long-term returns to his shareholders that only a handful of companies (Buffett's Berkshire Hathaway is one) could top. Greenberg also made himself seriously rich. His holdings of AIG stock alone were worth more than $3 billion, and he ranked No. 47 on the Forbes list of the 400 richest Americans.

Given his accomplishments, it may seem somewhat surprising that Greenberg isn't routinely ranked in the Parthenon of business titans, men like Henry Ford, Alfred P. Sloan, and Samuel Colt, or at least among lesser heroes of the modern age, like Warren Buffett, Walter Wriston, or Louis Gerstner. The reasons for so few accolades are several. First, Greenberg's stellar success came in insurance, and insurance is inherently recondite and dull (even if it wasn't dull as practiced at AIG). More important, Greenberg's innovations weren't ones that are readily transferable to other industries or even, it appears, to other insurance companies. Many AIG executives left for other insurers over the years to apply what they had learned from Hank, but none managed to duplicate what he had wrought.

Greenberg's remarkable, sustained success at AIG and his consummate skill at manipulating situations to his advantage make his downfall all the more surprising, as we shall see, but the way he achieved his victories may actually have made his comeuppance all but inevitable in the post-Enron era. To say that Greenberg ruled AIG understates the measure of control he kept over the company. He was an archetypal autocrat, one who knew every detail of the company's operations and, incredible as it seems, persisted in trying to micromanage the business even as it grew to nearly $100 billion in annual revenues. He was demanding, exacting, and frequently explosive with subordinates, so much so that he drove two of his sons out of the company after they had risen to its highest ranks, by all accounts on merit rather than favoritism. Nevertheless, those who tolerated his frequent sarcasm and occasional tirades, and also delivered the goods in terms of growth and profitability, were rewarded more richly than CEOs at other large companies.

Over the decades, Greenberg worked indefatigably to be recognized as the smartest, canniest, and most successful insurance executive in the world, the brilliant exception in what normally is a numbingly mundane business. Insurance, after all, is the domain of actuaries, people who are said to choose their profession because they lack the personalities to be accountants. Greenberg's brilliance manifested itself in several departures from the normal course of the insurance business—none all that revolutionary on its own, but dynamite in combination—in relentless execution of his strategy, and in demanding that his people regularly achieve goals that others treat as mere aspirations.

Throughout modern times, the insurance industry periodically has had a plague visited upon it known as the underwriting cycle. The cycle works like this. As competition heats up, especially in commercial coverage, insurers cut their premiums (the price of their services) to maintain or increase market share. Inevitably, it seems, premiums across the industry drop to imprudently low levels, ones insufficient to cover the subsequent claims. When those claims—and losses—materialize, typically from a rash of natural disasters, the freshly scorched insurers jack their prices back up and walk away from business that they fought over the year before. Then, as profits recover, the insurers once again bid premiums down to potentially ruinous levels. Many insurers are willing to let their income from investing the premiums cover the difference between the premiums and the claims they later have to pay. Not Greenberg and AIG.

Greenberg, who spent his entire career in insurance and understands its economics as well as or better than anyone, knows that success depends absolutely on getting adequate compensation for the potential loss one is underwriting—and preferably getting a premium that is much more than just adequate. AIG always wanted a bigger book of business than its competitors, but not if that meant suffering underwriting losses that ate into the investment returns from its premium income.

One way to reinforce pricing discipline was to eschew the lines of coverage that other insurers were chasing most aggressively. Another was to insure risks that others didn't want, business where the lack of competition enabled AIG to keep premiums quite comfortably high. As a result, AIG became the leading seller of directors and officers liability coverage, which insures corporate officers and directors against claims for personal malfeasance. Few companies actually file claims under the coverage, but no prudent executive will accept a board seat without it. AIG also has been the leader in kidnapping and ransom insurance for First World executives posted to Second and Third World operations in places like Colombia, Mexico, and the former Eastern bloc. Greenberg once commented that many executives are kidnapped each year, but many, many more aren't kidnapped but do buy insurance.

While one part of the Greenberg profit formula was to charge high premiums, another was to pay as few claims as possible. To that end, AIG has always had a notoriously tough claims department that is famous for finding reasons to send policyholders away empty-handed. The company was so tough, in fact, that some portfolio managers joked that they loved to buy AIG stock, but they would never consider buying an AIG policy. There is nothing wrong with that approach, of course, provided that it isn't carried to such lengths that it drives business away. Management's first and foremost obligation is to make as much money for its shareholders as it can. Its only real obligation to policyholders is to honor the contract.

Another of Greenberg's signal innovations was in the area of incentive compensation. A congenital quandary in any business is how to motivate salespeople most effectively. How do you get them to focus on the true profitability of what they sell rather than just top-line sales? Too often, salespeople will give away the store—in the form of price cuts, promises of extra service, or generous payment terms—in order to land the business and collect a commission. The problem is particularly acute in fields like banking and insurance, where the ultimate risks— loan defaults or policy claims—are not truly knowable until long after the sale is made, and often do not happen until the seller has moved on to a new territory or even a new company.

Greenberg's solution was a unique compensation scheme, one that "differentiated AIG from all other companies and created a culture that was unique in corporate America." He rewarded AIG's top producers with interests in two outside companies called C.V. Starr and Starr International (SICO), both named after Cornelius Vander Starr. (It was their papers that AIG would not let Greenberg remove from his office.) The two entities owned significant blocks of AIG stock and C.V. Starr did lucrative business with the company, but they were technically independent of AIG. Participation in SICO for good performers, and in C.V. Starr for the company stars, acted as both a long-term incentive and a highly contingent form of deferred compensation. The power of these incentives to feed the bottom line of AIG hinged in part on the fact that SICO and C.V. Starr prospered only so long as AIG prospered as well. The participants got some current cash from the entities, but the real payoff came from the appreciation in the companies' holdings of AIG stock. If AIG did not do well, neither did the participants.

The myth of AIG with its founding in China, the belief in its uniqueness and the thought that it could never fail created a cadre of true believers. They believed in the company, were assured it would always be a success and had confidence they would be well taken care of as a result. And many were for a long time. But AIG's near collapse in September 2008 was a stunning blow to many.

One was Jack Lancaster, a charming, brilliant Bermuda custom officer who rose to the Presidency of AIU and whose son is married to Norman Mailer's daughter. Jack is not despondent, but he will never have the wealth he had before. One of many believers in the company knocked for a loop.

That was just one of the wrinkles in Greenberg's system. Another was that the actual ownership of interests in the two entities did not vest until an executive reached the age of 65. Anyone who departed before then forfeited his or her interest, leaving more money in the pot for those who stayed. What's more, the participations were not fixed. If the business a person wrote ultimately went sour, or if profitability faltered in one's division, Greenberg could, and did, adjust the participation downward. The system forced managers to focus on sustained, long-term performance and provided ample motivation to deliver the "three 15s" that Hank demanded—15 percent revenue growth, 15 percent profit growth, and 15 percent return on equity. And the costs of the compensation didn't show up on AIG's income statement. The rewards for those who delivered year after year were truly enormous: Many in the C.V. Starr club became centi-millionaires, and one in addition to Greenberg reportedly is a billionaire. Indeed, C.V. Starr was known within AIG as the billionaires club (although as several current AIG executives pointed out to me, more money could be made out of SICO). When it came to everyone else, though, Greenberg was a classic skinflint. AIG was famous for paying its rank and file substantially less than the norm at other large insurers. Even basic pay for its executives was low. They made up for it with stock options and participation in the private incentive plans.

AIG's famous aggressiveness as a competitor has been matched by an equally aggressive approach to government and politics. Few industries are as regulated as insurance. Each of the 50 states has its own insurance department, with its own rules governing companies doing business in its territory. More important, AIG also had to deal with governments and regulators in more than 100 countries around the globe. Its middle initial, after all, stands for International, and AIG's roots are abroad. The company started not in the United States, but in Shanghai in 1919, and virtually all its operations were outside the United States for the first 30 years of its existence. One senior AIG executive insists that Greenberg was a liberal Democrat until McGovern was nominated. Then he became a conservative Republican. Hard to believe.

From its inception, AIG had to court regulators and politicians to win permission to do business in their countries. Even when it succeeded, it still had to wrangle again and again over specific business practices, over moving profits out of the country, and at times over

attempts to expropriate its businesses. As the company grew, it developed
a highly evolved culture of political exploitation. Step one, wherever
possible, was to cultivate critically important relationships with political leaders. Step two was to fortify its influence abroad by cultivating
even stronger relations with the U.S. foreign policy establishment. One
manifestation of that was Greenberg's leadership role with the Council
on Foreign Relations in New York. His interest in foreign affairs plainly
is genuine; the head of a company as far-flung as AIG has to care deeply
about world affairs. Fortunately, his very active role happens to be one
that served the interests of AIG as well.

The tight relations with U.S. policymakers gave AIG the genuine
clout to pursue a take-no-prisoners policy when cajolery failed to get
what it wanted. If a country threatened to seize AIG's assets, as various
nations did over the years, AIG could credibly respond with a coun-
terthreat of U.S. trade sanctions against the country. All this was done
quietly, of course, but quite effectively. AIG even secured legislation in
Washington that could cut off a country's textile exports to the United
States if it denied insurance licenses to U.S. companies. AIG played hard-
ball at home as well. One famous case involved the Delaware Insurance
Department, which in the mid-1990s was investigating whether a sup-
posedly independent Caribbean reinsurance company was actually controlled by AIG and should be consolidated on its books (a question very
similar to ones Spitzer was asking in 2005). AIG responded by having
private investigators snoop on the snoopers in Delaware.

A real asset in advancing AIG interests abroad was Hank Greenberg
himself. His contacts around the world are legendary and are sorely
missed by the new AIG management team. Whenever he went to the
Philippines in the 1970s and early 1980s, he dined with President Marcos
and then was debriefed by the CIA, part of the continuing symbiotic relationship with the intelligence community that started with Starr and continued with Youngman, Tweedy, Greenberg, and others. The
New York Times magazine once ran an interview with CIA Director Bill
Casey in which he commented on the few individuals outside government
he tapped most often for advice. One was former Nevada Senator Paul
Laxalt. Another was Hank Greenberg, who, needless to say, was absolutely

furious over the article. "How in the hell," he asked me, "can you possibly conduct covert operations when you end up in the *New York Times*?"

One consequence of AIG's intense political involvement, and of having to live in a world defined by myriad rules, was an odd sense of entitlement. When possible, AIG shaped the rules to its interests; when not, it bent them to its purposes. On occasion, it flouted the rules. In many cases, it operated as close to the edge as it had to in order to achieve its business goals. Given that mind-set, it hardly is surprising that Greenberg may have pushed the envelope on finite insurance contracts or stretched accounting principles to report the earnings he wanted. If someone did object, the company could defend, rationalize, or explain away just about any action. Greenberg would make his stock reply to almost every criticism ("You don't understand insurance"), and then the lawyers and lobbyists would make the problem go away.

Whatever the case, the actions in question cost Greenberg dearly, and not just at AIG. The scandal compelled him to give up his leadership positions at some of the nonprofit institutions that are an integral part of the New York power structure and had been an important source of prestige and influence for both Greenberg and AIG, but where he would now have to deal with some of the same directors who forced him out of his own company. He quit the board of the American Museum of Natural History, an organization to which the Starr Foundation, which he chairs, gave $35 million and whose president, Ellen Futter, is on AIG's board. He also resigned from the board of the Asia Society. Hank used to head that board, but it now is chaired by former U.N. Ambassador Richard Holbrooke, another AIG director.

One board seat Greenberg did not relinquish was at the Council on Foreign Relations, the old-line bastion of the foreign policy establishment. Greenberg served as its vice chairman for many years, and was elected an honorary vice chairman when his last term ended. When the scandal broke, the council quickly amended the Greenberg biography on its website, euphemistically describing him as the "retired" chairman and CEO of AIG. Less kindly, the council quietly removed the flattering portrait of Greenberg from the gallery of current and past leaders in the Rockefeller Room of its East 68th Street headquarters.

Something I had never noticed was pointed out to me by a high-powered member. All the other portraits—from David Rockefeller to John J. McCloy—show conservatively suited dignitaries seated in a library or what looks like a library, while Greenberg is standing outside on the top balcony of his headquarters at 70 Pine Street with a view of Manhattan behind him. It not so subtly conveys his powerful role in the business capital of the world—a striking contrast to the other leaders in the room. He looks dynamic, attractive. The woman who pointed this difference out to me claimed she heard Greenberg had demanded this distinctive portrait. Did he really demand this painting? Les Gelb, president emeritus of the council, says absolutely not. He explained that when a picture is commissioned, the honoree is given several artists to work with. Greenberg picked one he liked and delivered this picture. It is certainly in stark contrast to every other painting in the David Rockefeller Room, and it is the only portrait of a vice chairman hung in the room. The rest are chairmen and presidents of the council. But, as Gelb points out, there are also portraits of lesser than vice chairmen in this room—such as past directors of the council.

When I told Les why Attorney General Spitzer considered "Greenberg the most powerful businessman in the world and his Council involvement was one reason," Les was quiet for a minute then said, "I am blushing." Spitzer had said, "The AIG CEO has relationships with leaders around the world that surpass relations any other CEO has. He was at the vortex of where many different streams merged. A very significant player with the Council on Foreign Relations and others."

Regarding his portrait at the council—it has been rehung. Les advised me to ask his successor, Richard Haass, how it came to be removed. Les said he asked and was told the Rockefeller Room was being shown to prospective renters of the room and it was decided there were too many pictures, which would discourage those who wanted to use it for events. Therefore, several were temporarily removed. Some speculate that the council precipitously removed it in the embarrassing heat of the Greenberg scandal, got considerable grief from those who felt Greenberg had done a great deal and been very generous to the council, and quietly rehung it. Haass's office told me he was uncomfortable about discussing council board members and could not meet with me.

He subsequently called and we met but the book was already at the printer. I promised to include the results of our interview in the paperback.

Haass described Hank as a model director who cares about the council, is interested in foreign policy, knows a great deal about Asia, and is generous with his time and resources. I learned from Les Gelb that the Starr Foundation, which Greenberg chairs, has given over $15 million to the council.

Regarding the photos, Haass stated strongly that for events like weddings, since the Greenberg photo was at that time on one wall overlooking 68th Street, it was removed for picture taking. (The picture is now on the opposite wall.) He said paintings only come down because of events where the council rents space or for physical protection if the room is too crowded.

As to whether it was rare for a vice chairman, as opposed to chairmen and presidents, to have their photo in the David Rockefeller room, Haass pointed out that for a number of years Greenberg was a close partner with Pete Peterson, then chairman of the Blackstone Group, who served as council chairman for some 15 years. They worked together in leading the council, so it was natural that Hank's picture would be hung in recognition.

We talked about the sensitivity of Hank being a director and working alongside Richard Holbrooke, Martin Feldstein, and Carla Hills, directors of AIG, which had ousted him. Greenberg is especially angry at Holbrooke and allegedly says he will give no money to the Asia Society, which Holbrooke chairs, until he leaves. Haass said that directors compartmentalize very well. They come to the council for council business and he has never seen their other agendas intrude on the council.

I noted a senior office of the council told me that whereas Gelb got on famously with Greenberg, Haass does not. Haass disputed this, noting they first met in the 1990s, when the council had a task force on U.S. intelligence policy, which Hank chaired and which Haass served as executive director. They have known each other since and work together well. He described Hank as a strong personality who talks very directly, something he (Haass) is comfortable with.

He summed up by noting the AIG story was one of the great American business stories of the second half of the twentieth century.

The great irony in the AIG affair is the apparently modest degree of accounting chicanery. In the other great scandals of recent years, companies manufactured profits out of thin air to hide reversals that effectively doomed the enterprises. Enron leveraged itself into extinction while pretending to be a money spinner. WorldCom and Adelphia were forced into bankruptcy reorganization and ultimately sold for just a few percent of their former values.

The AIG numbers sound almost as big. The board's report at the beginning of May said that reversing improper accounting entries since 2000 would knock $2.7 billion off the company's net worth. That sounds like a lot, but not if you consider how enormous AIG is. The figure comes to only 3 percent of the company's equity capital, and substantially less than a single year's earnings. What's more, corrections of other accounting errors in those same years would add back $2.4 billion, so that the net change came to just $300 million. The net figure is chump change for AIG. Even the bigger $2.7 billion number is not large enough, by itself, to have a material impact on the value of the business.

Legal or not, Greenberg's actions were nothing like those of the other boardroom bad guys, who tried to fool investors by grossly distorting their numbers. Instead, if Greenberg did anything, he was simply injecting a little Botox into the balance sheet and fine-tuning the earnings reports to maintain the image he found so supremely important. Not so long ago, that kind of earnings "management" rarely brought more than a modest reprimand. The rules changed after Enron, of course, but Hank must have assumed that the changes, like so many other regulatory annoyances, weren't really relevant, or if they did apply to him, he could bluff his way through them as he had so often in the past.

The bottom line is that Hank Greenberg was forced out of a great company, one of a kind—a company with a dramatic and unusual history, very different management practices, an innovative offering of products, traditions unlike those in other businesses, and an extraordinary system of compensation.

The company was founded on a shoestring in Shanghai, China, before American businessmen really thought of going abroad, by an unusual entrepreneur, C.V. Starr, a young man who had very limited insurance experience but a great deal of self-confidence, moxie, and affection for the Chinese people. Starr's operating philosophy was not that you needed to know insurance. In fact, that was the least of his concerns. What you did need was to be ambitious, hungry, hardworking, creative, and dedicated to his company. Thus early on he attracted a group of talented people who knew nothing about the business. Among the founding fathers were Russian refugees and Chinese scholars. They would have to learn the business as they went—and they did.

True winners in the Starr companies were the real risk takers. Not only risk takers on what they insured, but risk takers in their other business decisions as well. Starr constantly took risks as he expanded his companies across Asia. Greenberg is the risk taker par excellence right up to the present by bringing lawsuits against AIG to recover $15 million in lost property and to protect $20 billion in stock owned by one of the AIG-related entities he still chairs and whose stock AIG claims rightfully belongs to it.

The company has always held great allure. It was swashbuckling and entrepreneurial, headquartered in Shanghai. Legends and stories naturally grew up around the company and soon were accepted as absolute truths. I get to the bottom of many of these legends in this book—some were bunk, some were partially true, others were absolutely true. Starr eventually had offices in Mexico City, Havana, Hanoi, and Paris and everywhere else exotic, but not in the insurance capital of America—Hartford. The company offered unlimited opportunity. It could grow and expand all over Asia (and later everywhere else). One lived in an exotic locale, places where anyone with even a modest income by U.S. standards could live like a king with a huge home full of servants, club memberships, and other perks of living abroad. Upper middle managers enjoyed a life reserved for only those at the very top of the wealth chain back home.

While insurance seems inherently dull from the outside (and generally is), this was insurance in the developing world, where nothing is routine or cut-and-dried. The company reinvented insurance in these countries. It came up with new coverages, operating without loss experience, without actuarial tables. It made insurance a very interesting business. Some would argue that if this disproves the allegation that insurance is dull, it suggests instead it is simplistic. The examples in this book of the kinds of previously unheard-of insurance coverages provided by American International, like expropriation insurance, refute this assertion.

A number of children of managers joined the company, making it one of those rare places where the second generation of management really was the second generation. The one glaring exception was Starr himself, who had no children. Perhaps the one thing drawing children of executives into the company was the very fact that there was no second-generation Starr to inherit the top spot. Even if they didn't get the very top job, at least they could have hope that their ultimate new boss would be someone who earned it instead of inheriting it. Or maybe the children were simply attracted by all the company's allure. Or it could be they saw the company as an "extended family enterprise."

Over time, the compensation paid to the top managers was phenomenal. Many millionaires and a few billionaires were created through a combination of stock options, involvement in Starr International (a Panamanian corporation that puts away AIG stock for participants), and becoming a shareholder of C.V. Starr, the owner of a number of insurance agencies.

In the end, AIG became the world's largest insurance company, the first reverse U.S. multinational, a company founded abroad by Americans that came to the United States only later in its corporate life, and the owner of numerous other businesses such as International Lease Finance Corporation, the world's largest airline leasing company.

There is no way to understand AIG today, and the trouble that Greenberg and the company got in, without understanding its beginnings and development over 90 years. It is an atypical history peppered with a cast of colorful characters of many nationalities that could be a lively movie instead of the story of an insurance company.

Chapter 2

Shanghai Starr

I n 1919 Cornelius Vander Starr walked down the gangplank of a steamship in Shanghai harbor and into the arms of the opportunity that had eluded him for the past decade. He arrived in November. On December 19, he launched his first insurance agency, American Asiatic Underwriters. Just two years later he started a life insurance company. Within 10 years he had insurance offices all across East Asia, had become a major land speculator, and was the publisher of two newspapers and a magazine. Starr probably would have succeeded wherever he settled, but Shanghai enabled him to prosper faster than he could have almost anywhere else. Shanghai in the decades between the world wars was the greatest city in Asia, easily eclipsing Hong Kong and even Tokyo. To some it was the wickedest city in the world, the "whore of the Orient." To others it was the Paris of the East.

The city was run by foreigners but it was not a colony; most residents were Chinese but it was not ruled by China. Shanghai had been carved up into foreign "concessions" after China's defeat in the opium

wars of the 1800s. The British were by far the most populous and powerful Westerners, followed closely by the French. The foreigners brought
with them their own military, courts, police, and even their own architecture. It was one of the most cosmopolitan places that ever existed,
full of growth, color, and life, and poverty and death. It was a haven for
refugees, rogues, and adventurers of all kinds and from all parts of the
world, fleeing wars, revolutions, and oppressive new regimes.

By the 1920s Shanghai was the most populous and industrialized
city in China, and a significant center of intellectual activity. There
actually were several Shanghais, with surprisingly little overlap between
them. Westerners lived in a Western city and had little need of contact with the Chinese around them. Very few ever learned to speak
even basic Chinese. Their world was based on the classic British colo-
nial model, with life centered around the racecourse and the club, the
church, and the trading houses and banks.

C.V. Starr, as he preferred to be called, began life in California,
where he had knocked about in a variety of callings. He was born
in the northern coastal town of Fort Bragg, where his mother ran a
boarding house from which she sold liquor to patrons of the lumber
town's nearby bordellos. His father, also Cornelius, was a Dutchman
who worked as a railroad engineer for the Union Lumber Company.
He died when Starr was only two. There were two brothers—John and
Ben. Starr took care of his mother after his early success in business
and apparently kept in touch with his brothers, who, like Starr, had no
children. Neither was particularly successful and one, Ben, seems never to
have amounted to much, according to Starr's cousin. Apart from occasionally mentioning that he came from humble beginnings, Starr did not
discuss his home life with anyone outside his closest associates. His drive
to achieve does not seem to have come from his mother or a mentor,
and certainly not from his brothers. Starr followed his own star from
Day One. He is a prime example of a business leader who succeeded
because of nature, not nurture. There is no obvious development in his
childhood that influenced this predilection, although from his early days
in school and working as a young man, he was always in a hurry.

Years later, as the Starr Foundation set up scholarship programs
around the world, none were in honor of his mother or brothers (much
less his father, whom he would not remember). They simply were

C.V. Starr scholarships. But then, the Starr Foundation was not established until 1955 and did not have much money. However, he was close to his mother and after his success he bought her a home in San Francisco. He also threw an 80th birthday dinner for her at the Waldorf-Astoria, but, according to his first cousin and former secretary, Marion Breen, he was not as absolutely crazy about her as others have asserted.

By the time Starr reached his 12th birthday, he began what became a constant throughout his life—working. Before he left grammar school, he took a job wrapping cigars, another sweeping out the local Odd Fellows Hall, and a third as janitor at the Baptist Church.

Starr apparently had no formal higher education, although he did tell one business colleague that he had gone to a law school in California where you could get a degree in one year. The memorial booklet published by AIG after Starr's death mentions that in "1910 he enrolled in the University of California at Berkeley, waiting on tables to pay his way. He left after a year telling his good friend, Clyde Ware, that he did not have time to spend four years at a University."

After moving to San Francisco in 1914, he read law at night with a San Francisco attorney, John T. Williams, and after several months passed the California bar examination, reputedly scoring the highest on the exam, and was admitted to practice in state and federal courts in 1915. This was a standard way of getting legal training without going to law school.

After his year at Berkeley, he returned to Fort Bragg and opened the first ice cream store with a soda fountain the little town had ever had. This is an early example of a Starr trait: looking for opportunity by finding things no one else was doing. This first entrepreneurial foray was successful, but it was neither stimulating enough nor big enough to hold him. So he sold it for $1,000 (according to the AIG memorial on Starr). With this unaccustomed prosperity, he purchased a Hupmobile, a popular mid-priced car made by the Hupp Motor Company.

Starr went from the soda fountain to the James Nelson Realty Company. Here he developed a fascination for the insurance business, telling friends, "There's a fortune in this business." At this time, realty companies were often in the insurance business as well. The company Starr first joined in China for a very short time, run by

Frank Jay Raven, was a realty company and bank that had an insurance arm. Starr obviously was a quick study because he successfully applied the principles of the Nelson Realty company to his own company in China a few years later.

In his off hours, Starr pursued an avocation that also would occupy him in Shanghai years later. When a new weekly newspaper opened in Fort Bragg, the *Fort Bragg Chronicle*, Starr, as city editor, wrote articles for it, taking a special delight in ribbing both the older established weekly paper and a neighboring small town. What is interesting about this is not what it tells us of Starr's interest in newspaper work, which clearly fascinated him, but it suggests a strong independent streak of not concerning himself with what others think. This probably explains why Starr was booted from the Rotary Club of Shanghai for speaking his mind many years later. It is one thing to speak your mind when you are financially independent; it is another when you are a paid employee. And that is what he was in Fort Bragg, the employee of a realty company that could have been upset by his mischievous journalism.

After he moved to San Francisco in 1914, Starr got a job selling automobile insurance—on the street—for the Pacific Coast Casualty Company. He asked his friend Ware, who had followed Starr there from Fort Bragg, to watch for new cars on the street, since each was a prospect. He then helped form an insurance brokerage firm, known as Shean & Deasy, running it until he enlisted in the U.S. Army as a private in March 1918, eight months before Armistice Day marked the end of World War I.

Starr did not get overseas in World War I, but even in the army his entrepreneurial bent manifested itself. Local merchants charged what Starr considered exorbitant prices for laundry. So he rented a delivery wagon, made a deal with an out-of-town laundry, and started clearing $400 a month, topping a major's pay. He was mustered out as a sergeant in 1919 (according to one AIG publication) or a second lieutenant (according to another). (More than likely he was a sergeant.) He was disappointed that he had not shipped to Europe, less for missing the action than the frustration over not fulfilling his yearning to travel, a trait often found among West Coast Americans of the era. Starr especially had a yen to go to the Orient.

As soon as he mustered out, Starr boarded a boat to Yokohama. He lasted half a year in Japan and was reportedly driven to leave within a few months of becoming a clerk at the Pacific Mail S.S. Co., a steamship firm, by a boss who insisted on buzzing Starr when he wanted him, even though they were together in a small office. He would not desist when Starr asked, so Starr departed for Shanghai, arriving with what legend has as just 300 Japanese yen in his pocket (a legend that is probably not true, since he had the modest returns from the sale of his insurance business, which helped start his business in Shanghai). While Starr had not absolutely decided China was the future before he arrived, he quickly reached that opinion.

The experience with the Japanese boss left a memorable impression on Starr that he often told others about. It helped push a born entrepreneur over the line and reinforced his determination to be his own boss, and it may have contributed to his strong belief in not only being fair to all his employees but in giving them participation in his ventures. When I was at AIG, his secretary, Marion Breen, was known to have substantial AIG stock. Whenever hosting a lunch in the famous AIG dining room, after the Chinese waiters left the room, I often commented: "That was probably a millionaire that just served you. Mr. Starr gave all of them stock. They keep doing this because they are fiercely devoted to his memory."

Extraterritoriality—the special right granted foreigners in China to do business and incorporate under the laws of their own countries— made for a promising business climate for an enterprising young man. Since the 1840s, a section of Shanghai had been set aside for citizens of foreign nations to live and trade in as if they were on their own native soil. This bursting international settlement was packed into a space half the size of Manhattan.

Once in Shanghai, Starr began to meet a legendary cast of characters. Fortunately for him, he mixed well and made friends easily. One colleague described him as quiet, unassuming, but very forceful. He went on to say, "He could sell anybody anything." Perhaps better said, he was quietly spoken, a bit gruff, and forceful, in contrast to his successor, who shares some of those traits but certainly is not quietly spoken. Shortly after his arrival, he called on Frank Jay Raven, a fortunate

acquaintance to make so soon. Raven was a wildly successful businessman with millions in real estate and financial interests.

A fellow Californian, Raven came to Shanghai in 1904, when the
foreign settlement was virtually all British. Early on he was lured by
the irresistible economic logic of Shanghai real estate. By 1914, the
Raven interests had reached some $70 million in assets, an incred-
ible fortune in those years. Like Starr, Raven was a bull on Shanghai,
and he frequently was elected as one of the two American members
of the Shanghai Municipal Council. He married Elsie Sites, daughter of
a missionary and a fervent teetotaler, and sent his three daughters to
school in Heidelberg. Years after Starr arrived, Raven's bank went bank-
rupt and he was sent to prison by a judge in the American section for
fleecing depositors and other crimes.

By one story, Starr took over the flagging insurance end of Raven's
firm. John Roberts, later AIG Vice Chairman, had always heard that
when Raven's insurance agency went broke, Starr bought it. By another
story, Raven created an insurance department in one of his banks and
put Starr in charge. Whichever it was, Starr very soon decided he would
do better on his own. Where he got the capital is unknown, although
he had some savings from selling his San Francisco insurance agency
and he may have borrowed from Raven or someone else. In any case,
in 1919, the same year he arrived in Shanghai, he opened an insurance
agency with two clerks in two rooms at the corner of Nanking and
Szechuan roads and called it American Asiatic Underwriters (AAU).
He invited Raven to be one of its directors. So the Starr enterprises,
later known as the American International Companies, were officially
launched when Starr was 27 years old, a very short time after arriving
in Shanghai that same year.

With AAU, Starr focused on the few American insurers already in
China, starting off as a subagent for Fireman's Fund and some others.
He made a trip to New York in 1921 to find a company that he could
represent exclusively, and landed a deal with Hanover. He met Charles
Highley, the president, who came out of the meeting and proudly said,
"Meet Mr. Starr. He is our representative in China."

Later, he added the National Union Fire Insurance Company
of Pittsburgh. This meant he did not insure for his own account but
received only commissions for writing business for these companies, or

as Tsuyee Pei, the former governor of the Central Bank of China, put it: "We [Starr and Pei] met on a boat—the Empress of Asia in 1920." Starr got the idea there that American companies shouldn't have to insure through British insurance firms. "He came back to the United States and somehow influenced a number of insurance companies to organize on a pool basis to underwrite general insurance for the Far East."

(In other words, all the business written by agents of these companies in China goes into a common pool and each company takes a predetermined amount of risk. So the American Home Company might, for example, agree to insure 10 percent of all the business Starr wrote.)

Nearly 40 years later, after moving to New York, Starr bought companies such as Globe & Rutgers and National Union as well as others he represented. In doing so, he fulfilled a dream to be not just an agent for these companies but to own them outright. More important, they gave him a domestic presence and an entry into the United States market. Meanwhile, in 1919, AAU started as an insurance agency that represented a number of American insurance companies in China, offering fire and marine coverage.

How many would have the self-confidence, at 29 years, barely two years into having his own business, to journey halfway around the world to New York and persuade insurers they should trust you, a neophyte in the business whom they did not know, to represent them in China? Not many.

C.J. Smith, Starr's colleague and friend of 50 years, whom he met in Shanghai in 1920, reminisced about what it was like for them to do business in China in the early days:

> Mr. Starr and I both traveled a great deal, living in dirty local hotels and making maps of the towns. I remember the first time I went to Soochow. I wrote back to . . . Starr, saying, We can't insure anything in this town. He said, You wait a while, maybe you can. So I stayed up there two weeks and we did write in that town and made money.
>
> I always carried a pistol when I traveled but never had the occasion to use it.

There were some kidnappings of foreigners, of course, but we were fortunate. We always said that if we were kidnapped we would never pay anything.

Our first branch was in Hankow about 600 miles up the Yangtze River. . . . Hankow was called the Chicago of the Far East. It took 3½ days to get there by boat and that was the only way. There were no roads or railroads. . . .

Mr. Starr was working all the time, scheming, traveling incessantly, and opening new branches. Within a few years, we had 14 branch offices in China, then we went to Hong Kong, further south to the Philippines, and to Bangkok and Saigon.

Later on Chinese insurance companies were formed that competed with us for the Chinese business. The British companies didn't compete very strongly for the Chinese risks because, well, if a merchant didn't do well he might have a fire before Chinese New Year, collect from the insurance company, and pay off his debts that way. But if we could prove it was arson, we just wouldn't pay. I think we were the first insurance company to start fighting it. . . . We had the reputation of being so tough that the crooks wouldn't insure with us.

This presages AIG's tough claims department set up by Greenberg years later.

Starr became friends with Singloh Hsu, a Chinese banker who lent money to him. When the Japanese began to expand their interest in China, Hsu was on a commercial airline between Hong Kong and Chungking that was shot down by the Japanese. Then, in a case of total brutality, they machine-gunned everyone but the pilot. Starr had apparently promised Hsu he would look after his son and he did. Even though he had never met him, he sent the son, T.C. Hsu, to Haverford College and visited him on his first Thanksgiving in this country. Starr kept him on as an employee of Starr businesses throughout his working life. For over 30 years, until 2000, T.C. Hsu was president of the Starr Foundation and did not step down as a consultant to the foundation until 2005.

The early years also brought Starr together with a group of White Russians who had fled the Communist Revolution since Shanghai was a popular haven for refugees in the 1920s. The Russians fled east to Vladivostock and Harbin, and then on to Beijing and Shanghai. They all had several things in common: They were well educated, sophisticated, hardworking, often entrepreneurial—and desperately in need of work.

One of these was Artemis Joukowsky, a former Russian diplomat. There are various stories of how Joukowsky came to hook up with Starr. Shortly after I joined AIG in 1973, I had heard what I thought was the absolute true story about Joukowsky, a White Russian in the foreign service when Lenin came to power. After a pound of beef was left on his desk once a week at the foreign ministry so he would have some meat in his diet during difficult times in revolutionary Russia, Joukowsky decided it was time to leave. He fled across Russia and landed in Shanghai. Thanks to meeting Starr he did not have to resort, like other White Russians, to being a chauffeur, instead becoming an early partner in what would become a gigantic worldwide business. And his wife never became a mistress to a Chinese mogul, which often happened because of a Chinese preference for White Russian women.

Version two of the Joukowsky story is a much different tale. Joukowsky, a graduate of cadet school in St. Petersburg, went into the foreign service. He was fluent in Mandarin, so he was posted to the Russian embassy in Beijing. When the Russian civil war between the Reds and Whites moved to Siberia with the famous General Kolchak leading the Whites, Joukowsky joined with the general and was part of the expeditionary force until Kolchak was defeated. Joukowsky ended up in a Russian refugee camp in Shanghai with nothing. Friends told him there was a strange American who wanted to hire foreigners who spoke Mandarin to market to Chinese. Joukowsky said, "but I don't speak English." They responded, "Starr talks all the time, anyway. You won't have to." So for about a week, they practiced key English phrases. Then Joukowsky walked into the meeting with Starr, said he had an infected tooth and couldn't speak (he had a bandage wrapped around his head), Starr talked a while, and then offered him a job. Joukowsky used the little English he had learned and said he would be honored.

A great story—except the person faking the toothache was George Moszkowski, a Polish cavalry officer who was a refugee from the Communists as well and ultimately had an illustrious career with the Starr companies. It was Moszkowski who spoke no English when he began, although it was attributed to Joukowsky in company lore. Starr apparently saw through his toothache excuse but admired his spunk and hired him anyway, expecting he would be very entrepreneurial.

But that story may not be correct either according to Moszkowski's grandson, Colin Fraser, who worked for AIG for twenty years. His mother, Helena, Moszkowski's daughter, refutes the toothache story. She says that he led a motor car expedition across the Gobi Desert for which he was well paid when he reached Shanghai. After enjoying himself for a few weeks and befriending a Russian banker, he tells him his landlady has told him to get a job or move on.

The Russian banker suggests seeing Starr. He does, speaking perfect English, and gets the job right away. After a number of weeks, the banker asked if he has booked any business. He says no, but is enjoying reading the paper, having tea, and other amenities. The banker gives him a giant piece of business handling the marine insurance for the Trans Siberian Railroad. This is three times larger than anything Starr's firm has ever written and endears him to Starr and starts his upward career.

A romantic story about his father, according to Artemis Joukowsky II, the son, who spent 30 years with the company, but not quite accurate. He explained that his father, a nobleman, came from a very aristocratic family. His grandfather was a colonel in the imperial guard in St. Petersburg and fought against the Ottomans in Bulgaria under Alexander II's leadership. Art has his grandfather's memoirs and they talk about Alexander being considered the liberator of Bulgaria.

Joukowsky, Sr., was educated at the imperial Alexander school, where the poet Aleksandr Pushkin was educated. He joined the ministry of foreign affairs in St. Petersburg. (Buck Freeman, son of another founder, called him the most cultivated of the Russians who joined the Starr organization—and there were a number of them.) The minister of foreign affairs asked him to be an assistant to Admiral Kolchak, the famous Russian military leader who was captured and executed in Siberia. Working with the admiral, he wore a uniform but was an intelligence officer, not a military officer.

Joukowsky, born in 1893, one year after Starr, blond and blue-eyed, was of Swedish descent from a family that immigrated to the Ukraine. He understood he was on the NKVD list for assassination but did not know why, so he went to Kolchak and said he preferred to work out-side the civil war area. He was reassigned as vice consul of Harbin in Manchuria, a major Russian city. Joukowsky met his wife there, the daughter of the chief justice. Joukowsky Jr. thinks it was ultimately his father's job to close the consulate when China withdrew recognition of the Communist regime. At that point Joukowsky moved to Shanghai, the destination for refugees.

Joukowsky, fluent in Russian, French, and English (of the Oxonian variety), took a job with an English insurance company. Since his family had never been in business but had been doctors and government ministers, this was a real change but something he had to do to sup-port his family. A British friend told him he would never succeed with the company because he was not English, and that he should look for opportunity with an American company. That is how he found Starr, and a career of two generations was launched.

Joukowsky, with his facility for languages, soon learned Mandarin. He initially became a marine underwriter but found it a struggle to expand into underwriting other risks because of a particular Chinese resistance to buying new types of coverage. For example, they did not want to insure damage from wind storms "because we don't know how to start a wind storm." There were many interesting incidents in developing the business. The Kuomintong, the nationalist army, owned a Chinese merchant fleet that was abandoned in the harbors when the Communists took over. The Chinese wanted to be paid for barratry, the wrongful conduct by a ship's crew that results in a loss to the owners. National Union was sued for payment of mortgages on the ships, but when it went to the Supreme Court, they didn't recognize the Chinese government.

Ultimately, Joukowsky worked to develop the Middle East oper-ations, was CFO, and ended up a senior vice president of C.V. Starr & Company, the senior company of the group.

By Starr's standards, Joukowsky, having worked for a British insurer, was practically an insurance veteran when he joined the young firm. More often, Starr hired men like him, generally Russians, who had no insurance experience or business experience of any kind, yet he gave them senior responsibilities, having absolute faith they would quickly catch on. They would grow in the company and make it not only their lifelong profession, but a lifelong obsession. Then their involvement and excitement would pass on to their children, who also made their lives within AIG. This would not have been unusual if their father was the CEO and they could expect to be the heir to the top job, but to be a son whose father worked in the business and choose to work there with little expectation of getting the top job was unusual. It suggests how stimulating, exciting, and lucrative working with Starr and his company was, an excitement that could be conveyed to sons by their fathers.

Sure enough, Artemis's son, also named Artemis, later joined the company. He saw it, and still does, as "exciting and romantic, a place where a young man could go abroad and run a company on his own. Then there were no faxes or emails and daily communications from the home office as there is today." The younger Joukowsky had numerous jobs—Milan, Beirut, Hong Kong, and others—but eventually became head of the Socialist country division (technically called the Special World Markets Division). There was great irony in this since Joukowsky, because of his family's experience in Russia, hated Communist regimes and everything about them. After 30 years with AIG, Joukowsky left to become vice chancellor at Brown University and ultimately chancellor. While he was at AIG, like the good trouper he was, he capped his career by working at building a prosperous business in Eastern Europe.

When the elder Joukowsky died in 1986, Buck Freeman and Hank Greenberg attended his funeral. This was a Russian Orthodox funeral with open casket and mourners all holding a burning candle throughout the service. At the conclusion, everyone files past the casket and kisses the body. "I don't know about you," Greenberg said to Freeman, "but I never kissed him when he was alive and I'll be damned if I'll kiss him when he is dead."

The same year Starr went to New York to line up additional representation, 1921, he formed Asia Life Insurance Company so that, different from other foreign insurers, he could sell life insurance primarily to the Chinese, not just to expatriates. Why did Starr have the wisdom to take this gamble that turned out to be a gigantic boon to his business and led to Starr owning the largest life insurer in Asia? Because he was American, not British? Because he saw the possibilities of growth?

Clearly, the latter more than the former. The bottom line is that this was characteristic of a trait Starr displayed throughout his career: He spotted the new thing, the new opportunity that others did not see.

Starr observed that many Chinese lived to a venerable age, and calculated that improved living standards would likely cause a further decline in the death rate. From an insurance point of view, the longer they live, the more money he makes. With the size of the Chinese community he could visualize a market without limits. Think of the possibility of insuring millions of Chinese compared to the limited expatriate community the other foreign insurers focused on. Scant competition and a giant marketplace, a business approach that would become an American International hallmark.

In launching Asia Life, Starr started what became a tradition of his companies as they grew and expanded around the world: the placing of locals in positions of responsibility and on the board. Starr invited several prominent Chinese citizens to serve on the board and started selling life insurance in Shanghai, with the most popular product being a 20-year endowment policy, something the British would not sell to the Chinese.

This is one reason why, over the years, Starr became a legend in China—Starr, the American with a special knack of working with the Chinese people. Yes, he wanted to build a business, but he had a respect, an affection, for his Chinese colleagues and for the Chinese people.

In 1924, he encountered someone who became a lifelong friend and colleague when he persuaded Mansfield Freeman to join him. Freeman, the son of a Methodist minister who had served in Shanghai, was a teacher of English and philosophy at Tsing Hua College in Peking. He was offered a job by the manager of Starr's Peking office but said no. Freeman was intrigued when the manager then suggested that he train some of his Chinese students to sell life insurance. There would be a team competition among students. As he explained in a seminar held many decades later at his alma mater, Wesleyan College, in Connecticut,

> That was a challenge. I put a notice on the bulletin board that attracted three or four students. I knew nothing about insurance, but I got a book on the subject and gave them a good course of lectures.

When summer came, I sent them out with applications to solicit their friends. They returned in a week or so, complaining, "We can't sell this; perhaps the instruction we got was faulty."

"Not at all," I replied, "it was the best you could have had. To prove it, I'll go out with you and show you how to sell." It was all bluff, of course. I'd never sold anything of the sort, but when they took me out, I sold the first prospect I went to see.

That summer Freeman and his team made what he calls "some sort of record." The directors of the company were impressed and its president, C.V. Starr, came to give the prize to the winning team. They said they owed their success to their teacher—Mansfield Freeman, so Starr visited Freeman and persuaded him to join the firm. "I got into the insurance business by the back door, but Mr. Starr was the reason I stayed in it. My initial confidence in him grew into real respect and love."

Starr and Freeman quickly developed a good relationship, and Freeman helped Starr recruit and train a local agency force, drawing on his teaching skills to do so. By 1924, Freeman was managing Asia Life's Peking branch. In a career of nearly 40 years, serving throughout China before moving to New York City in 1941, Freeman had a variety of responsibilities until he retired in 1960 as vice chairman of the board of C.V. Starr & Company. It is said that prior to Bill Youngman's arrival and elevation to heir apparent many years later, Freeman was the most influential member of Starr's team. He died in 1992 at 97 years old.

Mansfield's son, Houghton (Buck) Freeman, like Joukowsky's son, joined the company and spent his entire career there, rising as close to the top as one could without displacing Hank Greenberg. Born in China, Buck Freeman speaks Chinese and Japanese. He retired to Vermont, where he set up the Freeman Foundation, the largest foundation in the state.

Both Asia Life and AAU operated with few precedents. Despite a minuscule amount of information compared to today's insurance company, the business prospered. Within 10 years, Starr had opened offices and agencies across China and in Hong Kong, Indochina, Jakarta, Kuala

Lumpur, and the Philippines. Starr was convinced this growth was fueled, at least in part, by his focus on hiring, training, and promoting local people to managerial positions, and putting Chinese people on his board. The practice of putting locals in high positions is still a hallmark of the AIG culture. This again is one of the Starr beliefs that have taken on the dimensions of a fable, a part of the folklore of AIG, passed down through the 90 years the company has been in business. AIG still practices it at all levels—from company manager to the public company board. Granted, there are countries, especially in Africa, where often an expat is put in charge, but this is rare.

There is simply not a history of significant black participation in the company. A retired senior personnel executive told me that in his experience, insurance had never been one of the industries where African-Americans saw opportunities. And clearly in AIG there was not an aggressive policy of recruiting them.

While I remember AIG as the most international of companies, with a mélange of nationalities wandering the halls, I don't remember blacks. After Greenberg left and new directors were added, the first in the history of the company, George L. Miles, Jr., President and CEO of WQED Multimedia, an accountant, was elected to the board. And in an AIG-sponsored two-page spread in the April 30, 2006, *New York Times* business section, AIG CEO Martin Sullivan is pictured with Executive Leadership Council CEO Carl Brooks. This organization promotes diversity in the workplace. So AIG is catching up at last.

age Rate
Rate

Chapter 3

Secrets to Building the Chinese Empire

Over the past 30 years a cult has developed within AIG, the cult of Greenberg. Not that it was fostered by Greenberg. In fact, he probably would be the first to disown it or even deny it exists, but it does. Everything is Greenberg this, Greenberg said that. Hank wants it done this way. Hank said to ignore this. Hank wants this license and we damn well better get it. The cult of Greenberg did not come about because Hank or anyone else, including his most passionate admirers, created it. It came about because of the force of his personality and a fierce determination to get his way, and because of longevity. He was CEO such a long time—37 years—that other ways of doing business were forgotten. Most of all it came about because of his phenomenal success building the largest insurer in the world, in growing from an estimated value just before the company went public of $100 million to a market cap of some $165 billion.

In essence, the cult of Greenberg has become the corporate culture of AIG. If you ask present and past executives about the culture at the company, they reply almost instantly and unanimously: The culture that drives AIG, the culture Hank created, is best embodied by Hank himself.

One may speculate how it will change now that Hank is gone and AIG has had three CEOs, with Martin Sullivan having the longest tenure. Under Sullivan, the noticeable change was a serious focus on transparency, an openness marked more by the new CEO's personality than anything else. One executive praised that openness. He said: "Hank's leaving had a liberating impact. You are no longer afraid to offer your own opinions. Maybe our creativity was stifled. I would argue a year from now this creativity will be unleashed." AIG is clearly a more pleasant place to work today than it was under Greenberg, but whether people will meet objectives and accomplish as much is another question. Time has suggested otherwise.

There also is a strict adherence to newly established governance rules (or at least AIG says there is). But what Sullivan will be judged on over time are earnings and the commensurate growth of the stock. The company has recouped $43 billion of the $59 billion in market value lost after Greenberg came under scrutiny in early 2005, but the stock is not yet back where it was. It will take quite a while to see what real cultural changes there will be given that the Greenberg culture was inculcated into the company for nearly 40 years. The phenomenal success the culture produced means one has to question whether one wants to change it. To maintain it, someone from on high must drive the Greenberg operating principles throughout the management of the company. That is a fine balancing act—maintain the competitive spirit of the company but rein in the excesses. Axel Freudmann, longtime AIG personnel chief, described the culture to me very simply: "It is a culture that rewards success, rewards profit, ignores background, creed, nationality, and puts up with a lot of individual idiosyncrasies as long as you produce."

While it may be understandable that Greenberg would set the tone for the culture given the combination of his force of personality, his years in power, and his astonishing accomplishments, the perception that Greenberg dominates all aspects of AIG distorts the history of the company and ignores a number of special people who have played remarkable roles. The founder, Neil Starr, given the time and place where he worked, was at least as formidable. If there had not been a Starr, there could not be a Greenberg. That cannot be forgotten. I suspect Starr would paraphrase that comment and say: "If there had not been a Starr and also a Mansfield Freeman, an Artemis Joukowsky, a K.K. Tse, and many others, AIG would never have achieved what it has."

All these executives and others began their careers with the Starr companies in China and continued working in China or the United States until their deaths or until they theoretically retired. I say theoretically because at times it seems no one ever really retires from AIG. They include executives like Ernie Stempel, who started with the company in 1939, was president of AIRCO, a major company that Starr created in the late 1940s, for many years. Ernie Stempel, listed in the Forbes 400, died at 92 in April 2009. He had an office in Bermuda, and New York and still went to work from time to time. Buck Freeman, formerly president of a large part of the organization and an AIG director who was retired, came out of retirement to move to Japan a number of years ago to "guide" Evan Greenberg, Hank Greenberg's youngest son, when he was made president of AIG Japan. Buck worked with Evan for several years until both returned to the United States. When I asked why he did it, Buck said: "This is the price I pay for my sins." The point is, top executives rarely really step down completely but become honorary directors or are given some such title.

Understanding the power of the Chinese connection is vital. To begin to grasp a company as complex as AIG, it is necessary to appreciate its unique Chinese origins—the role, almost mythological, China plays within the culture of the company. It's not that China contributes so much to earnings—although the expectation is that it will, and there is already premium revenue of over $1 billion. It is the evangelical belief embraced by AIG employees that they had a beginning like no other company, which is true, and that they have a special affinity with China and understand it like no other, which is largely a delusion.

China has played and will continue to play a unique role in the life of AIG not only because of the belief that it should and that it always has (except for a quarter of a century interregnum from the time Mao came to power until his successors began to open to the West) but because of a real conviction that China will be a huge economic power where AIG can make a ton of money. Tom Friedman writes in his bestseller *The World Is Flat* that in the eighteenth century, China had the world's biggest economy. So, although few of those currently enthralled with China's phenomenal growth realize it, in some ways history repeats itself.

As noted, a major reason for AIG's growth has been its willingness to insure what others would not. The premiums are higher and the competition is less, or nonexistent. Back in the 1970s, Greenberg had the idea that AIG would write political risk insurance—insurance against expropriation, currency inconvertibility, and the like, something unheard of for a private insurance company. He thought the federal government's Overseas Private Investment Corporation (OPIC) should be AIG's reinsurer and sent me on a mission to persuade them to do so. While we made a strong case, it came to nothing. So we created a political risk insurance company subsidiary (which today has the rather uninspired name of AIG Political Risk Insurance Company, Inc.) that set about competing with the government and made money in the process.

This practice started in China with Starr. American Asiatic Underwriters was willing to insure a wide assortment of risks—from a baseball team wanting protection against rainstorms to the cargo of a Czech ship carrying refugees from Vladivostok to Europe. What Starr insured is less remarkable than the fact that the companies he represented in the United States allowed him to do it. Starr ran an insurance agency. He was authorized to sell insurance for these companies, but was not the actual insurer, so his company was not the one bearing the risk he was insuring. He was committing the capital of one of the U.S. companies he represented or risks were written on a pool basis among all the companies. A very persuasive young man, indeed.

This was the standard way agents representing companies worked. They would have withdrawn from the pool if they had not done well with Starr. None withdrew, so they must have made money.

One of Starr's longtime friends was Henry Luce, the China-born founder of Time, Inc. Luce summed up Starr's approach to the life insurance market: "Neil Starr started out in Shanghai with a very simple calculation. He figured that with the coming of modern hygiene to Asia, the life expectancy of the Chinese must inevitably go up, so he

went into the life insurance business when rates, based on a life expectancy of less than 30 years, were immensely high. What could be simpler
or more obvious than such a calculation? Well, most businesses are built
on simple calculations."

While a flattering comment from an immensely influential friend,
this does not do Starr justice. There was much more to what he did
than a shrewd business calculation. He fervently believed he was doing
good things in China for those who never had the opportunity to
be insured. "Never forget the little man," Starr was often heard to say.
From all we know today, Starr was convinced that he was helping his
customers because he saw life insurance as a kind of self-philanthropy.
To him, life insurance provided the discipline, and the security, that
enabled poor working Chinese to accumulate assets that they otherwise
never would have had. As one of his associates explained years later: "As
a great admirer of the late Sir Winston Churchill, who described insurance as 'the magic of averages that works wonders for millions,' Starr
made this vision a reality in a land of great suffering and hardship."

The never-questioned wisdom among foreigners in Shanghai was
that you couldn't do business with the Chinese because they would
cheat you; or if you did, you had to watch them like a hawk. This belief
was especially true in the insurance community, which is not very surprising given the frustration over not knowing how to start a wind
storm. One wonders how many fortunes were never made because of
adherence to the notion that you can't deal with the Chinese because
they will cheat you. Starr, again showing remarkable insight for a newcomer to China, rejected the belief outright. He stated unequivocally:
"Chinese fraud was no more to be feared than Western fraud." It was
fortunate for him that others hewed to the conventional wisdom with
a timidity that allowed him to operate with few competitors.

Atypical of other foreigners, he believed in the Chinese, and
believed that Shanghai, foreign concessions and all, would eventually
revert to the Chinese. He put Chinese citizens high in his organization,
such as K.K. (Koong-Kai) Tse, his chief accountant, who worked at a
partner's desk opposite Starr for many years and continued to work in
Hong Kong and New York through the 1980s. Starr promoted Chinese
employees to very senior positions, and some ended up at the headquarters in New York after the Communist takeover. Not only did K.K.

divide his time between New York and Hong Kong, but his son, Steve, like the sons of White Russians and Americans, made a career in the Starr enterprises and became vice president for investments at AIG.

K.K., commenting on his work with Starr during the early years of the firm, said: "Our desks faced each other for years. We worked closely together, not only in the office, but often during quiet dinners together or just sitting down for chats. He knew me and I knew him." K.K. remained a quiet but powerful figure. He was a partner of C.V. Starr. I had an office near his and would see him during his annual New York sojourn, long after Starr died. That's when I realized firsthand Starr had a real gift for relating to the Chinese (and virtually any nationality), since I found K.K. charming and pleasant but somewhat inscrutable. Not so his son, Steve, whom I felt I knew better, but I suppose he had more exposure to the American way of thinking from an early age.

Steve bemoaned to me one day that thieves had come across the roof of his Manhattan townhouse, broken in, and stolen his multimillion-dollar jade collection. I commiserated but said, "Well, you work for AIG. At least it will be fully insured," to which Steve replied, "Insurance. I don't have insurance. Why would I pay the outrageous premium it would take to insure my jade?" I chuckled but didn't voice what I was thinking: "The family fortune comes from insurance but that doesn't mean he would buy it himself." Those of us who knew of the incident were discouraged from relating the story to outsiders. It certainly wasn't a marketing plus.

To sum up Starr and the Chinese, Starr judged people both by their own moral standards and by his personal measuring sticks of integrity, intellect, competence, and performance. With these as guiding principles, he developed a deep and genuine admiration and affection for Asians and proved it by giving them major responsibilities in his businesses. If there were ever those who objected, Starr would gladly have welcomed their departure.

To do business in China, foreigners hired compradores, a Portuguese term used to describe a local, or Chinese, operative. They were, in effect, businessmen who filled a liaison role between the Chinese and the foreign managers, most of whom spoke little or no Chinese. Zao Pah Siu, a highly respected compradore, heard that Starr was opening his office. He came to Starr and said that "if they worked together Starr would be the greatest insurance man and he would be the greatest compradore." Indeed, he brought so many clients to Starr that the company was able to begin business without using the line of credit that had been extended by Raven's bank. In essence, Starr internationalized his business decades before it became the "must do" of business elsewhere.

It was 1926 when Starr opened his first office on U.S. soil, setting up American International Underwriters in New York to write insurance on American risks outside the United States, but again as a general agent for U.S. insurers. This "home foreign" business, as it was called, was modest at first, but provided the Starr enterprises with their first important diversification of business risk. One of its purposes allegedly was to explain Chinese business methods to Westerners and encourage them to do business in China. It was something of an oddity, in fact, a rarity—a subsidiary of a U.S. company headquartered in China. It was the first step in becoming America's first reverse multinational company, and eventually provided the firm a place to relocate to because of the war in Asia.

By the 1930s, the U.S. location took on added importance as the Starr enterprises started to buy American insurance companies. The first was the United States Life Insurance Company, which in turn acquired another small company. U.S. Life was eventually sold, a sale which years later caused Hank Greenberg considerable frustration because he was trying to move into the domestic life insurance market and needed a vehicle with which to do so. Hank bewailed the loss of this now large U.S. life insurer. The proceeds from the sale of U.S. Life were used to buy Globe & Rutgers, somewhat of a sentimental purchase, since it was company that had given Starr his first insurance representation in China.

As Starr's insurance firms grew and prospered, he began to branch out into other businesses. Typical of other foreigners in Shanghai, Starr had a passion for land speculation. He owned the Metropolitan Land Co. outright, together with a chunk of the Asia Realty Company, owned by his friend F.J. Raven. Raven's fortune in 1914 was worth $70 million, so by the late 1920s and 1930s it would have been immensely larger. Starr had some small percentage of that if it was not seized when Raven was thrown in jail for running a defunct bank.

A more striking passion that shows the protean range of Starr's interests was the continuation of an interest he first manifested in Fort Bragg, California—journalism. As a young man, not only had he written for a weekly newspaper in Fort Bragg, but even earlier he had taken a special delight, as his longtime friend Clyde Ware noted, in writing articles in high school. Starr was such a people person that journalism was natural for him. So in 1930 he bought the English-language *Shanghai Evening News* for the princely sum of $2,500 and changed its name to the *Post*. Later he bought the British-owned *Mercury* for $10,000 and hired as editor Randall Gould, a Far East correspondent for *Time, United Press*, and the *Christian Science Monitor*. Starr had the only American-owned papers in China. From 1931 until shortly after the Communist takeover of Shanghai in 1949, save for the wartime interruption by the Japanese, Starr published them as one joint endeavor—the *Shanghai Evening Post and Mercury*.

During the war between the Communists and Nationalists, the paper served as a clandestine front for Chiang Kai-shek, according to one senior AIG executive. This did not take away from its standing as a solid newspaper, however.

"Newspaper work," says Gould, the kind that "in its purer form is hard to come by nowadays, had fascination for Neil. He was a good publisher, a good editor, and a good reporter." Gould, an exacting reporter himself, states that Starr "would never have taken . . . a newspaper job for the same reason (besides the incessant buzzing by his boss) that he left Japan after discovering how meagerly his shipping office boss was paid."

Gould had doubts about his publisher at first. His office was several blocks from Starr's, so they communicated frequently by "chit coolie" (one who fetches and carries, an expression that originated in a volume called *The Unexpurgated Diary of a Shanghai Baby*). The chit coolie nimbly maneuvered through the crowded streets. When a telephone was installed, Gould hired a pert Chinese-Portuguese female operator called Jimmie. She wasn't shy in her dealings with callers. One day,

Starr, impatient to reach Gould, couldn't get past Jimmie's insistence that the editor was busy.

"This is Mr. Starr who wants to talk to Gould," snapped Starr's operator. Jimmie responded, "You can just tell Mr. Starr to keep his pants on." Starr cut in saying, "This is Mr. Starr. I have my pants on, I mean to keep them on, but I do want to talk to Mr. Gould." Just then, Gould switched in and heard Starr laughing. Says Gould, "I thought, here was no stuffed-shirt publisher, but a real newspaperman, the kind of man I liked to work for."

Starr, starting in 1933, also put out a Chinese-language edition of the *Post*, *Ta Mei Wan Pao*, meaning Great American Evening Newspaper. This was not simply a Chinese-language version of the *Post and Mercury*, but an original paper, written and edited by the Chinese. In size, but, more important, in influence because it was in Chinese, this grew to be perhaps the most important of Starr's publications. However, Buck Freeman, who was in the military in China during the war and afterwards located with the company to Shanghai, was not aware of it. Another senior AIG executive, still high up in the company, does not believe there was a Chinese-language newspaper, but he joined the company much later. Yet the information on this paper was reported in the memorial to Starr published in 1968, another example of the stories associated with the company's history that take on a life of their own. I believe there was such a paper.

For a while, Starr also owned *Norte,* a feature magazine with illustrated articles. He also bought and published *East, The Newsweekly of the Orient*, which was modeled on *Time* magazine. John Ahlers, a C.V. Starr executive and author of a book about old Shanghai said: "I think Starr was attracted to publishing by the thought that he would have made a good writer if he had tried, and that his good friend Luce was successful in publishing. Starr thought he could do with his left hand what Luce could do with both. He could not, of course."

These became sound enterprises—as Starr demanded of nearly all his investments—but it was clear that his own interest transcended that of profit alone. He was very engrossed with publishing and writing. Starr seems to have taken the proper hands-off attitude an editor wishes an owner would take. Ted Thackery, former editor of the *Post and Mercury*, as well as *East*, said: "In the operation of *East*, I never recall receiving a single order from Starr—suggestions yes, but always in the mildest tone. He was eager not to interfere with what he felt was a satisfactory operation, and not to second-guess those who ran it."

As Starr expanded his publishing activities, he began to cut quite a swath through Shanghai society. The January 1935 issue of *Fortune* magazine, founded five years earlier by Luce, features an article titled "Men of Shanghai," with brief profiles of six expatriates and Chinese movers and shakers. Luce's friend got great treatment—Starr's is the first profile in the package, and the longest. Even then, journalists recognized that insurance as practiced by AIG was different: "His insurance career has not been the dull, routine-ridden affair that is so typical of this profession in America.

"Were the total assets of Mr. Starr's companies to be tabulated they would seem midgetlike beside those of Metropolitan Life," *Fortune* wrote. "But Mr. Starr's income is fat—perhaps as big today as any U. S. insurance income. This money is earned upon a sociological premise, that the standard of living and hygiene of the Chinese middle classes are improving, with a consequent decline in the death rate. Indeed, since Chinese statistics are all but nonexistent, the success of Mr. Starr's American Asiatic Underwriters, and of its various subsidiaries, is perhaps the best available proof that the death-rate decline in China is a reality."

The article observed that Starr had never bothered to become proficient in Chinese, but his knowledge of China was encyclopedic, and he was famed in the foreign community for his uncanny ability to work with and through the Chinese people. *Fortune* explained he was expelled from the Rotary Club for speaking his mind. There is no record of what he said but I would wager it was his pro-Chinese stance, either his belief in their integrity and honesty or his conviction the foreign concessions would revert to the Chinese. In any case, his expulsion probably became a badge of honor to Neil Starr.

Fortune called him Shanghai's most bullish tai-pan. "But like many of his modern associates, he is bullish in finance rather than in goods." Interestingly, the article describes an insurance operation with one characteristic that became a hallmark of AIG under Greenberg: "His operations form a vast and intricate web, the outer limits of which no one knows."

The article concluded: "His is a machine-gun mind, tactful at times, but often tough. At the psychological moment he will thrust out his jaw, which, with his glasses, is the most prominent feature of his face. He is forever on the go—Shanghai to New York, New York to London, London to Singapore. He goes with, and in quest of, ideas, talks insurance everywhere, spreads his interests out through Asia. . . . In his rare periods of quiescence he lives with a maiden aunt on the eighth floor of the North-China Building, No. 17, The Bund, where Asia Life and American Asiatic are also housed. He belongs to the usual Shanghai clubs, dines out, drinks sherry flips solemnly in corners of hilarious night clubs. He is not really social. And he has never married."

The maiden aunt was Nelle Vander Starr, who served as secretary of the Asia Life Insurance Company. She had been trained in the life insurance business in Chicago and joined Starr in 1923. She very efficiently managed both Asia Life and his household. When he traveled on business, she sometimes disallowed portions of his expenses, telling him he spent too much. Ultimately, Starr moved to Shanghai's Broadway Mansions, across the Huangpu River, and had the penthouse apartment there until the war. (Today it is a four-star hotel.) He also had a house on Hungjao Road, about seven miles from The Bund. The Russian delegation lived in it for some years and the Chinese probably do now. It was a European-style house and he added to the gardens and built tennis courts.

A few years ago, AIG reopened the offices at No. 17, The Bund, taking its board of directors over for the ceremony. It was an emotional moment for Greenberg, other executives present, and those board members who could appreciate the AIG history and the remarkable development of going back to where you were founded over 80 years ago in a country that has been through war with the Japanese, a civil war, the Communist Revolution, and nearly three decades of isolation from the West.

Chapter 4

Starr and "Wild Bill" Donovan Use Insurance to Fight the Japanese

As Japanese influence increased in the 1930s, and especially after Japan invaded China, Starr began to use his newspapers as vehicles of his own opinion. He was outspoken in his opposition to the Japanese and their Great Southeast Co-Prosperity Sphere, but found he had to endure more than the slings and arrows of outraged subscribers. Incredible as it seems now, the swell of European opinion in the Far East supported the invaders. As Gould put it, Starr's *Post* "did a lot of kicking, squalling and upbraiding."

Starr did exercise some measure of caution, since he knew that strong opinions that lacked power are best kept quiet. On July 7, 1937, the Japanese attacked China, sending in thousands of troops and warships. They occupied Beijing and later occupied parts of Shanghai and

in December took Nanjing, the Kuomintang capital. But Japan was not
at war with the United States. According to Samuel Eliot Morrison,
History of United States Naval Operations in World War II, the bombing
of the *Panay*, a small river gunboat that patrolled the Yangtze River in
order to protect American commerce and American nationals during
the Chinese civil war, was deliberately planned by responsible Japanese
officers.

When Japanese forces were approaching Nanking, Chiang Kai-
shek's foreign office notified the American Embassy it must prepare to
evacuate. It did and the *Panay* was attacked repeatedly by shore batter-
ies who wanted to eliminate civilian influence from the Japanese government. On December 12, 1937, a series of Japanese Navy bombing
planes flew overhead and released bombs. A few minutes later, 12 more
attacked. Surprisingly, there were not many deaths or injuries.

The promptness and apparent sincerity of the Japanese apology,
with an offer to make reparation, turned away U.S. wrath. An inquiry
found a face-saving explanation and said it was all a mistake. U.S. sentiment was to avoid getting embroiled in the war.

In 1939, after the Japanese had occupied Shanghai, the offices of
the Chinese edition of the *Post and Mercury* were bombed and its editor, Samuel Chang, was gunned down in a café. One reason was the
paper's influence. *Ta Mei Wan Pao* had run its circulation up to 100,000,
the largest in Shanghai.

Starr marched grimly in the front row of pallbearers but took to
riding in a bulletproof limousine since he, as the newspaper's owner,
was threatened as well. Houghton (Buck) Freeman remembers Chang
as being a friend of Starr's (but not the proprietor of the newspaper);
in any case, Starr led the pallbearers to show solidarity. He didn't back
down an inch in his resistance to Japanese encroachment.

When the Japanese attacked the Chinese in Shanghai, the Starr
memorial booklet reports, incredibly, that many of the British and
French, and even many Americans, took the Japanese side. Starr stood
out like a sore thumb in this group and said the Japanese would swal-
low them all. The *Post* carried a front-page editorial headlined "To
Those Who Have Abused a Trust—Get Out!" Randall Gould noted
that one of the Japanese embassy men remarked to him, "Your paper is

very hard on us, but it is fair." Gould responded, "Neil demanded that things be that way."

With Japanese armies sweeping across Asia, Starr moved his headquarters to New York in 1939. Others followed. But many did not get out in time. A number of American International employees such as Clayton Seitz, a longtime executive, along with their families were interned throughout the war. Starr sent messages though the Red Cross: Your salaries will be continued and jobs await you when the war is over. Two years later virtually the entire Far Eastern operation was brought to a halt by the Pacific War. One old friend of Starr was Lucino Reggio, head of Shanghai's fascist party. He had a magnificent home with beautiful gardens and took the valuables of Americans in concentration camps and buried them in his garden in Maxwell House coffee cans.

After the Japanese occupied Shanghai, they put their own supervisor into the Starr office to wind up the business. Starr's chief accountant, Koong-Kai (K.K.) Tse, with an eye toward the future, persuaded them to put the firm's files and records into storage. He then convinced them that the bank next door should take over the furniture and equipment, as well as most of the ex-employees.

That is the AIG version of the story, as recounted in the Starr memorial booklet, only it's not true. Buck Freeman's version is one that AIG employees have heard for years as the gospel. The day after Pearl Harbor the Japanese entered Shanghai, and by Freeman's account, K.K. Tse took all the records and buried them in his backyard. Freeman does not know of a bank next door to the office, and if there was one it likely was closed, along with the rest of the banks, by the Japanese.

Eventually, the Japanese took control of his publishing enterprises, a while after they invaded Shanghai. After the Japanese attacked Pearl Harbor, Starr and Gould decided to publish a New York edition to help counter the Japanese propaganda that began to appear under his paper's respected logo in Shanghai. In the first-known Starr enterprise cooperation with U.S. intelligence services, something that became a tradition with AIG, in December 1942, Starr offered the *Shanghai Evening Post and Mercury* to the OSS (Office of Strategic Services) as a cover to gather intelligence and conduct operations against the Japanese. As a senior OSS special intelligence officer reasoned, "Newspapermen everywhere are expected to stick their noses into everybody's business. No suspicion attached to their curiosity. A newspaper is therefore automatically almost indestructible cover for the collection of information."

So on January 1, 1943, the OSS took up Starr's offer and started the New York edition of the *Shanghai Evening Post and Mercury* as an intelligence-gathering operation. On October 21, 1943, the Chungking edition was also started in the city that was General Chiang Kai-shek's headquarters. These two newspapers were to last until the end of the war as an OSS intelligence project, at which time the OSS had spent $350,000 on these two publications. By July 1944, 18 months after it became an OSS project, the *Shanghai Post* was a great success. From the China and New York bases, "data on over 5,000 individuals had been assembled and carefully edited covering . . . many nationalities who were collaborators."

When the war ended, Starr's news management returned to Shanghai but it wasn't but a few years before the coming of the Communists and the introduction of even more censorship. "If we can't have a free American newspaper we'll just stop the newspaper," Starr said. So ended a fifth of a century of trying to bring a free press to China.

But early in the war, Starr was visited in New York by "Wild Bill" Donovan, the founder of the OSS, the precursor to the Central Intelligence Agency. Donovan, who earned the Medal of Honor in World War I, wanted to use the Starr organization as a means to gather information. He recognized that the Starr organization was everywhere. For example, Mansfield Freeman was asked by the navy to supply all his family pictures taken at the beach. There were amusing nonintelligence incidents. Some of the AIU people doing intelligence work came to see Freeman in Beijing, where he was attached to the U.S. naval attaché office. What they wanted was not intelligence but cigarettes from the ship's store, since they could not find them anywhere else.

The really intriguing scheme only recently came to light when President Clinton declassified some intelligence documents with the intention of speeding the identification of Nazi assets. This was reported in 2002 in the *Los Angeles Times* by Mark Fritz in "The Secret (Insurance) Agent Men."

This article describes a World War II unit gathering underwriters' data, such as bomb plant blueprints. "They weren't just secret agents. They were secret insurance agencies. These undercover underwriters gave their World War II spymasters access to a global industry that both bankrolled and, ultimately, helped bring down Adolf Hitler's Third Reich." The unit was both OSS operatives and Starr's people, although driven by operatives.

These newly declassified U.S. intelligence files tell a remarkable story of this component of the OSS, and its elite counterintelligence branch X-2. "Though rarely numbering more than a half dozen agents, the unit gathered intelligence on the enemy's insurance industry, Nazi insurance titans and suspected collaborators in the insurance business." The unit mined standard insurance records for blueprints of bomb plants, timetables of tide changes, and thousands of other details about targets, from a brewery in Bangkok to a candy company in Bergedorf.

"They used insurance information as a weapon of war," said Greg Bradsher, a historian and National Archives expert on the declassified records.

The OSS insurance unit was launched in early 1943, long after it had become alarmingly clear that the Nazis were using their insurance industry not only to help finance the war but also to gather strategic data. Germany had 45 percent of the worldwide wholesale (reinsurance) insurance industry before the war began and managed to actually expand its business as it conquered continental Europe. As wholesalers, or reinsurers, these companies covered other insurers against a catastrophic loss. In the process, they learned everything about the lives and property they were insuring.

The motives of the OSS unit's founder were both patriotic and pragmatic. "This story is incredible because the unit begins as part of the desire of American insurance interests to contribute to the war effort and exploit it for future economic gain," said historian Timothy Naftali, a consultant to the Nazi War Criminals Interagency Working Group created by Congress.

The men behind the insurance unit were OSS head William "Wild Bill" Donovan and California-born insurance magnate Cornelius V. Starr.

This Insurance Intelligence Unit found that the Nazis did business through countries such as Switzerland and laundered transactions through South American affiliates, particularly Argentina.

Starr's people and other insurance executives had intimate knowledge of the people involved in the global insurance business, so they were able to track potential collaborators. The unit also investigated Americans. One report showed that an Argentine company owned by the American Foreign Insurance Association (AFIA), Starr's principal competitor overseas, had a known Nazi collaborator on its board and reelected him after it promised it wouldn't.

The unit had problems in the field, since agents operated without the knowledge of local American embassies, in places ranging from the Far East to North Africa. "One operative, a Starr insurance man named Bob Smith, traveled throughout China (generally those parts under nationalist control) and appeared in several local newspaper accounts as—what else?—a traveling insurance executive named Bob Smith."

The cables he sent back showed a man under heavy suspicion, often anxious to leave his post and uncertain of how to deliver his information. At one point, posing as an insurance man on a humanitarian visit to a leper colony, he stumbled on Japanese positions in South China. He subsequently speculated that he wasn't shot at because the enemy was too busy laughing at Smith's pratfall-plagued attempts to flee through a thicket on a bicycle.

As the war neared an end, U.S. intelligence officials focused greater attention on the ways the Nazis would try to use insurance to hide and launder their assets so they could be used to rebuild the war machine. The newly released OSS files show just how hard it is to track a paper trail through 50 years of mergers, acquisitions, secret deals, and silent partnerships. The files show that American insurance premiums almost certainly wound up in Nazi banks, and German brokers were secretly covering London establishments under attack by the Luftwaffe.

"It makes you wonder if a German insurer insuring an American ship went to the German military and said, 'Don't bomb this ship!'" Greg Bradsher said.

Starr sent insurance agents into Asia and Europe even before the bombs stopped falling and built what eventually became AIG, which had its world headquarters in the same downtown New York building where the tiny OSS unit toiled in the deepest secrecy. (AIG is currently headquartered at 70 Pine Street, previously the Cities Service Company headquarters. This location probably refers to 102 Maiden Lane, which was AIG headquarters earlier.)

Chapter 5

Turning the War to Advantage

T he war in the Far East obviously was a terrible setback for Starr, and could well have brought the entire business down. Instead, it provided the impetus for Starr to accelerate the diversification that he had begun a decade before, laying the foundation for today's global AIG. Not one, but two unique opportunities presented themselves during the war, and Starr immediately seized upon them. The bottom line: The Second World War, terrible as it was, was propitious over the longer term for the Starr enterprises.

Starr had turned his attention to Latin America back in 1932. At the time, Latin America's insurance markets were ruled by insurers from three countries: Italy, Germany, and, running a distant third, England. Starr first ventured there by acquiring the Central American operations of an American insurer that was shuttering its foreign operations. The man he put in charge was George Moszkowski, another refugee (this time from Poland) who landed in Shanghai shortly after Starr first opened shop there and found Neil Starr soon after Starr established his business. Starr transferred Moszkowski to New York in 1929. Three years later he negotiated the purchase of the Central American business. Later, John Roberts recalls George Moszkowski being designated liaison in New York because the chairman of Texaco, American Asiatic Underwriters' biggest account, said American International needed a liaison office in New York, since we can't always depend on communications with Shanghai.

The war created a vacuum that an aggressive company like AIU, Starr's non-life company, could fill. Moszkowski relocated to Cuba in 1941, where he ran the Latin American operations until his death in 1952. Cuba was AIU's biggest operation by far, but Moszkowski opened businesses in half a dozen Latin American countries in rapid succession. The business was spectacular. By 1945, in only four years, premium income for AIU (the non-life company) in Latin America surpassed the Asian revenues it took 20 years to develop when Starr started American Asiatic Underwriters in 1919.

Someone like me, who had in his AIG job description 30 years later to do what Moszkowski made look like a piece of cake in the 1940s, can only be envious and realize that in some ways it would have been easier to live in a different era. The Latin American environment of the 1970s and 1980s was far different. In the earlier era the mood was not as nationalistic and was fairly pro-American. So while AIU in the 1940s was opening offices, getting a good manager and staff, and making tons of money, by the 1970s the manager needed to be not only a top salesman but also a diplomat who understands government and relationships. His primary job is to protect the company from nationalization or partial nationalization, or being forced to sell the majority of ownership, from currency controls, and general harassment. With the change in Latin America, AIU could never be duplicated again. So the existing franchise has a great advantage over competitors.

The second diversification move was in Europe. Before the war, AIU's European operations had been confined to small agencies in Belgium, France, and Holland. But the war fundamentally transformed these markets and the European economy in ways that facilitated AIU's expansion. First, the war left the large European insurers financially strapped, short of the insurance capacity needed by recovering European industries. Second, as American commerce went overseas, there were enormous opportunities for AIU. There is an old axiom in the insurance business about insurers "following the flag." This was a perfect example.

AIU used the same model to enter both Germany and Japan in the same year, 1946, having one ostensible purpose—to serve American troops. There is little a defeated country can do to object to an invitation from a victorious country to one of its insurers to come in to serve its troops. What started as a limited franchise eventually became a major operation serving the entire market.

About this time Starr sent a newcomer perceived as rising star, John J. Roberts, to work in the brokerage houses of London and in a Lloyd's of London syndicate before moving on to France to develop new business. He and Buck Freeman were among the first sent to London to work with Willis Faber and other brokerage houses. Roberts went on to serve in a number of executive positions but initially he went to France to help develop business resulting from the Marshall Plan. DeGaulle nationalized a number of French insurance companies, which provided AIU the staff they didn't have.

This was a difficult time to be in France because of food and housing shortages. Generally, Roberts and his family did okay in selected hotels and restaurants. He was told to see a man often called the last American aristocrat, David K.E. Bruce, Andrew Mellon's son-in-law, who was the Ambassador for the Marshall Plan. There were opportunities because the French had little foreign currency, especially dollars, and wanted to import everything. So John and his colleagues talked to agents all over France with the intent of insuring imports and paying for losses in dollars.

When this assignment was over, Roberts was sent back to New York to report to AIU President Jimmy Manton for a new assignment. His wife, Nan, was expecting a child at any time and he said: "Have it on board the ship and it will have three nationalities: French, English, and American." It didn't happen. By the time he reached New York, he had been selected to be the general manager of Italy. He had worked for the company, starting as a trainee, and slightly less than two years later, he was a country manager.

He visited Starr before leaving and asked for advice—advice that Roberts gave out to trainees ever after: "I expect you to be honest, hardworking, and treat the company as if you own it. You won't make too many mistakes."

In 1956, he was made AIU's regional manager for Europe and the Middle East. He worked closely with Artemis Joukowsky, Sr., who was Roberts's boss for Europe and was responsible for opening Pakistan and India. The Middle East operations started with an Aramco contract, and AIU put a claims operation there. Starr visited Beirut on his way from the Far East and was very enthusiastic. It reminded him of the beehive of Hong Kong, and he launched an ALICO (formerly Asia Life) operation.

This period was one of tremendous expansion and illustrates how a young man can catapult ahead dramatically.

AIU expanded in Europe, the Middle East, North Africa, and Australia. By the end of the 1950s, AIU was represented in approximately 75 countries around the world. Roberts ultimately became chairman and CEO of AIU, an AIG director, and its vice chairman of external affairs.

People would often remark that John Roberts looked like the chief executive officer. Placing him and diminutive Hank Greenberg together was like the Mutt and Jeff characterizations in the old comic strip. John, 6'4" or so, erect, full fleshed, with wavy white hair. Hank, 5'7" or so, trim, straight-backed, with eyes that would burn through you. John was the perfect image of what a CEO is supposed to look like. Nevertheless, it was clear that Hank was in charge. If you had any doubt, Hank would tell you.

While opening business in Germany and spreading across Europe, Starr made the reestablishment of the Far Eastern business his first priority. American International was the first foreign company of any kind, insurance or otherwise, to resume business in Shanghai. K.K. Tse was at the center of this reopening as he had been at the center of the shutdown. The day after V-J Day, K.K. dug up the files in his backyard. He then rehired the employees and bought equipment to operate again. Less than two weeks after the Japanese surrender, he cabled back to New York: "We are ready to go back into business."

Starr chartered a plane for Shanghai, bringing with him a suitcase full of greenbacks. Inflation was rampant in the city, and the U.S. dollars bulwarked the enthusiasm of the employees and gave the Chinese clients a much-needed sense of security. Starr also brought along a large supply of medicines, an almost forgotten commodity in a city that had long been sealed off from the world.

While Starr had become wealthy as he built his companies over 20 years, he had not accumulated the kind of capital he needed to really expand and grow the company. However, the Starr companies are true risk takers, and a highly risky opportunity presented itself at the end of the war. There was a flotilla of boats, about 20 in all, sitting in Shanghai harbor waiting to take people out of China and back home, but nobody would insure the boats. Nobody but Starr, that is. He had them checked closely for safety, watched them nervously until they reached their destinations, and collected an insurance premium of $1 million per boat. If just one of the fleet had sunk, Starr could have been out of business since he had no reinsurance on the transactions. All told, he made about $20 million on this one transaction. Insuring this fleet gave Starr his first really significant capital.

Mansfield Freeman returned with a number of colleagues about this time to ascertain what was left of the business. They found all their records not only intact but also "neatly labeled by the Japanese and left in apple-pie order." Obviously, there is a conflict between this explanation and the story of K.K. Tse burying the records, unless the life and general insurance operations were totally separate. Freeman traveled the area and was flabbergasted to discover that in Saigon, where the companies remained open throughout the war, they had made a tidy profit. Since they had had no contact with the office for several years, they were astonished.

Starr also visited there, where the general manager was Basil deBordesky, a Russian naval cadet who was kicked off his ship for being against the Russian Revolution and ended up in Saigon. He ran the office and operated it during the war with French-American flags on the stationery. At that time, the French easily gave citizenship to people like him, which was called a nansen, an international passport. And the Japanese left him alone during the war. Starr asked where all the money was, and Basil took him to the back room where it was stored in a safe.

Starr next moved to reopen in the Philippines. This had been Asia Life territory, but in 1947, in a gesture of confidence for the brand-new, war-scarred republic, he incorporated Philippine America Life Insurance Company. A sign that the company had arrived was the kind of high-profile political talent Starr attracted from the beginning. The chairman was Paul McNutt, a former governor of Indiana and U.S. ambassador to the Philippines. Starr recruited Earl Carroll, an American prisoner of war in China who married the wife of another prisoner, as president. General Jesus Vargas, who later became secretary-general of SEATO, was another high-level executive.

Earl Carroll became a legend in the Philippines and a star at American International. He was an absolutely extraordinary salesman. Within a decade, the company had 60 offices throughout the island nation. It was recognized for its enlightened practices that helped the country recover from the war and grow. Philamlife endowment policies provided Filipino farmers and small merchants with a means to build their savings in areas where banks were not to be found. The company in turn utilized these policyholder funds to promote national development, investing in key local infrastructure projects. Philamlife received international attention for developing middle-income housing in the early 1950s, a period of acute housing shortage in the island nation.

Starr thought long and hard about what would be good investments for a company to make with its reserves in a foreign country, especially a developing country. He chose mining, agriculture, banking, and glass. Stocks were risky, but because his companies developed close contacts in government, they had an inside track in local commerce, and the Starr companies did all right in the local stock markets as well. Starr's policy on investments was followed throughout the region.

Until you visit the Philippines you cannot accept just how visible and well-thought-of Philamlife is and how much of an impact the company has had. It sounds like corporate propaganda, but the company truly is viewed very favorably by Filipinos. I can testify to that from my visits to the islands. The derogatory comments commonly made about American companies are rarely heard. The company seems to have offices everywhere. Also, it continues to attract powerful leaders.

Cesar Zalamea, a Filipino, just retired after many years of leading the company and taking on much bigger roles as well. At one point some 20 years ago, President Marcos decided he wanted Zalamea to leave Philamlife to head the Central Bank. We cheered in New York, but Zalamea put up a mighty resistance. However, saying no to Marcos was very tricky business, so he finally took the job. Cesar returned to Philamlife after his stint in government.

Philamlife built a large, magnificent auditorium, carved of a local wood in a traditional Filipino style. It is used frequently, generally for cultural events and the occasional political affair, having nothing to do with the company's business. It serves as a public reminder of the company's role in the life of the country.

In 1943, John Roberts, still in the army, was hired by Brock Park, of Starr, Park and Freeman. He was paid nothing but told to report to duty when the war was over, and he did in 1945. The thriving business in the Philippines was at the center of the only serious attempt to wrest control of the company from Starr. There would not be another succession fight until Starr was near the end of his life. The creation of Starr, Park and Freeman, a partnership consisting of Starr, Mansfield Freeman, and Brock Park, was formed in China but heavily focused on the auto business in the Philippines. Park, like most of Starr's colleagues, was not trained in insurance but apparently was involved with the OSS in southern Europe. Park's second wife was the daughter of one of the senior people in Sedgwick Collins, a prominent insurance broker in Europe. Starr wanted to expand to Europe but Park, perhaps to protect his father-in-law's business, opposed the move on the grounds it would be too expensive. A more important issue was an automobile insurance agency the company had set up in the Philippines. Starr found this a very dirty business, especially in the Philippines, where there were lots of kickbacks and unethical practices, and he wanted out. Park liked the profits and wanted to keep the agency going.

When Starr was out of the country, reportedly in Brazil, Park tried to enlist others to mount a coup against him. Starr was alerted and returned promptly, but there was very little support for Brock, anyway. Starr generously bought out Park, who went to Manila and eventually retired to Bermuda. His first wife, Helen Graham Park, was close to Starr and was the company decorator for many years. Later in the 1940s, after this incident, Starr established C.V. Starr and Company, which became the senior company and repository for true control of the group throughout his life.

The strategy for the rest of Southeast Asia was similar. Starr had acquired a minority interest in a relatively small life insurance company, the International Assurance Company, before the war. In 1948, he took over majority interest, added the prefix "American" to its name, and assigned it the entire territory of Southeast Asia. Clearly, putting "American" in your company name was a big plus immediately after the war. While the United States is no longer held in such high favor, AIG companies have established such a reputation that American International is still a good marketing tool. Most citizens would rather have their insurance with such a company.

American International Assurance Company took off under the leadership of G.M. "Barney" Hughes, an American with extensive experience in the Far East. Written premiums doubled within a year of Hughes's arrival. It expanded from its Hong Kong base to Malaysia, Singapore, and Thailand. Today, AIA is the No. 1 life insurer in Southeast Asia.

General MacArthur, commander of forces in Japan, wanted an American insurer to insure American military occupation troops. Starr had tried to enter Japan before the war, but only one American company, the AFIA, was there and Starr could not get permission. Starr knew General MacArthur, had good contacts in Washington, and had people like McNutt to advance the cause politically. By 1946 he had an invitation from MacArthur to open shop in Japan with the specific and limited authority to cover the insurance needs of the American military. The Japanese government had barred new foreign insurance ventures after the great earthquake of 1923 and said they would continue to be barred until they were properly compensated. It took until 1951 before the ban on foreign companies underwriting general insurance was lifted. Afterwards, AIU began a period of tremendous growth and today Japan is AIG's largest overseas property-casualty market.

Showing his usual astute real estate judgment, Starr found a piece of property on the edge of the grounds of the Imperial Palace next to the Tokyo Hotel. Some AIG employees believed this was property of the emperor and that Starr bought it to get on his good side. This is a myth. The hotel belonged to a keiretsu that was closed down by the occupation and never recovered. The catch with the property was that it had a dormitory that housed employees working in that area. Thus no one else wanted it, since it was almost impossible to get them out. Starr's people hired an ex-gangster—some would say not just an ex-gangster—to "vacant" the building. One by one he negotiated with the employees and found them locations elsewhere in town. The great majority was evacuated, except one group—the employees of the Hotel Tokyo refused to move. So he took off the roof. They sued and claimed their belongings were ruined. The courts ruled they would have to move but held the Starr companies responsible for damage to their belongings. Still, this was a rather inexpensive cost in securing such prime real estate. Today, the AIG building stands on this site, overlooking the Imperial grounds in a very desirable part of a major business district in Tokyo.

Again and again, Starr made similarly astute real estate judgments, buying and developing properties that returned many times their cost to AIG.

Besides the new ventures in Asia, the old business picked back up in the rest of Asia and was as strong or even stronger than before the war, with one exception—China. While business was okay, it never regained its prewar status and importance. Especially slow was life insurance, which dragged throughout this period. This was strange, since the combination of the return of Western countries and the fear of the relentless progress of the Communist Party should have made the Chinese more receptive to life insurance, especially life insurance sold by a foreign-owned company.

One of the few misjudgments about the Chinese that Starr ever made concerned the advent of Mao and the Communist Party. In 1949, as they advanced on Shanghai, Starr took the view these were really agrarian reformers whose greatest interest was the countryside and that he would be able to do business with them. He was clearly in a one-man minority among his colleagues. One of the Russians he had hired adamantly stated: "I am getting out of here. A commie is a commie."

This man was in Shanghai with his wife and mother-in-law, who was stateless. He and his wife could go to the Philippines but the Philippine government wouldn't allow the mother-in-law to enter the country. So he went to Bob Miller, one of the senior people in Shanghai, and said he would give him $5,000 to marry his mother-in-law. "You don't have to consummate the marriage," he said. "Just take her to Vancouver and leave her on the docks." Miller demurred. As resourceful as the other Russians Starr had hired, he found another way to get the mother-in-law out and ended up in Rio de Janeiro, where he became AIG's chief underwriter and moved up in the company.

Within four years, the advance of the Chinese Communists closed the entire operation, which by then included a number of businesses besides insurance. As the Communist advance became more threatening, on January 1, 1949, K.K. Tse transferred the regional headquarters to Hong Kong and airlifted out 40 employees and their families, along with the company records. The local operations in China continued until voluntarily closing in late December 1950.

Buck Freeman was intimately involved with these final days in China since he followed in his father's footsteps, working for Starr. Buck left Wesleyan to enter the navy and spent a year of language training in Japanese. "They heard I'd been born and raised in China and they believed that anyone who knew one Oriental language could easily pick up another, which isn't true." Freeman spent most of his war years in intelligence activities within China. Freeman remembered his boyhood years when American International only had about 10 executives and many would come to his house for lunch on Sunday. He remembers Starr, a former high jumper, teaching him to jump. After graduation in 1947, Starr took him to lunch and asked him to join the company. He jumped at the chance, feeling a special affinity from having grown up in the American International family and thinking it was a great opportunity. He joined American International Underwriters and was sent to England to be trained at Lloyd's of London. When he sailed home a year later on the *Queen Elizabeth,* he brought with him an English bride, Doreen.

His first posting with the company was in Shanghai, Freeman's boyhood home, but his tour of duty was cut short when the Communists took over the city in 1949. When K.K. Tse and most of the company's staff transferred to Hong Kong, Freeman and a small crew stayed in the hope that business could be done with the Communists. It soon became apparent that the Communists wouldn't let them sell insurance in Shanghai, but the company had other interests—a bank, the newspaper (the *Shanghai Evening Post and Mercury*), a real estate company, an apartment building, and franchises for both General Motors and Chrysler automobiles. This suggests just how extraordinary an entrepreneur Starr was. The small insurance operation he founded 30 years earlier now included businesses in six industry sectors.

Since the Chinese Communist takeover, AIG has embraced another company belief of mythological proportions, that, alas, is not true. What is true is almost as colorful. I had always heard that the paper had continued for some time until the editor, Randall Gould, got on his soapbox and started making speeches about freedom of speech. Then he was jailed and it took Starr's personal intervention to get him out of jail and out of the country. That is not the way Buck Freeman tells it.

Gould was very pigheaded and wrote a scathing editorial about free speech the very first day of Communist rule. And the newspaper was the first of the Starr enterprises to be closed. When the authorities closed it down, the workers, 150 strong, their relatives, everyone but the paper's reporters, vociferously demanded payment of their wages from Gould. His office was a few blocks from the AIU office and he hid there, but the workers found him and blockaded the building. This was not only the workers but relatives, grandmothers, everybody. After some days, he was getting very hungry. In an effort to help him hold out, Freeman and others consulted a doctor, who told them to feed him a rich and nutritious chocolate drink that would enable him to last a long time. So Freeman and his colleagues put it in the tube container that held the toilet paper in the men's room and told Gould to go to the bathroom and he would find it in the third stall on the left. He didn't know their baths and was ranting and raving that he couldn't find it, and the Communist guards in the building found it first. Ultimately, he capitulated and paid a settlement to the workers.

"Gradually, they moved in on all our enterprises and we had to close shop," says Freeman. The next thing to fold was insurance. The language of insurance had nothing to do with the Communist system, at least at that point. Later, Communist countries put in their own state insurance enterprises. The basic approach at this time, however, was that whoever has the most money pays the other. So if AIU was insuring an auto in an accident, the other guy is always right and AIU pays.

The final straw came when AIU insured a Chinese-owned cargo ship going up and down the coast from Hong Kong to Shanghai. This was a dangerous voyage because nationalists on Taiwan bombed everything they thought was Communist. The insurance excluded war risk because the owner declined it as being too expensive. The nationalists bombed and sank the vessel. The owner told the captain to go see Freeman and he would pay his salary. Bob Miller and Freeman were handling the last days of the company in Shanghai and decided to leave the decision to the people's court in Shanghai. They foolishly thought it might be internationally minded and know international law. Because of this, both were restricted to Shanghai and couldn't leave. Since most policies ran a year, they had to wait them out, anyway. So they closed the office, played tennis, and waited.

Freeman's daughter, Linda, was born during these uncertain days. "When Doreen went to the hospital, it was being managed in true Communist style, with the costs borne each day by those patients who happened to be in it. If there were 100 people in it on a given day, the costs were incurred by 100; if there were three patients, the costs were divided by three. Linda was a $10,000 baby, a lot of money in those days."

Freeman secured passage for himself, Doreen, and 10-day-old Linda on a refugee ship headed for Hong Kong, but they came very close to missing the boat. "A claim had been made against the company in the people's court," he recalls, "and no one was allowed to leave the country if any litigation was pending. The ship was due to leave on a Friday. On Thursday, the summons arrived. We were assured that only our testimony was required, and once it was given in court, we could leave.

"The proceedings started about 6 P.M. The judge opened the proceedings by asking wasn't Shanghai a wonderful place. I said yes,

I spent 20 years here and grew up here." Then the judge, who had never before been in a big city and was not really a judge, began with a panegyric to the Shanghai skyline, asking Freeman if there were any buildings in America taller than those in Shanghai like the Park Hotel. "In Shanghai, the tallest buildings were about 13 stories high," says Freeman, "so I told him that in New York City probably two-thirds of the buildings were at least twice as high. He didn't believe it. He said, 'In America, your problem is that your workers are all oppressed.' I said, 'Yes, if owning their own homes and automobiles is what you call being oppressed.' By then he was frowning, and he said, 'You have a great deal of difficulty in the United States with the Ku Klux Klan.' I finally realized what I had to do and I said, 'Yes, we certainly do.' Then he beamed like a Cheshire cat as we'd found a topic we could agree on. So then we talked about the case and we gave him the information he needed and he gave us permission to leave.

"It was 10:30 before I got home that night—but what a relief!"

When they boarded ship the next afternoon, nobody could bring much baggage, but, Freeman says, "Everyone brought booze—the best scotch and brandy they could find. There were a lot of young men from the oil companies, like Texaco and Standard Oil; they all got tight that night and, up on deck, they began singing the Nationalist anthem, "San Min Jui." That made the Communists onshore absolutely furious, of course; they stormed onto the ship and refused to let it sail until the captain found the perpetrators.

"You never saw people sober up so quickly. The hero of the occasion was the captain, who hustled all the singers below and told them to stay out of sight, then somehow managed to appease the Communists and calm them down."

Starr left Charlie Miner, the senior executive in Shanghai, to close up the rest of the business. They had to pay people on the bombed cargo ship some $300,000, which was heavily reinsured with Lloyd's, and it covered most of the costs. Freeman explained they had to run off their insurance policies such as fire but they were only in effect for one year. Starr was not back in the life business yet, but there was life insurance outstanding before World War II and AIA paid off all they could find. They ran ads in the newspapers but never found many of the insureds. The payment was in local currency.

K.K. was in Hong Kong meeting with the unions with each entity having a union bargaining for their people. Banks went down next, then the real estate company, but the Chinese had expropriated it all, anyway. The auto agencies were closed and spare parts were sold off to pay the employees. Starr had to send in about $500,000 to pay off final amounts due. Starr did not have to do this but chose to. Nobody thought about filing an expropriation claim. The main concern was to pay off or extradite employees and leave the country with as little pain as possible. It was about 1½ years before Charlie Miner completely closed down the operation and exited to Hong Kong.

Starr had already found a perfect manager for his new but limited Japanese operations. It was Mansfield Freeman's son. Buck's facility with languages served him well during his long career in the Far East. The ship took the Freemans to Hong Kong and then to Japan, their home for the next 20 years.

This was September 1949, and in that postwar economy, everything revolved around the military. Primarily, they filled the military's insurance needs. "It was a fascinating era. Japan was just beginning its reconstruction. There were no factories making automobiles, there was no electronics industry, they hadn't started making transistor radios. Taxis were running on charcoal. The only vehicles people could get were those discarded by U.S. military personnel. The Japanese patched up heaps that we would have considered total write-offs."

American International Underwriters wanted to get into the Japanese market itself, not just cover American soldiers, and, after many years, made a breakthrough with automobile insurance. In those days, under a typical Japanese policy, the owner of a car had to bear 25 percent of any loss from an accident. "Japanese companies didn't have claims departments," says Freeman, "so the driver, after he ran over somebody, would have to jump out of his car and negotiate with the victim.

"Like everybody else, the Japanese preferred to have someone else do such talking for them, and we provided that service. We became the most popular company in Japan for automobile insurance and soon . . . [others] began to copy us. Now they have overtaken us in the automobile field, but we're still the largest foreign company for general insurance in Japan, far and away."

When he returned to the United States in 1970, Buck Freeman was first put in charge of all the company's operations in the Far East and Japan; later he took over direction of all overseas operations, which accounted for 40 percent of the company's business. Then he became president of American International Underwriters and a director and senior vice president of American International Group.

Chapter 6

Business Is Pleasure and Pleasure Is Business

Mary Starr may not have been everyone's favorite even if she was the boss's wife, but she was beloved by many if the number of AIG people attending her memorial service in New York after her death in Paris in 2005 is any indication. Starr married Mary Malcolm in 1937 when he was 44 years old, later in life than most. She was born in China, the daughter of a Canadian missionary. It was Starr's only marriage and the second for Mary, who previously had been married to a British regimental officer. Mary would have been in her 20s, some 20 years younger than Starr, and would marry once again to a difficult but accomplished artist.

Neil Starr was a complex man. He grew up to be a scrappy, instinctive entrepreneur, but was raised working class, without advantages, in a small town in California. From his teenage years, he was eager to succeed. He tried law, college for a while, real estate, insurance, had an ice cream parlor, dabbled with journalism. He seemed to always be looking for something he could grab on to, always with a view to climbing the ladder to wealth, importance, and prominence in society.

And he did. He succeeded as his dreams told him he could. "He suffered his greatest defeat," as John Roberts, former chairman of AIU, put it, "in his marriage."

Starr married very late for his era. Most married in their early 20s, even though the war delayed marriage for a few years. Back then you were considered old at 55. Starr was a late bloomer romantically. But he fell head over heels in love. And he was in love with only one woman his entire life. He indulged her, was devoted to her. Yet he held on to her for only 15 years. And what a bittersweet loss. She left him for a man whose vocation was his avocation. If Starr had a failure, it was this one—failure to hold on to a woman he really cared about, a failure that saddened him the rest of his life.

Roberts's explanation is that he overmanaged Mary, who was one of three sisters from a sweet, lovely, gracious family. A beautiful woman, artistic. John suggested I had seen some of her work—usually flowers or scenes of Paris—at AIG or Morefar. Starr should have let her career blossom, but got her into the dress business with Elinor Garnett instead of simply setting her up to paint.

When she left from St. Anton to go to Paris, she left everything. Money, the Rolls Royce, everything. She simply said she was leaving and wasn't interested in "things."

In the years before he married, it is doubtful Starr had the time (much less the inclination) to be a ladies' man or enjoy the nightlife of Shanghai, the Paris of the East. He worked constantly and loved to travel. He had his friends and ways he liked to relax. The need for women did not seem a part of his makeup. This is not atypical of the American International family. Most executives are married, with one or two exceptions. For those who are, marital indiscretion is not part of the unofficial corporate culture. It is a fairly straightlaced bunch, who, while enjoying generous expense accounts, puts business first. To Starr, from the time he married in 1937 until the painful split (painful to Neil at least) 15 years later, the couple seemed to have a wonderful time, with extensive world travel and a rich and satisfying life. Marion Breen, Starr's first cousin and secretary for nonbusiness matters, later to become vice president and a director of his foundation, tells about her first year working for Starr. He had visited her in Chicago and persuaded her to come to work for him. Right after she arrived in New York, Neil, Mary, and Marion left on a round-the-world trip that lasted an entire year. Marion said Mary seemed to love the trip and the couple was happy, traveling constantly. Starr was clearly restless and loved to travel, but, according to Marion Breen, so did Mary.

No one knows why there were no children or if they could have even had children. Many have commented on Starr's love for children but others have said he really preferred young adults. What he seemed to appreciate was young people he could converse with, learn from, and give advice to. In fact, providing scholarships is the principal priority of the Starr Foundation, to which he left his estate. In any case, the separation was a blow Starr never recovered from. One executive close to Starr, Ernie Stempel, president of AIRCO, grew to hate Mary Starr for the effect her leaving had on Neil. She was a beautiful woman, but, according to Stempel, was indiscreet in her life in Shanghai. Another executive agrees with that assessment. Nevertheless, even Stempel said the one thing he sympathized with Mary about was that everything with Starr was business. There would almost always be business acquaintances around, even if they weren't discussing business. On the trip around the world with Marion Breen, most meals would have been Neil, Mary, Marion, and one or more business associates. She might have wondered about Starr's affection and certainly questioned his priorities. She might have craved other diversions.

Starr was at Lookout, the picturesque house above the beach in Hong Kong, with Stempel, when he got the word from Mary that she wanted a divorce. He was so distraught he could hardly speak one moment and was raging angry the next. He felt the same years later. As Stempel put it, "Starr was truly a one-woman man." Mary Starr was the woman he loved and always would. Starr asked Stempel to talk to Mary in St. Anton, Austria, where she was. From Hong Kong to St. Anton was not the easiest trip, but Stempel did it only to find Mary had departed shortly before his arrival.

Mary Starr left Neil Starr for Constantine Kluge, an artist who had been raised in Shanghai. Ironically, they met because Starr hired Kluge to paint a portrait of Mary in New York. It is not clear whether they knew each other before then. Starr and Mary had moved to New York years before. Ultimately, the portrait fell into AIG's possession and when

Ann and Clare, two daughters of Gordon Tweedy's, who later would become chairman of C.V. Starr & Co., tried to obtain it (presumably for Mary), Greenberg refused but let Ann Tweedy see it. Today, the presumption is that it is stored in the bowels of AIG headquarters at 70 Pine Street in New York.

Kluge was born in Riga, Latvia, of Russian parents, in 1912. His family was well educated and came from an aristocratic background. Kluge's father was drafted into the Czar's army in 1914, but then the chaos of the 1917 Bolshevik Revolution completely uprooted the family. They moved frequently, but always eastward, until they ended up in the French concession of Shanghai in 1925. Kluge finished high school there and was an active member of the Shanghai Art Club. His parents decided that pure art was not a dependable career, and in 1931 Kluge left Shanghai for Paris to study architecture. He graduated in 1937 with the title of French government architect. He stayed in Paris for a while but then returned to China to practice architecture. He also began to paint seriously and concluded that painting could offer him a livelihood. Kluge remained in Shanghai throughout the war and was convinced he avoided trouble with the Japanese occupiers because of their respect for painting. In mid-1946 he accepted an architectural post in Hong Kong but continued to paint. The rumor that the Chinese Communists might invade Hong Kong convinced him to leave Asia for good and return to Paris. From that time until his death in 2003, two years before Mary Starr died, he was a successful painter and won numerous awards.

Mary joined up with him in Paris and became a painter herself, reverting to her maiden name for her work—Mary Malcolm. They married but divorced after some years, primarily because Kluge was a manic depressive. Mary remained in Paris the rest of her life and lived a comfortable life, thanks largely to Neil Starr.

Starr sent both Artemis Joukowsky and Gordon Tweedy to help him settle with Mary and clean up their affairs. Joukowsky's son tells of his father "having some 20 suitcases of clothes to deliver to her, but she didn't want them"—just as she had apparently not wanted a Rolls Royce or numerous other things Starr tried to give her. Starr genuinely loved her, but this gesture also reflected a trait that came out late in life when he seemed to be trying to buy friendship and love. For example, Starr spoke to Joukowsky Sr. about setting up a place for him at

Morefar, Starr's spacious estate in Brewster, New York, "because his place in Larchmont was too small for a man of his accomplishments." Joukowsky politely declined.

There are various notions as to what Starr did for Mary, including setting her up with a million-dollar endowment, but whatever it was, it was generous. A document written by Starr's lawyers refers to a trust for "Mary," which must be Mary Starr. His 1954 will notes that he had already provided for his wife but she abandoned him and forfeited her rights.

That same 1954 will left all his personal effects to Youngman, Mansfield Freeman, and Tweedy and provided for the establishment of the Starr Foundation. Neil Starr, as bitter and distraught as he was, though, generously provided continuing support for his wife that enabled her to live comfortably. Mary never brought a claim against Starr. She could have, even though she had left him. Ironically, when Neil and Mary were first married, he had taken steps to help her parents, who were in financial difficulties. Over the years, Mary grew close to Guy du Saillant, the AIG president in France, who was the brother-in-law of the president of France, Valery Giscard d'Estaing.

On one of my first visits to Morefar I noticed a large painting, a still life, in the room off the kitchen. I was told it was by Starr's ex-wife. At the time, I was too new to understand how sensitive Starr was about what happened. Later I wondered if the painting was there when he was alive and lived at Morefar or if it had been retrieved from storage later. From what I could intuit about Starr, I suspect it was there all along.

After the divorce Mary kept in touch with her friends from AIG through lunches and dinners in Paris, visits in New York and Paris, and exchanges of letters. Starr was amazingly tolerant as long as it was not flaunted at him, seemingly proud that he had had such a splendid wife that others hated to give her up. During a visit Mary made to New York around 1990, Howard and Clare Tweedy McMorris, Gordon and Mary Tweedy's oldest daughter and her husband, gave a dinner in her honor that included a number of AIG people, including several Chinese people. Mac (Howard) noted how the minute she entered the room, "it was as if she assumed the role of the chairman's wife. She reverted to Mandarin, which she spoke well because of her birth in China, and displayed a gracious and commanding presence."

Speculation on what would have happened to the Starr Foundation if the marriage had not ended is tantalizing. Created by Starr in 1955, the foundation was worth some $4 billion before the crash of AIG, larger than the Rockefeller Foundation, and one of the largest foundations in the country. Since Starr created the foundation several years after his split with Mary, would it be nearly as large or would there even be a Starr Foundation if he and Mary had stayed together? Would Starr have seen the need for a foundation if he had an heir? My guess is yes because of Starr's passion for helping young people attain the college degree he never attained. Clearly, more of the funds that went to the foundation would have been kept for Mary and the children. Probably, since Starr's death preceded Mary's by many decades, Mary's will would have been designed so that some or all of her assets reverted to the foundation.

Starr picked up his life after the divorce and carried on, dedicated as always to his business, but also to obsessive travel, by plane, steamship, train, riverboat, or whatever other means were available. Presumably, the travel was business related, but not all of it was necessary. Starr simply loved travel and felt at home wherever he went, but he also was driven to wander out of loneliness. During these years he also focused more than ever on helping young people, and continued to develop his interest in architecture and art. He also dedicated himself to the one sport he was passionate about—skiing—including developing a ski resort. While he had exhilarating moments—in business, on the slopes, with business friends and young people—associates say he was always sad and seemed lonely, even when people were around. This sadness remained with him the rest of his life. One of his young protégés, Raymond Bonham Carter, the father of actress Helena Bonham Carter, said: "He seemed to be a lonely figure who found it difficult to have many real friends among his contemporaries." As before, almost all his friends were colleagues from his company, except for the young people he sponsored.

How Starr found these youngsters was a bit of a mystery to his friends. At that point, the Starr Foundation was small so they all were financed from Starr's own checkbook. Starr's love for Asians was reflected in the number of recipients from that part of the world. Others came from different places where he would meet students—on tennis courts, ski slopes, or wherever. He liked having these young people around and he wanted to help them. "He was not always, I think, very discriminating in his choice of young people whom he befriended," says John Chancellor, an Englishman whom Starr helped when he was a student. "He found a great many of them on the ski slopes or in English universities. Is it possible that he romanticized the products of these environments? . . . Nevertheless, I was very fond of this kind, lonely, and brilliant man."

Many of these young people were invited to visit his estate in Brewster. Starr called this form of philanthropy "corrupting." One of his protégés, Daniel Ley, from Cambodia, says, "It was such a luxurious corruption that no young individual of limited means would ever think of refusing. . . . Many other people wished they were included on his list of corrupted minds. But I feel there were occasions when his influence was resented by those who were affected."

Another beneficiary was Wen-Shi Yu, whose father had served Starr as a steward. Starr showed his gratitude for faithful service by financing her education in physics. "He had the strange power of drawing the hearts of people, especially Chinese people, toward him as a magnet attracts a bit of metal," she says. On Starr's 74th birthday, a large group of his "corrupted" young friends sent him a silver tray. T.C. Hsu, his old friend from China and first of that group, selected this inscription from Aristotle:

They who educate children well are more honored than they who produce them; for these only gave them life, those the art of living well.

Whereas Starr came prodigiously early to some things, such as launching what would become a worldwide business when he was in his mid-20s, he came late to others. He didn't take up skiing until 1938, two years after his marriage. He soon developed such a passion for the sport that he was driven to find a convenient, comfortable place to ski near New York. As always, Starr was motivated by economics, the economics of skiing, as much as by his passion for the sport. At the time, skiing was in its infancy and, among other problems, it was not easy to get up the mountain you wanted to ski down. In most ski areas, people clung to machine-driven ropes that yanked them up the slopes.

Mt. Mansfield in Stowe, Vermont, had the largest and highest chair-lift in the United States, but the queue was interminable. Starr thought the business arrangement with separately owned lift, ski school, hotels, and land was pure business anarchy. So he and Sepp Ruschp, the Austrian ski school director at Mansfield, started buying up the pieces in the later 1940s. By 1950 the ownership of the various elements was all under the Mt. Mansfield Co. For an investment of $1 million, Starr launched the prototype of the modern ski resort. (Starr owned a house at Stowe, Brook House, which Greenberg always used after Starr's death. Mary's older sister, married to a man known as The Admiral, lived in Brook House for a while. Since C.V. Starr is the corporate entity that owns that house and that is outside AIG, Greenberg continues to use it.)

Starr later did something similar at St. Anton in Austria, the site where modern skiing was virtually invented. He built two double chairlifts capable of hauling 700 people an hour to the top and tried to persuade the locals to invest in the company. Whenever Starr would go to Anton, he always had a special place, as did his successor, Greenberg. Late in life, he decided to give the lifts to the citizens of Anton. As benevolent a move as this seemed, it struck his business colleagues as madness. They finally talked him into selling the lifts instead, but he tried to get the citizens of Anton, who made him an honorary citizen, to buy shares in it.

S tarr did not particularly like the opera, though he always kept a box to entertain a constant flow of guests ranging from business colleagues to a company secretary to Japanese diplomats. Mary Starr liked both the opera and the social occasion associated with it, but didn't want to go alone. So Starr found colleagues like Ernie Stempel, who liked the opera or would do it for Starr, had them to his penthouse for dinner, and then they would escort Mary to the opera; Starr would meet them afterwards. One could argue this was an example of how Starr was setting himself up for marital failure.

What Starr did like—loved, in fact—was the Orient. He cared for the Orient as it really was, not as Westerners thought it was. When he agreed to underwrite a new production of Puccini's *Madame Butterfly* in the 1950s, he insisted that it depict more of the real Japan that he knew and less of the mythical Japan that the opera had helped promulgate.

Miss Toshi Suzuki, the interior decorator, said Starr told her it was not to be the prettied-up versions that had traditionally been presented in the United States but an authentic production.

To get this underwritten and done the way Starr wanted, Rudolf Bing, general manager of the Metropolitan Opera and a strong personality in his own right, had to adjust himself to Starr and to Starr's schedule. He found it somewhat maddening. When Starr returned from a trip to Japan with at least two complete productions of *Butterfly* in sketches and swatches of gorgeous material, Bing was sold. They loved the simplicity of the set by Motohiro Nagasaka. Then came doing it. To have all the sets, props, costumes, and accessories made to order and shipped in time was a feat. After a successful opening, Starr invited everyone to a wonderful party where he put on Haori and Hakama (Japanese formal costumes).

Starr was always interested in art and architecture. He generally bought what he liked, although sometimes he would buy to help an artist or art dealer. Naturally he had an eye for Oriental art but he liked Occidental art as well. In his later years he loved the Fauve art and as he became more experienced with art, he developed a genuine interest in sculpture. If a sculptor he bought from did not come to see where Starr had placed the piece, it was the last piece he would buy from this sculptor. Starr's purchases are spread among American International facilities around the world, and some have appreciated tremendously in value—a Van Gogh, *The Stream at St. Remy,* and a Vlaminck, *Bords du Rivere,* among them.

What Starr could really put his arms around, however, was architecture. The time and involvement Starr devoted to the construction of a company building was extraordinary for the CEO of a significant corporation. His attitude was more like that of a small company CEO whose firm was going to put up its first building. Starr would think about it, sweat over it, picture the finished building, try to understand the history of the country and its architecture. Helen Graham Park, the first wife of the former business partner Brock Park, who actually tried to take over Starr's company, was the company decorator. In fact, she decorated most of the overseas offices. Starr's relationship with her and his affection for her was not the least bothered by the dispute with her ex-husband. She had a home at Morefar as well. Starr put up structures in Wilmington, Kuala Lumpur, Manila,

Karachi, Dhaka, Penang, Bangkok, Beirut, Guyana, Hong Kong, and Singapore.

In speaking about his striking building in Beirut, she noted that "he insisted that all his buildings . . . must look as though they belonged to the culture." Starr envisioned a horizontal building recalling the columnar repetition of the historical ruin of Baalbek. "That building is the showpiece of the Middle East and a deeply gratifying solution."

But Starr's building ambitions were often divisive in his own organization. Youngman argued with Starr repeatedly about a proposed building that would be ALICO's headquarters in Wilmington, Delaware. Even if ALICO were to be headquartered there, Youngman posited, the building Starr had in mind was unnecessary. Of course, Starr won out and hired the distinguished architect I.M. Pei, whose father, Tsuyee, was a governor of the Central Bank of China and director of a Starr company in China, to do the work. It took a long time to build and there were millions of dollars in cost overruns. Pei said about Starr: "He was a perfectionist. He wanted both utility and beauty. He came close to being an ideal client. . . . His buildings all look advanced, not hidebound, and they represent a progressive approach. . . ." There were similar arguments over building in Malaysia. Starr went to Kuala Lumpur and personally selected the largest and most open plot available. He was criticized for building more than could be rented. Today this building is rented, and another office block of the same size could easily be rented as well.

Helen Graham Park summed it up well: "He often said that he felt like a frustrated architect. . . ."

John Roberts sums up this remarkable man: "He was a great visionary, a very generous man. His perception of people was very discerning. He made some mistakes like a lot of people will. One of the most honorable men I ever knew. Great love of beauty, architecture, art, landscape. A very unusual man. A modern renaissance man."

Starr's lifestyle and habits were very expensive: sending youngsters to schools around the world; extensive travel; estates in Brewster, Hong Kong, and elsewhere; collecting art; pushing for expansive architecture construction worldwide; launching a ski resort; settling an ex-wife; and maintaining his penthouse at 930 5th Avenue (bought by Woody Allen after his death). Among his expenses was a continuing generosity to friends. Marion Breen has lived at 930 5th Avenue since 1948 and has full-time help and a cook. I would not be surprised if Starr gave the apartment to her and made provisions for her expenses. While some of this would have been costs borne by the company, those revenues weren't limitless, and some of these expenses caused dissent in the company.

I reviewed several summaries of Starr's federal tax returns from the late 1950s and early 1960s. As best as I could tell, the returns had only the deductions you would expect—mortgage, state and local taxes, and the like. Starr's annual federal taxes were only about $75,000, a remarkably low figure for a businessman of his stature and success! It is estimated that his taxable income was between $125,000 and $140,000 a year. Yet he had large expenses.

Some were legitimate business expenses—architecture, art purchases for offices, Mt. Mansfield—but the rest were not. Apparently, the way Starr covered these expenses was with money from C.V. Starr & Co. It is a private company and Starr was the major shareholder, but this would have caused considerable consternation from other shareholders like Bill Youngman and probably Hank Greenberg, Ernie Stempel, and Gordon Tweedy. Remittances to Starr meant less for them, especially if he took out more money than his share percentage of ownership justified.

This same striking disparity was revealed after Starr's death. He was the principal shareholder in a number of companies—AIRCO, SICO, C.V. Starr & Co.—and owned Morefar, Lookout, and other entities, yet his estate was valued at about $10 million. While this is not to be laughed at, especially for a man who landed in China 50 years earlier with a very small stake, it is not the estate you would expect a man of his success to have, even in 1960s dollars. He left most of his estate to the Starr Foundation, which today is worth nearly $4 billion. If Eliot Spitzer is correct and the correct values were not paid for foundation holdings sold to C.V. Starr and SICO by executors of the estate, it is worth $10 billion. The point is, most of the growth of the Starr fortune has been in the past 37 years under the formidable drive of Hank Greenberg. Starr began it and left an extraordinary franchise for Greenberg to build on, but it was Greenberg who drove that franchise to become a mammoth enterprise.

The remaining years of Starr's life were unhappy, painful, and frustrating. Many entrepreneurs have found it difficult to turn over their empires to someone else. Starr was no different. During the last years of his life, Starr was sick, still grieving over the loss of Mary, and yet trying to hold on to running his business, as well. Bill Youngman was the designated successor, and even before Starr became sick with emphysema, Starr would constantly override his decisions. Bernie Aidinoff, until recently an AIG director but a tax counsel to the company at the time, said Starr regularly overruled Youngman. This happened before his debilitating illness but continued after he was sick.

Youngman prepared a rather remarkable memo to shareholders of the privately held C.V. Starr about the situation in the spring of 1968 and asked that these issues be addressed at a shareholders meeting. It is striking in its frankness, although Youngman says he had asked to retire, so he apparently had decided that if he did not get total authority he would leave. Writing such memos was a Youngman habit. Maybe they helped him arrive at a decision. Maybe he just preferred to communicate by memo and not face to face.

Some extracts from the memo:

> I now say that I believe he is today too sick to have good judgment or to continue his management role. . . . I am sorry to say "the time has come." . . . at which I think he should get out of management completely.
>
> . . . but he has gone on setting salaries (viz. Donnally's $20,000 bonus for nothings, and Davis's children's scholarships) . . . and spending and giving away our company money (once more $30,000 plus to the Opera this winter, for example) without consulting us.
>
> Mr. Starr's flirtation with Fleming failed though he built for him a six-or-seven-hundred-thousand-dollar house in the outskirts of Beirut. [This at a time when $125,000 would buy a mansion in Greenwich or Darien, Connecticut.]
>
> Then there has been the matter of the Wilmington building—supposed to cost one or two million dollars, "never three," as he wrote to Youngman. Now it is costing eight and one-half million without completion or a tenant in sight.

AIRCO has a fundamental problem which Mr. Starr has con-stantly made worse—the more so now that he can only work a few hours a day—overhead is piled on overhead. . . . there is the Bermuda AIRCO staff; then there is Mr. Tweedy and the CVSCO life insur-ance . . . staff; then Mr. Starr, the Senior Director and staff; then Mr. Youngman, the Chairman of AIRCO, and staff; the New York Real Estate, Life Production and Finance Committees described below.

He has promised PHILAM stock to almost every PHILAM employee in sight. In Carroll's, Zalamea's, and my presence a year ago in Honkkong, he told Ferry, a relatively new employee, he was making him a millionaire in the lousy automobile business.

The proposal to build the Tokyo building, on which close to a million dollars has been spent on a half dozen different architects, is another serious problem. . . . Basically it is a proposal to take AIRCO land currently said to be worth some eight million and put up a nineteen-million-dollar building on it. (In recent years this has grown from a 4 to 5, to 6, to 8, to 10, to 12, to 15, to 18, to 19 million U.S. dollars and my guess is that it is still growing.)

Another sign of the effect of Mr. Starr's illness on him has been his tendency lately to criticise severely or attack almost everybody with whom he works. In recent months, he has criticized Greenberg for being greedy, rough and Jewish; Manton for being stupid; Ahlers for being narrow, bad with people and endangering the UBank in illiquid Latin American investments; Tweedy for being weak and run by Mrs. Tweedy; Roberts as being inadequate to run AIUO worldwide, hence he should share it with Buck Freeman; Freeman for not knowing the business; Stempel for being merely a caretaker and one who could not run and should not run AIRCO; even K.K. he says is no good in recruiting and training people or building replacements. . . . I would hate to hear what he says about "yours truly."

Another sign of Mr. Starr's illness is the ineptitude in participat-ing in recent negotiations. In the Seaboard Surety matter he contra-dicted Mr. . . . Mr. Starr did the same thing in the National Union Negotiations. . . . Mr. Greenberg did well to negotiate the price down below what Mr. Starr indicated was the value. In a luncheon with Superintendent Stewart of the New York Insurance Department, Mr. Starr denounced the Department and all regulation.

Starr's unhappiness and illness caused him to reach out for new friends. He periodically would hire someone new and unnecessary for the Starr companies. He would give out money indiscriminately. Psychiatrists say this represents a kind of insecurity. Who knows—he had his setbacks, but the principal one was his loss of Mary. Maybe that made him feel the way he did.

There was a dispute over a promised gift of shares from Starr to Tommy "the Cork" Corcoran, the famous Washington attorney who was a Roosevelt aide and longtime lawyer to Starr, which Youngman and Greenberg had to settle. Starr offered Bob Youngman, Bill Youngman's son, 10,000 shares of AIRCO and then apparently forgot about it. These traits are described by one person involved at the time as a desperate need to buy friendship. In any case, Youngman's effort to bring the situation under control failed. He said he loved Starr and that if he pushed too hard it would have killed him.

Thus on August 19, 1968, an article appeared in the *New York Times* announcing Starr's and Youngman's retirement, with Gordon Tweedy to succeed Starr as chairman of C.V. Starr & Co. and Maurice Greenberg to succeed Youngman as president.

Just before Christmas, on December 20, 1968, Starr died at his home in New York City. After memorial services held simultaneously in New York City and St. John's Cathedral in Hong Kong, the New York mourners debated whether they should go ahead with the Christmas party Starr had arranged for them at Stowe, Vermont. It was classic Starr—gifts for all, skis, the works—so the decision was made that they should go ahead with the party. There was one hitch—at the last minute, the customs and immigration people seized the Chinese who were to help serve the party. So the executives themselves played that role. No doubt, Starr would have been irritated at this interference with his plans, but delighted at the good spirit his friends had shown.

Chapter 7

Preparing to Be a
Public Company

S hortly after the war, Starr began taking the steps that would ultimately lead to the launching of a public company, American
International Group, although Starr would die shortly before this
happened. Over time, Starr realized he had a franchise that was immensely
more valuable than even he and his colleagues understood and would be
even more so as American business expanded overseas. Yet he did not
envision going public. What the American International companies were
missing was the ownership of domestic insurance companies, something
that had always been Starr's dream. With these, Starr would be able to
supply the needs of American multinationals domestically and internationally, and a potential powerhouse would be created.

To help him plan what needed to be done, he could draw on the
solid legal minds in the company—Bill Youngman, Gordon Tweedy,
Duncan Lee, and Frank Mulderig, who was a member of the in-house
law firm of Lee, McCarthy, and Mulderig. Later Mulderig would

become a director of C.V. Starr & Co. Most of these attorneys had
been at the company only a couple of years but had earned Starr's confidence. In any case, it was Starr who knew what he wanted to do.
They simply helped him carry out his strategy.

The one existing company that he decided to reorganize was Asia
Life, his oldest life company and the second company he founded
when he first opened in China in 1919. So in 1951, 30 years later,
Asia Life, after being relatively inactive for a decade, was renamed
the American Life Insurance Company (ALICO). Besides replacing the
old Asia Life offices in Asia, it aimed its sights at the unchartered areas
of the Caribbean, the Middle East, and Africa, following exactly the
strategy that had earlier given Asia Life its success in Asia: It offered life
insurance to locals whom national companies and expatriate companies had not been interested in. The company grew as the economies
of these countries grew.

Later, in the 1970s, ALICO followed AIU into the industrialized
markets where AIU was already established, opening offices in France,
Germany, and the United Kingdom. In 1972, again following AIU's
lead, ALICO was granted a full yen license in Japan, which in time
would become ALICO's largest territory. But like AIU's expansion in
general insurance, most of ALICO's expansion would occur within
countries where it already operated except in Africa and Central
America, countries that ALICO pioneered.

Today, over 50 years later, ALICO, domiciled in Delaware, has life
operations in approximately 60 countries and is the largest U.S. international life insurance company.

S tarr's big loss during this period was Cuba, where AIU had a huge
operation, its largest in Latin America. When Castro took over in
1959, this enterprise was expropriated, something that would happen
often to American International over the years. Yet Starr and especially
Greenberg often found ways to turn these expropriations, if not to their
outright advantage, then at least so that they were less harmful, such as
managing the nationalized industry. Often the company was invited
back years after the nationalization.

Regarding Cuba, Starr called in his chief executive for the region
and said: "Look, what is our business? It's no more than a guarantee, a

piece of paper. What it boils down to is people. And we look after our people. We tried to in the Far East. We'll do the same thing for our Cubans. Anyone who wants to come out, we'll either give a job to or support until we get him a job." Some 70 families were brought out and housed in the United States and either went to work for AIU or were taken care of until they found another job.

Greenberg operated according to the same principle during my years at AIG. No stone was left unturned, and money was never an object when our people were incarcerated or could not get out of a country. Some examples of this will be discussed later. Starr's statement that our business is "no more than . . . a piece of paper" seemed to have been heard by our diplomats, for it was turned against AIG by the U.S. government until it sparked the company to lead a major legislative change that drastically altered the concept of international trade.

One of the heated criticisms people have made about AIG for many years, and especially since the company confronted its accounting and related crises, is that it is too complicated. When Starr was alive there were fewer than 100 companies, many offshore. By the time Greenberg resigned, there were hundreds of companies, again many offshore. Some would argue it is not only complex, but impenetrable to an outsider, and especially to insurance regulators. That has its advantages. Good for dealing with regulators, bad for investors, especially in this age of transparency. Yet to someone familiar with the corporation, the maze really is not so complicated, and Starr clearly was not trying to make it more complicated, especially since the regulatory issues of the 1940s were not what they are today. The overriding issue is that because so many of the companies are incorporated and domiciled offshore, it makes regulators suspicious, and it is true that the elaborate corporate organization chart could provide the means for chicanery.

By 1948, Starr saw it was time to consolidate the far-reaching organization he had created. He decided to split the company operations into domestic and international groups. The domestic business would be headquartered in New York, and the international business would be based in Bermuda. He began by establishing two offshore entities based in Bermuda: American International Underwriters Overseas, Ltd.

(AIUO) (which was later renamed Starr International Company or SICO) and American International Reinsurance Company, Inc. (AIRCO). The former became the parent for all of the AIU agencies established overseas, like AIU Hong Kong, AIU Argentina, AIU France, and so on; the latter owned the life insurance companies, managed their investment portfolios, and acted as a reinsurer for them.

The next year, Starr set up American International Underwriters Association (AIUA). This was an unincorporated partnership made up of the American insurance companies represented overseas by AIU, some owned by Starr, some not, 11 in all, which pooled business in agreed percentages and shared assets retained overseas to meet local requirements. In other words, X company would cover 10 percent of all risks the company wrote overseas regardless of the countries in which they operated, and would provide 10 percent of the assets they had to leave in a country to meet regulatory requirements, again, regardless of the countries in which they operated.

Starr realized there was a major flaw in this structure that could, in effect, put him out of business, at least temporarily, in a country or in a number of countries. If any of the member U.S. companies in the association gave notice to withdraw from his group, he could no longer operate in any country where that company was the only company licensed. The way around this was to have another company in the group licensed. Over the years, getting a company licensed to sell insurance had become more difficult, if, indeed, it could be done at all. This made it even more imperative to own at least one of the companies in the group he represented and enter it in as many country markets as possible, for his companies would not be pulling out of a country. Better yet, why not own them all? That would not only correct the flaw, it would give Starr a vital domestic operation. He vowed to do just that.

In 1952, AIRCO, his company that owned life insurers, acquired a majority interest in Globe & Rutgers Fire Insurance Company, a U.S. fire insurer that had once been represented by AIU. While AIRCO's purpose was to own and deal with life insurers, AIRCO had a broad enough charter to do whatever it wished. One reason AIRCO would become the company that purchased so many other companies is that it was cash rich because it was legal at that time to bring back to Bermuda the reserves a life company had to maintain in the various countries it operated in. In other words, the life companies did not have to keep all their investments in the country where they operated. So AIRCO became the Starr company that had the money to make purchases of other companies.

Ernie Stempel was chosen to manage AIRCO's new general insurance operations. Stempel had joined AIU in 1938 while attending law school at night. He vacillated for years about staying at AIG, earning a master's degree in law, and even after deciding to stay with the company he earned a Ph.D. in law. Stempel was introduced to Starr by his uncle, Max Stempel, who came out of an insurance background in Panama. Max was reputedly offered the No. 2 job under Starr. Ernie Stempel ultimately became president of AIRCO, responsible for its worldwide operations. He is one of two former AIG executives in the Forbes 400 list of wealthiest people in America.

But Greenberg always watched stock sales by his executive team. So when Stempel sold hundreds of thousands of AIG shares, Greenberg had a notable reaction. He called him, yelling and asking, "What are you doing?"

Stempel replied he had to have money to give his new wife, and that he wanted to buy a Jaguar. Every year thereafter, on the anniversary of the purchase of the Jaguar, Greenberg called Stempel and said: "Ernie, your Jaguar is worth X, if you still had the shares, they would be worth Y."

Stempel died in 2009. Before, he was 92 and going strong, still having an office at AIG and in Bermuda. A widower, Stempel got married again a few years back to an AIG employee. His new wife was concerned that they go to confession, not exactly a regular habit of Ernie's. When the priest asked Stempel how long since he had made a confession, Stempel replied, "Fifty years." The priest was stunned speechless but managed to mumble, "Maybe you should say a few Hail Marys."

Once he owned it, Starr proceeded to have Globe & Rutgers and its subsidiaries licensed in as many places overseas as he could. Globe & Rutgers served a second Starr objective: It launched his company for the first time as a participant in the purely domestic insurance market. Other companies would follow. With the Globe & Rutgers

purchase came a subsidiary, the Insurance Company of the State of
Pennsylvania, the second oldest stock insurance company in the country, and the American Home Assurance Company. In 1954, Globe &
Rutgers merged with American Home, and American Home was the
surviving name.

Years later, as American Home consistently fared poorly domestically,
Hank Greenberg, who reputedly resisted at first, was appointed president of the company. This was only a few years after Milburn Smith, the
Continental Casualty president, suggested during a meeting in Hong
Kong that Starr consider a young star, Hank Greenberg, as someone
who could meet Starr's desire to export the accident and health business
to overseas markets. Greenberg was doing well with this assignment,
but the company now had one that was even more important—fix
American Home. What Greenberg did with it was an absolute career-
maker. It changed the course of Greenberg's career and helped elevate
him to become Starr's eventual successor.

W ithin two years, Greenberg's unorthodox formula worked, and
American Home had favorable results. That led to other companies in the AIUA group turning to the Starr organization for help
with their own business problems. By the time Greenberg was finished,
American International had acquired many of the companies that Starr
had represented overseas through AIU. The first to join was New
Hampshire Insurance Company, which had a problem with a threatened unfriendly takeover by a major shareholder who wanted to move
the company to New Orleans. New Hampshire appealed to American
International for help, and Greenberg negotiated the purchase of a significant block of the company's stock from the dissident shareholder in
1966. Greenberg was very tough, firing over 10,000 employees,
although mainly agents, in a short time. New Hampshire prospered
over the long run.

Next was National Union Fire Insurance Company of Pittsburgh,
which AIU had represented overseas since 1927. It was in real trouble,
with underwriting losses threatening its solvency. Worse yet, this threatened the smooth functioning of the association of overseas agencies
Starr managed. With the approval of the National Union management,
American International purchased a controlling interest in 1968 and

applied the American Home formula to fix it. With National Union came a subsidiary, a Boston company, Lexington Insurance Company, which is a surplus lines writer (an insurer not admitted to write insurance in a jurisdiction but that insures what licensed insurers in a state are unable to insure—for example, a priceless Van Gogh or insurance on a home being built but not yet completed). In other words, a surplus lines insurer writes unusual and difficult risks. Today Lexington is the largest surplus line writer in the country.

Other acquisitions in the 1960s were Commerce and Industry Insurance Company and the Transatlantic Reinsurance Company. Not only had the flaw in AIU been fixed, in that American International owned most of the companies it represented abroad and the withdrawal of one company from the group no longer threatened the entire group's well-being (in 1976, AIU stopped writing business for insurance companies other than those it owned), but, in addition, Starr had found his entry into the domestic insurance market. His dream of 40 years had been realized—he owned the companies he represented overseas.

S tarr was not political in the way Greenberg is political. But neither was he politically naïve. In 1947, a year before Bill Youngman signed on with him with one of his primary responsibilities being to help with political matters, Starr started what would become a revolution in the way Bermuda regulated insurance companies. He visited the island and launched a series of changes that led to Bermuda becoming a global haven for the offshore insurance industry, so that today the insurance industry is a major employer and has more than $200 billion in assets. Currently, there are 1,600 insurers incorporated in Bermuda, or about 1 for every 40 residents.

It started in 1947 with the passage of the American International Co. Ltd. Act, developed especially for Starr. The law created an exception to Bermuda's local ownership requirement and exempted American International, which would become AIG, from taxes on income that came from outside Bermuda. Two years later Bermuda extended these provisions to other foreign insurers. American International quickly became a major employer. Then, in 1951, Parliament passed a law making American International the first foreign company allowed to purchase island real estate. Thereafter, American International began to build and expand its operations in Bermuda.

Starr died in 1968 and Greenberg succeeded him as CEO. As the *Wall Street Journal* of September 20, 2005, recounted, onto the scene walks L. Michael Murphy, tall, athletic, disheveled, engaging, with a warm smile. I worked closely with Mike over the years and remember the cover photo of *Sports Illustrated* showing him jumping through the air grasping a rugby ball. He had taken up rugby in college and became a champion.

Mike worked on international tax matters at the IRS before coming to AIG in 1972. In 1973 he was named corporate secretary of Starr International (previously AIUO), a Panamanian corporation operated from Bermuda. In the mid-1970s, Murphy helped island politicians draft a new insurance law for Bermuda that made the colony even more attractive to U.S. companies and insurers, according to David Gibbons, a former Bermuda premier, and Mansfield "James" Brock, a former financial secretary. Mike advised the government on the standards it would need to successfully attract business from the United States and avoid antagonizing American regulators.

In the end, the Bermuda Insurance Act of 1978 made Bermuda a much less demanding host than American states, which regulate insurance in the United States. It did little to regulate insurance rates or company conduct, and it set minimal requirements for the capital insurers in order to operate. Yet American regulators accepted the looser standards, in part because Bermuda required that insurers document their solvency annually. The 1978 act also created the Insurance Advisory Committee, which has the effective clout to prevent any further regulation opposed by the industry. From 1980 through 2001, a member of the committee was Joseph C.H. Johnson, another veteran AIG executive. For much of the 1980s, one of his duties was to help oversee which companies received government permission to form new companies on the island—an area of great interest to AIG, which was the sponsor of a number of new firms.

Another role Murphy played since the mid-1970s was shuttling to Washington to protect AIG's interests there. I worked closely with Mike on this effort. Washington lawyers and lobbyists said that Murphy helped persuade members of Congress and their aides to establish a new rule for determining which jurisdiction's taxes applied to underwriting income.

Mike's soft-spoken, easygoing, unthreatening ways, coupled with his encyclopedic knowledge of insurance taxes, made him brilliant in these efforts. I remember one incident when staffers on one of the Congressional tax-writing committees said they would give us the legislative amendment we wanted, but in return they wanted to pick Mike's brains on complex tax matters for a few hours. Pick they did, and we secured our amendment. I am sure Mike was helpful, but I am equally sure he gave up no information that would hurt AIG.

In 1986, Bermuda faced a competitive threat when Barbados signed a treaty with the United States exempting all premiums paid by American companies to insurers in Barbados from American taxes. Premier John Swain of Bermuda recruited AIG to help secure a similar privilege. Messrs. Murphy and Johnson served as advisors to the Bermuda government during negotiations in Washington that in 1988 produced the treaty.

All in all, over a 30-year period, AIG, started by C.V. Starr and carried through by various executives, shaped the regulation (or, some would argue, lack of regulation) to a form that is very attractive to the insurance industry.

During this period, AIG established one insurer that became emblematic of the problem that Attorney General Spitzer accused it of—placing reinsurance with a company you control. In 1978, AIG established Inter-Hemispheric Insurance Co., a $50 million joint venture with reinsurer Munich Re. Inter-Hemispheric was one of the first firms to offer a form of reinsurance known as finite-risk insurance. Many critics argue that some finite-risk policies are little more than disguised loans, which allow purchasers to prettify their books temporarily without transferring real risk to the reinsurer.

In 1986, Inter-Hemispheric was renamed Richmond Insurance Co. AIG was buying millions in reinsurance protection from Richmond but, according to the *Wall Street Journal*, continued to tell New York State regulators that Richmond was an independent company. AIG told these regulators in the late 1990s that it owned just 19.99 percent of this offshore company and didn't control it. In 1999, the company filed with the New York State Department of Insurance a form known as a "disclaimer of control" related to Richmond. Spitzer and the insurance commissioner, Howard Mills, allege that AIG omitted critical facts: An AIG unit managed key Richmond operations and Richmond's purportedly independent outside investors—Munich Re and others—were guaranteed against loss by an AIG unit.

In March 2005, AIG acknowledged to regulators that it should have accounted for Richmond as a company it could control and made adjustments.

In 1943 AIUO, a Panamanian corporation, was created. It later changed its name to Starr International (SICO). In the 1940s, Starr had put all the overseas agencies under SICO. In 1970, Starr International voting shareholders voted to exchange its vast network of managing general agencies and insurance companies outside North America for a substantial equity position in AIRCO. This overseas operation was a very valuable franchise indeed. It was also the principal business of Starr International.

With this exchange, Starr International became a substantial indirect shareholder of American International Group, a Delaware public corporation that had been created just two years earlier by AIRCO to hold shares of the domestic companies (AIG first was named American International Enterprises, but the name was discarded as unsuitable). AIRCO was the majority shareholder of AIG. Starr undoubtedly knew about these developments and consulted with Greenberg about them before he died in December 1968, since Greenberg was the driving force in getting them accomplished. Starr must have been excited that the small venture he had launched in China 50 years earlier was about to become a public company.

Eight years later, in 1978, Starr International became a substantial direct shareholder in AIG by virtue of AIRCO's merger with and into AIG. The subsidiary absorbed the parent. Prior to the merger, both AIRCO and AIG were listed on the Over the Counter Exchange; AIG didn't move to the New York Stock Exchange until 1984. Employees were shareholders in both companies, and many of us had options to buy AIRCO as well as AIG. Mike Murphy, one of the few who stand up to Greenberg, argued forcefully with Greenberg about the adverse tax consequences of merging AIG and AIRCO. The matter was put to rest when Greenberg closed the debate: "I am not going to let tax implications drive my business decisions."

Considering how much AIG has grown and how many times the stock has split and then grown to the pre-split price in the last 25 years, Greenberg made absolutely the right decision. The market cap on the day AIG went public was about $915 million. The day Greenberg left, the market cap was $165 billion. This constitutes an 1800-fold stock increase or 180,000 percent. This is a 24 percent annual increase, an absolutely remarkable return. But investors would never have understood the company—one-half onshore, one-half offshore. Nor would they have understood a company whose parent was a Bermuda company (AIRCO), also listed on the exchange.

AIG went from a private company holding part of the shares of domestic companies—American Home, National Union, and New Hampshire—to a public company owning all the shares of these companies, since AIG shares were used to buy them in a swap when it went public. By the time AIG and AIRCO merged, the combined company would include all of the companies around the world as well. Together, it was a potentially formidable company, something that time would bear out. It would be Hank Greenberg's charge to grow the company in the next 30 years the way Starr created and grew it in the first 50.

Chapter 8

A Nobody Beats the Ivy Leaguers

By 1960, C. V. Starr & Co. was a relatively small but well-established company with significant international reach. It had offices throughout Latin America and in a number of European countries. It was the first foreign insurer to reopen in China after World War II, and while it had to shut down again when the Communists came to power, it had established offices around the rest of Asia, including Japan. The company now had a modest U.S. presence as well. In 1952 Starr had acquired a majority interest in the Globe & Rutgers Fire Insurance Company and its subsidiaries, including American Home Assurance Company.

As he approached his 70th birthday in 1962, Starr made the decision to slow down at work. The driving factor behind this decision was ill health. He had emphysema, and Wang, his Chinese valet, followed him everywhere with oxygen during the last years of his life. He no longer came in every day, and when he did, his days did not start early or end late.

He was ill enough that he simply could not handle it. In effect, he was retired or semiretired, although all the major decisions were passed by him. Even though he had no choice, Starr felt he could safely take it easy because he had attracted well-credentialed executives to oversee day-to-day operations. His second-in-command was William S. Youngman, formerly a named partner in the law firm of Corcoran, Foley, Youngman, & Rowe. The managing partner of that firm, Thomas "Tommy the Cork" Corcoran, had become a legend in the 1930s as a multipurpose hatchet man, errand boy, and fixer for Franklin D. Roosevelt, and declared he would become Washington's first super-lobbyist when his former mentor, Felix Frankfurter, persuaded Roosevelt not to appoint Corcoran solicitor general. He did just that.

Corcoran was Starr's lawyer and principal lobbyist in Washington, and Neil Starr was well pleased with his work. It didn't hurt that the Corcoran firm—and Corcoran and Youngman, particularly—had strong China connections. They were close to Claire Chennault, founder of the famous Flying Tigers (years later Anna Chennault was alleged to be Corcoran's mistress; at the least he was her escort around Washington). After Youngman served as general counsel to the Federal Power Commission, Corcoran suggested to President Roosevelt that Youngman should run China Defense Supplies, which was Lend Lease for China. Youngman was also an OSS operative in Asia during the war. Youngman was close to Chennault's partner, Whiting Willauer, who cofounded the Flying Tigers, formed China Air Transport with Chennault after the war, and was ambassador to Honduras in the 1950s.

"Wild Bill" Donovan, head of the OSS, may have introduced Starr to Youngman. In any case, Starr met Youngman in China, and after the war, in 1948, when Youngman was back with Corcoran's law firm, he recruited him to the Starr companies. It wasn't hard for Starr to recruit Youngman, who was weary of practicing law, was driven crazy by Corcoran's wild antics, and saw a chance to be his own man and make a lot of money in the process. The question of whether he knew anything about insurance did not concern Starr or Youngman (but it would be a sore point with Greenberg later). After all, the company had a history of recruiting successful executives with no insurance experience—Joukowsky and Freeman, to name two. Youngman was recruited to make or utilize his political connections around the world, or be a "connector of people." As a first step, Starr took Bill Youngman and his wife, Elsie, on a world tour to meet American International people and convey the importance Neil Starr gave to the Youngman appointment. Youngman quickly became assistant to Starr in Starr's role as president of C.V. Starr, the senior company in the group, and he moved north to New York.

Starr, who had started poor and never received a college degree, must have been impressed by Youngman's family wealth and impeccable blue-blood credentials (Youngman's wife was a Boston Brahmin), including Harvard College and Harvard Law. Attracting someone with this background would help give his company the stature and credibility he was sure it deserved. The white-shoe image got some added reinforcement when Youngman and Starr recruited Gordon B. Tweedy, a product of Yale University and Yale Law School who, like Youngman, had a China connection. He had worked for the China National Aviation Corporation in Calcutta during the latter part of World War II while also serving as an OSS operative under Youngman. He was married to Mary Tweedy, a respected correspondent for *Life* magazine. The Tweedys had one adventure that took on legendary proportions. Early in 1945, while Mary was in a state of advanced pregnancy, she and Gordon took a flight from Delhi in a U.S. military aircraft headed for Kashmir. Halfway there the pilot got lost and they all had to bail out. They were rescued and finally made it back to Calcutta. General Hackett pinned a gemmed caterpillar on the diapers of the girl (Clare) subsequently born to the Tweedys and she became a member of the Caterpillar Club (a club formed in the 1920s whose requirement for membership was that you had jumped out of a disabled plane).

Starr loved this story. It probably reaffirmed his belief that his firm clearly had arrived if it could attract a personage with Gordon Tweedy's credentials. Youngman worked for the OSS during the war and had a number of operatives working for him, including Gordon Tweedy. So it is not clear who attracted Tweedy—Youngman or Starr. In a company like Starr's, he would not have come aboard without Starr's approval. But since Tweedy had worked for Youngman, he would have been the deciding factor, even though Starr had met Tweedy in China. Tweedy was to serve as a counsel in the company but was basically reporting to Youngman. In any case, with the addition of two men of the stature of Youngman and Tweedy (and a wife as formidable as Mary Tweedy), C.V. Starr & Co. was a firm to be taken seriously.

Youngman and Tweedy were at the front of a line of American International executives involved with intelligence agencies. It started with Starr, who, as reported previously, worked with "Wild Bill" Donovan, head of the OSS, during the war. A number of Starr's employees served as agents. In the case of Youngman, basically he had a string of six or seven operatives like Tweedy. A controversial employee was Duncan Lee, a friend of Youngman's, who was not one of his operatives during the war. While working at C.V. Starr, he had to be smuggled to Bermuda by Youngman because he was targeted by Senator Joe McCarthy in his Communist witch-hunting. Lee, a descendent of General Robert E. Lee and a Rhodes scholar, was born to missionary parents in Nanking, China. He graduated from Yale and returned to Yale Law School after Oxford. He joined the law firm of Donovan and Leisure, and followed World War I hero "Wild Bill" Donovan (holder of a Medal of Honor) to Washington. He was fingered in the book *The Haunted Wood* as being a Soviet spy. In the early summer of 1942 Lee was appointed confidential assistant to Donovan, chief of the OSS. Lee was employed by the OSS from 1942 to 1946. A decryption from June 1943 lists six Soviet agents working in the OSS. One of the Soviet sources was identified as Duncan Lee. Lee allegedly supplied the Soviet Union with a list of OSS employees suspected of being Communists or Communist sympathizers, and informed Moscow of the impending D-Day invasion in 1944 and operations in China and Japan. Decoded Soviet intelligence cables show Lee reporting on British and American diplomatic strategy for negotiating with Stalin over postwar Poland, American diplomatic activities in Turkey and Romania, and OSS operations in China and France.

Elizabeth Bentley, a Vassar graduate descended from *Mayflower* passengers, testified before the House Un-American Activities Committee that Duncan Lee and others such as Alger Hiss were Soviet spies. But Lee was never prosecuted.

Later, he privately admitted that he and his wife had joined the Communist Party while they were students at Yale. In 1944 his wife discovered he was having an affair with another Communist courier, Mary Price. He subsequently remarried and moved to Bermuda but fervently denied that he had ever done anything in the least revolutionary. When Lloyd Cutler, former White House counsel, was interviewed for a biographical oral history project, he described Lee as a McCarthy victim who was quite visible and very interested in China. Cutler's interviewer said he was a Soviet spy. In any case, Youngman was totally supportive of Lee and backed him throughout the ordeal, as did Starr. He later returned to New York and finished a successful career at the company.

All told, Youngman brought at least four of his former OSS operatives into the Starr companies, including Betancourt, Weinbrenner, and Tweedy. While this meant there were lots of executives with loyalties to Youngman, this was not a threat to Starr, although it may have been to other ambitious executives. All these former OSS operatives prospered at American International, which, again, was commensurate with Starr's notion that you did not need to know insurance to do well in his company. Later, Greenberg would perform a similar service, although generally at a higher level, when he would brief the CIA after his overseas business trips.

One AIG director does not remember the exact details but says that Greenberg was involved with the CIA when the North Koreans shot down the U.S. commercial airliner.

Greenberg recruited Frank Wisner II, former ambassador to Zambia, Egypt, Philippines, and India to be vice chairman of AIG, although after a few years, Greenberg asked him to step off the AIG board. Wisner is married to Christine de Ganay, former wife of Pal Sarkozy and thus the former stepmother of French President Sarkozy. He recently retired from AIG. But his fame comes from his father, Frank Wisner, the head of CIA covert operations and a famous spy with a long history of accomplishment for the OSS and CIA. After a bout with depression, Wisner committed suicide in 1965. Through the Wisners there is a definite CIA connection, and some assume that Wisner II worked for the agency. Whatever the case, there is a continuation of involvement with intelligent communication and Greenberg's love for that work.

It was always alleged, but never confirmed, that AIG insures CIA facilities around the world, although about their only property would be airplanes.

S ome 12 years after Youngman and Tweedy arrived, Starr brought a
very different kind of man into the company, someone whose background was worlds apart from the aristocratic circles of Tweedy and
Youngman. Starr had become interested in the market for personal accident insurance, and he sought advice from J. Milburn Smith, president
of the Chicago-based Continental Casualty Company, in 1959. Smith
recommended that Starr have a talk with one of his bright young stars,
Maurice Greenberg, whom he described as a whiz at selling personal
accident insurance.

Greenberg was born on May 4, 1925. His father, who owned a
candy store on Manhattan's Lower East Side, died when Greenberg was
seven years old. His mother then married a dairy farmer and Greenberg
grew up in the town of Swan Lake in New York's Catskill Mountains.

While this is in his official bio, the following was in a recent
Fortune cover story. He was born in New York City but moved to
upstate New York after his father, a taxi driver, was killed in an automobile accident. Greenberg was only 6. His mother, Ada, a beau-
tician, remarried a farmer, Hyman Mushkat. In 1942, 17-year-old
Greenberg lied about his age to join the army, became an Army
Ranger, and landed on Omaha Beach on D-Day. His unit, the
Fifth Ranger Battalion, helped liberate the Dachau concentration
camp in 1945. Greenberg received the Bronze Star. After the war,
Greenberg attended the University of Miami, where he met his future
wife, Corinne Zuckerman, and then went to New York Law School
full-time. He received his law degree in 1950, only to be recalled
for service in the Korean War, where he rose to the rank of captain.
Greenberg says he was given a choice: serve two years in a desk job
or 17 months in a combat unit. He chose the latter so that he could
get back to his bride and finally begin a career. He was assigned to the
Judge Advocate General's Corps and won a reputation for winning so
many acquittals for the soldiers he defended that the army switched
him to the prosecutorial staff.

In 1953, his military service behind him, Greenberg walked into
the offices of Continental Casualty in lower Manhattan on a whim
and talked his way into the office of the personnel director. He got
such a rude reception that he stormed into the office of a vice president and told him that Continental's personnel director was a jerk.

Audacious as the action was, anybody who has dealt with Hank Greenberg can easily imagine him doing that. He was rewarded with a job as a $75-a-week underwriting trainee. In 1959, he was elected vice president, the youngest vice president Continental ever had. He had done an extraordinary job in building their accident and health insurance business. In 1960, Mil Smith, during a conversation in Hong Kong, recommended Greenberg to Starr in response to Starr's question about finding an executive who understood the U.S. accident and health business.

Greenberg, then 35, jumped at Starr's offer of a vice presidency at C.V. Starr & Co., seeing a world of limitless possibilities at the Starr companies.

His appointment was announced by Youngman on December 16, 1960, to be effective January 1, 1961. A driving force behind Greenberg's move was a statement made to him by Milburn Smith (who was considered more of a mentor to Greenberg than Starr) that a Jew could never become president of Continental Casualty. This may be one reason Smith was willing for Greenberg to leave. But anti-Semitism wasn't an issue at a company owned by a self-made man from humble beginnings who prided himself on attracting the best talent, regardless of ethnicity or race. Years later, when Greenberg became CEO and AIG became a public company, Greenberg thanked Smith for recommending him to Starr by putting him on the AIG board.

Shortly after Greenberg joined the company, Starr took him to a board meeting with the intent of introducing the man he hoped would be his new star employee. Youngman, who was presiding, apparently felt so confident of his position that he lit into Starr. "What is he doing here?" Youngman demanded. "He doesn't belong here. This is a board meeting of our company, not a social gathering to introduce new employees." The meeting left a bad taste all around. It created permanent resentment between Greenberg and Youngman, and it caused Starr to wonder if he should have Youngman succeed him.

During the next couple of years, Greenberg worked at his specialty in accident and health (A&H), giving special focus to the international business. Once again, Starr had an insight that proved correct, which is the reason he was looking to hire someone like Greenberg. With the coming of jet travel, greater personal mobility, and more widespread affluence, he sensed that the lifestyles of many people would be changing.

In countries with expanding economies, there would be greater concern with keeping hard-won gains and more interest in safeguarding against more hazards. So in the early 1960s, Starr steered AIU toward writing accident and health insurance abroad for the first time, because he felt that growing numbers of people were ready for it. He believed he could create demand for an accident and health product. Through Greenberg he did, and the company's A&H business boomed.

Meanwhile, Greenberg stayed as far out of Youngman's way as one could in a company as small as Starr's. Then, in 1963, the pair had another run-in. A group of executives was meeting to discuss what to do about American Home, their primary domestic company, which was losing up to a million dollars a year, a lot of money for the company back then. This so-called find-a-solution meeting turned into a gripe session. "It's not like our international companies," someone said. "We are captive to what these agents send us," said another. "It's a dog. Let's sell it and stick to the cream—our international business." Greenberg, exasperated and out of patience, interrupted and said, "If you weren't all such goddamn fools, we could do something with American Home. None of you understands the basics of insurance."

Youngman saw his chance to set up Hank for failure. "Since you think you are so damn smart," he said, "you are today officially the president of American Home. It better not be losing money next month like it is today. The meeting is adjourned." Youngman must have regretted his impulse a thousand times. This decision was one step toward sealing his doom.

Greenberg acted quickly. First and most important, he got rid of the insurance agents who wrote the business for American Home and converted American Home into a brokerage company. That meant brokers would bring the company business it could accept or reject. Agents, in contrast, were empowered to commit the company to a policy on their own. Greenberg took other steps, including focusing on larger industrial and commercial risks, but this was the heart of the change. He also developed substantial reinsurance facilities, enabling him to write large shares of major risks and thereby control pricing. Within two years, American Home's losses were turned to a profit. This caught Starr's attention in a big way. Marion Fajen, a secretary in the company, the corporate secretary of AIG, and a director (all at the same time), said Starr took an instant liking to Greenberg, seeing him as "the son he always wanted." Other AIGers are not as comfortable with this comment. But the two men grew closer, and Greenberg was edging into position as a candidate to succeed Starr, something which, until now, had been Youngman's alone. Starr liked Greenberg and his determined drive, respected his obvious talent, and, not incidentally, was losing some of his enthusiasm for Youngman.

Once a year Youngman made a trip around the world, visiting the American International offices, reviewing operations, making appointments, giving salary reviews. When he returned from this journey, all too often he found Starr had overruled a number of his actions. Youngman might raise someone's salary in Japan to $35,000, only to have Starr visit Tokyo after him and give the executive a second boost to $40,000. If Youngman made a decision that a new building in Tokyo or Wilmington or elsewhere would be 10 stories high, Starr would change it to 12. Sometimes, Starr would come back and tell Youngman about the changes he had made. Other times Youngman would only hear about them from others. This second-guessing only worsened as Starr became more ill.

So Starr manifested the classic characteristic of proprietors: an inability to give up control of what they had created. He said he would turn over power, but he could not. He was an unhappy man, and the company was all he had.

Greenberg reported to Youngman but often went around him to Starr, disagreeing with Youngman's position on a business matter. Having said that, in a company as close-knit and freewheeling as American International, it was not only to be expected but somewhat encouraged. The give-and-take among principals was considered positive.

An issue developed over the election of directors of C.V. Starr. These eight wise men in essence controlled the company, and shares were allocated according to their power. Starr, for example, had the most—24 percent. A debate arose between Starr and Youngman over two candidates: Greenberg and Tweedy. Youngman was opposed to Greenberg joining the board, but wanted Tweedy, his top aide, to be a C.V. Starr director. Starr differed. He wanted the exact opposite. One reason was apparently because of a moralistic streak that Starr would manifest occasionally. In Starr's view, Tweedy was drinking too much, and he didn't like it. The end result: Both Greenberg and Tweedy were elected directors of Starr. Starr got his pick and Youngman got Tweedy onto the board.

Starr clearly manipulated his top people and played them against one another. He once asked Stempel if he would like to succeed him, and Stempel apparently said no, the job was too consuming. Others of the "Big 8" would have opposed him succeeding Starr, anyway. He allegedly told Joukowsky that he should succeed him but could not because he was Russian and that would be bad politically, although Joukowsky's son strongly denies this. Later, he told Joukowsky, "We are both getting to be old men. Let's retire." He told the same thing to Mansfield Freeman. They both listened and retired, but others didn't, including Starr, who didn't really retire until he died. Joukowsky retired in 1956 but was around for certain meetings. Youngman wanted the top job and clearly had been designated his successor, but Starr second-guessed him constantly on decisions. Yet with all the manipulation and indecision, he cared about each of them and took generous care of them financially.

As Starr became sicker, taking morphine a good bit of the time, Youngman anguished over his future. Those who were close to the situation say Youngman cared deeply about Starr. They traveled together and skied together, Starr had made him rich, and he felt obligated to Starr. But the countervailing pressures—Starr's countermanding his decisions and Greenberg's pushing for aggressive business actions, including buying more companies—made him wonder if he wanted to fight for the keys to the kingdom. He spent many hours walking the golf course at Morefar, where he had a place, Yopang House, and wrestling with what to do. Youngman also bore another burden in Starr's moralistic eyes—he liked women, especially young women. He had a series of affairs and one serious mistress, Hilda Babin, who lives in Vero Beach, Florida. She was introduced to Youngman by Silvan Coleman, CEO of brokerage firm E. F. Hutton and a director of American Home. He would take her to the company enclave at Morefar (which Youngman's Brahmin wife, Elsie, had no interest in visiting). Starr did not appreciate this, especially his bringing her to Morefar.

By some accounts, Youngman decided on his own to abandon the fight for succession. Confederates say he told them at the time that he thought a confrontation would kill Starr. He also was weary of battling Greenberg over the direction of the company. Greenberg wanted to grow the company aggressively and make many acquisitions, and didn't shy from pursuing his vision by confronting what he saw as excessive conservatism on the part of Youngman and Tweedy. A different version of what happened, told by a very senior officer of the company, is that Starr bought off Youngman to get him to leave. In any case, Starr and Youngman negotiated an exit. Starr agreed to buy Youngman's stock in various parts of the companies, including American Home and AIRCO, and both would leave the company. This was face-saving for Youngman and something Starr presumably thought he should do. On August 16, 1968, Starr sent an internal announcement that both he and Youngman were retiring. Youngman would stay on the C.V. Starr board and the AIRCO board, and serve as chairman of American Home Assurance Company. Starr would remain a director of C.V. Starr.

On August 19, 1968, the *New York Times* reported that "C.V. Starr & Co., Inc., the international insurance managers, announced the election of Gordon B. Tweedy as chairman and Maurice R. Greenberg as president." It said: "Mr. Starr is retiring but would remain a director of the company." It also noted that Youngman would remain a director of C.V. Starr and AIRCO and chairman of American Home Assurance Company. This suggested that Youngman would stay active, something that did not happen, probably because of a company stock sale he made that the others bitterly opposed. The article carried photos of each and did not address who was the top executive. Youngman, whatever his disagreement with Starr, had taken care of his personal No. 2 on his way out the door.

Since both the company announcement and the *Times* story are vague about who really was the new boss, I raised this issue with Greenberg in February 2006. He insisted that he was the new top executive, that Starr had picked him, and this was not made clear in the release only because Mary Tweedy, Gordon's wife, wrote it. Her authorship makes some sense, since Mary was a former *Life* correspondent and at the time was president of the Starr Foundation. She was the seasoned and respected journalist in the company and close to

Starr and top management. Such an arrangement that the press release implied would not have been all that unusual. Some companies had a chairman who was the corporate statesman—the Mr. Outside—while the president actually ran the business and had greater decision-making authority, and neither had the formal title of CEO. This happened even when both were full-time employees. But since the news release would have been reviewed by all players, it is hard to believe it could happen unless it happened accidentally, or Greenberg et al didn't read it carefully, or indeed Mary did write it her own way, revising it after everyone reviewed it.

A memorandum that Youngman wrote for the directors of C.V. Starr several months earlier sheds some light on Youngman's thinking. Youngman had recommended that the president of C.V. Starr *no longer* be chief executive officer, but serve as operational leader. Since Youngman himself was president of Starr at the time, his memo suggests that he was at least de facto CEO during his eight years in the presidency (with Starr always ready and able to overrule him). It sounds like he had a plan to handle succession whereby he would be chairman of C.V. Starr and the chairman would be CEO. We do not know whether the Starr directors acted on this memorandum or even saw it.

The truth of the matter can only be found in AIG's archives, which it will not make available. If Greenberg did not immediately ascend to the top spot—and if Youngman ever was the true CEO—then AIG will have to amend its official history. The company has maintained for several decades now that it had only two CEOs until 2005—Neil Starr and Hank Greenberg (though, of course, Greenberg was the arbiter of that official history).

A fascinating letter was written to Paul Steiger, managing editor of the *Wall Street Journal*, on March 22, 2005, after Greenberg was forced to resign. The letter, from William S. Youngman III, notes: "While you and a great many other members of the media have erroneously printed, time and again, that Hank Greenberg was the first and only hand picked successor to C.V. Starr, the founder of what is now AIG, this was not the case.

"As the enclosed press release of August 16, 1968 . . . clearly indicates, for a number of years prior to Mr. Starr's death and before his own voluntary retirement, my father, William S. Youngman, was the hand picked successor of Mr. Starr and was, in fact, the CEO of all that today is AIG."

During this last period, as Starr neared death, Greenberg was treated as the successor by Starr himself.

Norman Crafts, the personal V.P. to both Starr and Greenberg, says that Starr sent him around the world to get a sense of what company executives thought. When he returned, he wrote Starr a two-page memo. The majority thought that Greenberg would succeed Starr. Starr told Norman Crafts that Greenberg was his choice.

Starr had trouble sleeping and called Greenberg at all hours, often asking him to come to his apartment. He would tell Greenberg who he wanted taken care of, like "Chick" Igaya, a Japanese skier he had sponsored in the Olympics and sent to Dartmouth, and who then was a managing director at AIU Japan but was not considered very good in his job. He wanted T.C. Hsu, who became president of the Starr Foundation (whom Greenberg reportedly did not like) looked after, and he wanted to make sure the company maintained Stowe, the ski resort. He also thought the company should give Philamlife to the Philippines, something Greenberg and others talked him out of. Greenberg took all these pledges very seriously and implemented them.

Additional stories told by AIG executives, mostly but not all retired, offer varying nuances of the retirement of Starr, the departure of Youngman, the rise of Greenberg, and the edging out of Tweedy. There was an incident that occurred at a meeting of senior executives in Bermuda. At a cocktail party, Youngman was ruthlessly teasing Starr, who Youngman allegedly thought was so sick he wouldn't know the difference. After the party, Starr told Ernie Stempel, the president of AIRCO and a Starr partner, that Youngman was finished.

This story, if true, is not inconsistent with what finally happened, only Starr let Youngman go graciously and Youngman may have genuinely desired to retire. Others involved with AIG have told me that some kind of rift definitely did occur between Starr and Youngman at that Bermuda meeting. Another story is that Starr announced that Greenberg was his heir and showered him with C.V. Starr shares, AIRCO shares, and other stock to make sure no one could interfere.

I suspect the story is much more complicated than this and could do justice to a melodramatic business miniseries like those witnessed on television a few years back. How the drama played out so that Greenberg came out on top is complex and also says something about Starr and his illness in his final years.

The most believable story is that at a Bermuda meeting, Starr raised the succession issue and mentioned he would die soon. He asked what they should do. Two of the directors—Youngman and Tweedy—pushed for liquidating, selling the company. Allegedly, Joukowsky, retired for many years, was there and he supported that. At the time, the company was worth about $100 million, a high valuation for a private company in 1968.

Greenberg countered with the notion of taking the company public and building a giant public insurance company, which at the time seemed like a grandiose idea. Starr did not make a decision and everyone returned to New York. Then Youngman and Tweedy started quietly organizing a move to liquidate and went to K.K. Tse, one of the most powerful people in the company, for support. He demurred and told Starr what was happening. That, apparently, is when Starr made the decision to support going public and began to lean toward Greenberg as his successor. When I spoke with Greenberg, he denied focusing on being a public company at this time, explaining he had too much to do with handling the National Union and American Home.

John Roberts says that Gordon Tweedy would never have been involved in this scheme. He was honorable, totally loyal to Starr, a real acolyte. John suspects it was the above-mentioned meeting of AIUO in Bermuda or a subsequent Bermuda meeting where Youngman crossed Starr. Starr related to the C.V. Starr board that he had been misled about Youngman's character.

When Youngman retired, he decided to relocate to his home state of New Hampshire, where he had aspirations to run for the Senate. When he went to sell his stock holdings back to the company as part of his settlement agreement with Starr, the company reneged, probably because it simply didn't have the money to buy the shares. Things got nasty because Youngman was angry that they had reneged on his deal. Youngman then threatened to sell his shares to Victor Hurd, chairman of Continental Insurance Companies, near the AIU's downtown New York City offices. At one point during this drama, Starr called in a young executive, related to one of the founding fathers, and seated him so that Starr had a window to his back. Starr was surrounded with a halo effect and the young executive was somewhat blinded by the light and awed by the leader's power. Starr asked the executive one question: "Bill has told me he has been offered more for the stock by Hurd than we offered him. What should I do?"

The young executive was flabbergasted and flattered to be asked this question by the founder and leader of the company. He hesitated a moment and replied, "I wouldn't pay more than you promised."

Roberts says that Hurd was an honorable man and came and told Starr about Youngman's offer. Ultimately, Youngman did sell shares to Hurd, and for the next few years, AIG executives lived in fear that Hurd would make a run at buying the entire company and possibly succeed. Ernie Stempel made a related point when he said, "If Youngman had become the boss, he would have sold the company." While I did not hear this fear expressed by others, they may well have felt it. At a minimum, they were afraid of Hurd's intentions.

Some weeks after Tweedy and Greenberg assumed the helm, a meeting of the investment committee of the company was scheduled. Both were on the committee. A discussion ensued about whether an investment should be made in bonds. Several parties, including Tweedy, argued that since interest rates were projected to go up and therefore bond prices go down, it made no sense. Greenberg took the other side, supporting John Ahlers, a C.V. Starr director and the treasurer of American International—someone whose support he wanted. The argument became very heated, with Gordon Tweedy standing and yelling. Greenberg finally replied, "Sit down, Gordon, and shut up. I'm in charge now."

Tweedy, dumbfounded and ashen, quietly sat down. He left the meeting, and in 1970 he left the company. Irene Sullivan, a secretary who was in the typing pool of the executive offices and was the wife of a policeman, recounted what happened. She said the daily practice was that a secretary put together two manila folders—one for incoming mail and one for letters to sign. Tweedy habitually signed all the outgoing mail without reading it. In that outgoing mail was his resignation.

This does not ring true except as a ham-fisted way to accelerate Tweedy's departure. I talked to someone at the investment committee meeting and someone who was told the story by Irene Sullivan.

Whether one could resign so simply and unknowingly from a company is questionable. Certainly, Gordon Tweedy, a first-class lawyer and an honorable man even according to those who did not like noninsurers managing the company, could have said he was defrauded and gone to court. On the other hand, he could have been worn down and decided it was not worth it, especially since he had made millions.

Another version of the story is that Starr picked Greenberg, either outright or by insisting the C.V. Starr directors had voted for him. If he was alive when this happened, since he had the largest block of shares and was respected by the others, this would have been easy. If he was not, he would have had to arrange it. One principal told me Starr arranged for Greenberg to be elected and at the meeting, K.K. Tse said, "Our leader has always had 24 percent of the shares, so Hank should have that many." In essence, he would have had to buy them, probably Starr's shares. If invited to become a shareholder of Starr, you buy the shares at the current price. However, C.V. Starr & Co. would loan you the money to do so.

Whatever happened, whether it was clear that Greenberg was CEO or not, Tweedy and Greenberg worked together for a number of months, including serving as executors of Starr's estate. One executive recalled how he and his wife were invited to visit the Tweedys at Morefar at this time, since they were favorites of Gordon's. He had the good sense to tip off Greenberg, who told him to enjoy himself and don't worry about it. Gordon would not be here long, anyway.

Greenberg asked Gordon Tweedy to exit the company in 1970, about 18 months after Starr died. Company executives argue that Greenberg had to get rid of Mary Tweedy, who was President of the Starr Foundation, as well. He did not want Gordon's wife running something this important. Mary's daughter, Clare, argues that this never came to pass because her mother understood she could not run a key organization that involved her husband and Hank Greenberg. So she voluntarily left.

A postscript about Youngman's views. While he was Tweedy's strongest friend in court, he clearly thought Greenberg should be the CEO. He felt that only Greenberg had the talent to run the company and he, Youngman, still had a financial interest, since he hadn't sold everything to Hurd. He used to visit Greenberg once a year to see how things were going.

The letter from his son to the *Wall Street Journal* makes the point clearly: "My father felt strongly that Hank was the right person and the most able of the various possible successors to take the helm after his departure from the company. . . . it [AIG] required an able hand to . . . exploit its potential. As he has proven by his outstanding record, no one could have done this better than Hank Greenberg."

Chapter 9

Life with Hank
Greenberg

My first day at AIG in 1973 was like Hank Greenberg's first day at C.V. Starr & Co., but the career similarities end there. Jimmy Manton, the English-born, self-taught, erudite chairman of AIU, recruited me from running the International Insurance Advisory Council (Association of U.S. Insurers Operating Overseas), where he was AIG's representative. The members of the council (some 25 insurers) had agreed not to try and lure me away, something that AIG, naturally, ignored.

Greenberg would have had to approve my hiring and although I thought I was reporting to Manton, I started reporting to Greenberg almost immediately. Among other things, Hank was very active in Washington, which was in my portfolio. The AIG board was meeting that day, so when I came to Jimmy's office he promptly took me down the hall to the boardroom and introduced me to the board. While AIG had only been a public company for four years, this was an amazing act of informality that led to Greenberg exploding at Manton. "What do you think you are doing bringing a new employee into my meeting?" he asked. The yelling rolled off Manton's back, but, of course, it unnerved me.

A few months later Greenberg called me in to discuss China. "With Nixon's visit, China is gradually opening up," he said. "I want us to be invited back. And I expect us to be the first invited back. Okay? Run with it." After leaving Greenberg's office, I began to wonder: Did he mean the first American insurer invited to China? Or the first American company invited to China? Rather than ask that question and get an answer I didn't want, I devoted my attention to getting an invitation by pursuing every avenue I could find. At that point, helping American companies crack China was already a cottage industry. Within a few years, it was a fast-growing service industry.

After several false starts I landed at the Chase Manhattan Bank, which worked on China projects like ours in combination with a San Francisco lawyer, Stanley Lubman. Ken Morse was running this section of the bank and soon took David Rockefeller to China. Following their guidance, we wrote a proposal from Greenberg suggesting cooperation between AIG and the People's Insurance Company of China (PICC). We were tutored to lay it on pretty thick, talking about enhanced cooperation and mutually beneficial relationships. Then, mistakenly, we played it cheap by having some of our Chinese employees in New York translate it.

Stanley was en route to Beijing to present the proposal but got off the plane in Hong Kong and called to tell us the proposal, as translated, was a disaster. It would not only fail to secure an invitation—it would set us back years. Seems our guys had used the Chinese they knew, but this was not modern Mandarin as spoken and written in China today. He gave one example: American International Group as translated in the proposal came out in modern Mandarin as American International "Clique."

So Stanley supervised a new translation in Hong Kong and resumed his flight to China, where he presented the proposal. Then we began the waiting game. Stan and Ken periodically would use their contacts to check on the proposal but were advised to wait. Finally, the first breakthrough came—an invitation from the People's Insurance

Company of China (PICC) to visit Beijing. Hank was excited, as were all those who felt the company's Chinese roots were important. A date for the visit was set several months in advance. I was excited about making my first trip to China.

Then I learned indirectly that Hank was taking only Buck Freeman, Jimmy Manton, and their wives with him to China. I was outraged, and found the occasion, in the privacy of his office, to let Hank know. Maybe I toned down my expression of disappointment—I'm sure I did. But someone as good at reading people as he is got the message. Hank told me he was taking those most relevant to China (Buck, I understood; Jimmy, I didn't, much as I admired and liked him). In retrospect, I realized that Jimmy, who was president of the company in his early 30s when everybody else was off at war, which, according to him, was the only reason he was promoted, was now getting up in years. This was like a swan song. Hank added that I was young and there would be plenty more opportunities. With that, the conversation ended. By this point my anger had subsided, but not my disappointment. While he didn't praise me or thank me for securing the invitation, I was sure he appreciated it (although I was also sure he was pursuing his own China connections while I pursued the one via Chase and Lubman, and he may have thought that he got the invitation). In any case, this wasn't worth sacrificing my career.

The first trip to China was successful. The Chinese wanted insurance arrangements with an overseas company, and AIG fit the bill. There would be a memorandum of agreement, and Buck Freeman, as the junior man, was to create it. They found an old typewriter, and Hank began giving Buck suggestions over one shoulder, Jimmy Manton over the other. I am not even sure Buck could type. It was translated into Chinese and accepted as the Memorandum of Understanding. The highlight Freeman remembers is that "the People's Insurance Company of China and AIG would continue to explore possibilities of a joint venture."

My opportunity to visit China finally came in 1980. I was invited to travel there for three weeks with an affinity group of others in similar professions. Frankly, it was a boondoggle, unless familiarizing yourself with an important country for AIG counts otherwise. Three weeks was a long time to be away, but I accepted, told Hank, and received a call from him wishing me a good trip before departing. I sometimes think travel and other perks substituted for salary at AIG.

The 1975 AIG trip to China was the first step in a strategy that took Hank there numerous times and led AIG to again become the best situated of any foreign insurance company in China. In 1975, when the first visit occurred, meetings were held with Song Guohua and other officials of the PICC. By 1980, the relationship had progressed so that meetings were held in Bermuda to sign the Shareholders Agreement forming the jointly owned China America Insurance Company, Ltd., the first partnership between the PICC and any foreign insurance company. In early 1985, China America opened a branch office in Hong Kong.

There were bumps along the way. For example, I remember one Chinese proposal suggesting they had too many insurance losses, and we should cover more than our reinsurance with them required. It seemed that we should have done this in the interest "of mutual cooperation and friendship." Needless to say, Hank rejected this.

In 1992, 17 years after the first visit to China, AIA was granted the first foreign life insurance license ever by the Chinese government. It is still the only one. Today AIG operates in eight Chinese cities. It generates $1.3 billion a year in insurance premiums in China including Hong Kong. And while that is just 2 percent of AIG's insurance revenue, its take from Chinese premiums will quadruple in five years, the way they are growing.

This end result came about because of a strategy of dedicating considerable time and resources to China, doing some things that could only be justified by a long-term view and long-term earnings projections. I asked Buck Freeman recently if we were well received by the Chinese because of the conventional wisdom within AIG on the topic: we got a warm welcome because in leaving after the Communists took over, we paid all our claims. In addition, some former Starr employees from pre-Communist days were working in the PICC. Buck said no, "the reason we were well received and made progress was simply because we could help the PICC meet some of its needs." Another AIG myth shattered.

The success in China came from dogged persistence. A joke inside AIG was that the company acronym stood for "All Is Greenberg," which is an apt description of the activities with China. They were closely directed by Greenberg, who shares Neil Starr's affinity for things Chinese. Over three decades, Greenberg made an enormous contribution to China's economy. He advised Shanghai's mayor and was founding chairman of his international business leaders advisory committee. He spearheaded the effort to build Shanghai Center in Tiananmen Square in Beijing, where the Ritz-Carlton is located and which was the largest building in China when it was completed. He directed the Starr Foundation to fund a children's hospital in Shanghai (which is the advantage of having the founders' independent foundation, in effect, serve as the AIG foundation). Perhaps most creative was the purchase by the foundation from a Paris antiques dealer of the original carved doors to Beijing's Summer Palace, which were then returned to China. He also had AIG help finance a giant Shanghai residential and commercial development. Finally, Greenberg lobbied for China's admittance into the World Trade Organization, which happened in 2001. But not before he fought for what he wanted. In 2001, as the Chinese were about to be admitted, the U.S. government handed off the final sticking point—access to insurance markets—to Greenberg. Greenberg put his demands in a letter to Chinese Premier Zhu Rongi, who, after reading them, angrily summoned one of his top trade representatives and, according to that official, declared, "I would never, never see this old man."

The vow was short-lived. In less than an hour Zhu reconsidered. It was clear to Zhu that Greenberg had been given extraordinary authority. So Zhu sent Long Yong-tu to the "Greenberg suite" of a hotel partly owned by AIG and the two began negotiating the final piece of a historic trade pact that, among other things, gave Greenberg what he wanted: the right to keep running wholly owned subsidiaries. Long Yong-tu, the WTO negotiator, has subsequently said, "AIG is known because of Mr. Greenberg."

I asked Greenberg recently why he gave so much time to China. Was it because of our unique company founding and ongoing connections or something else? He responded—somewhat defensively, I suppose—that he "did not give it a lot of time but thought a place with over 1 billion people would be important." I suspect that, like Starr, he has a passion, although more muted, for China.

In the middle of his problems with the U.S. authorities, Greenberg, nevertheless, left for China to accept its prestigious Marco Polo Award for his contributions. He stayed at the government's official guesthouse in Beijing. He was forced to resign as chairman of the company by the time he returned. In an op-ed he authored in the *Wall Street Journal* on October 20, 2005, five months after leaving AIG, he cautioned, "The Chinese have always responded far better to patience than to pressure." Seventeen years of waiting (for an insurance license) is a great deal of patience indeed, especially for Hank Greenberg. This is very different from AIG's actions in other countries where it has difficulties getting what it wants, but China is a very special interest for Greenberg and for the company.

The relationships he developed can only be built over time. That became strikingly obvious in a *Wall Street Journal* article reporting on a meeting in China that both Greenberg and Martin Sullivan, AIG's new CEO, attended. The Chinese swarmed around Greenberg and left Sullivan standing alone with aides. After all, the Chinese have spent 30 years getting to know Greenberg, and they do not abandon such relationships easily. Post-AIG, Greenberg has stayed in close touch with Chinese officials, visits China, and has kept his various honorific posts, now using the title of chairman and CEO, C.V. Starr & Co., instead of chairman of AIG.

I n the mid-1970s I became acquainted with Jack Howell, chairman of Schroeder's Banks and a member of AIG's board. Jack was impressed with my knowledge of international trade and asked me to be a speaker at a meeting of the Pacific Basin Economic Council that was to be held in the Far East. Without missing a heartbeat, I accepted and took my wife along for the speech and a three-week tour, my first, of our Asian offices, something I thought I should do and certainly more defensible than simply visiting China for three weeks. Midway through the second week I received a fax from Greenberg: "I am single-handedly running your department here. I need you in New York." A mild enough statement, but I could hear the tone in which it was said. I cut the trip short and rushed home.

On my first day back in the office I was a nervous wreck, probably because I had no justification to feel indignant because I was flat
wrong. If I were Greenberg, I probably would have fired me. But he
did not. I was not summoned for a meeting, but when we were in a
meeting together he frowned at me—nothing more—and never said
a word.

My wife had a word, used with a somewhat bittersweet taste I think,
that she used to describe how Ken Nottingham (a close friend who
was chairman of American Life Insurance Company, the major overseas
life operation of AIG and has recently passed away), I, and a few others
passed our time on international business trips: as megaconsumers. Ken
would have the head of our operations in Pakistan get me a nice Persian
rug. Artie Joukowsky would buy paintings from Yugoslavia. I would buy
some jade in China. We would trade off Senegalese wooden carvings for
Nigerian ivory carvings. And on and on. I explained we just did not go
overseas and work and hang out in bars like so many businessmen—we
were in the rare, cultivated business of collecting, collecting some items
that might some day be impossible to get. About all I got was "you're an
addict—enjoy yourself, megaconsumer."

When I was recruited to AIG, I considered myself fairly sophisticated in the ways of power and government relations, especially
in Washington. There had been some successes for my business constituency not only in D.C., but some abroad as well. Soon I would learn just
how naïve, by AIG standards, I was. Shortly after joining the company, a
group of us went to Buenos Aires, led by Jimmy Manton, an elegant
Englishman who began his career with no postsecondary education as a
"clark" in England but before he retired was knighted for using some of
his many millions to become the Tate Museum's second biggest bene-
factor after Sir Henry Tate. Also along was Paul Butler, head of AIG
operations in Latin America, and several other AIG executives. The purpose was to attend the Hemispheric Insurance Conference held every
two years, a confab intended, when it was founded by U.S. insurance
executives, to bring American and Latin American insurers together for
like-minded causes. By the time we went to Argentina, however, the
conference had degenerated into a political football where Latin
American nationalists used it as a platform to push their point of view.

In this, my first experience as a business insider (and not just a trade association representative of various business interests), I attended the plenary sessions, the surfeit of social events, including the overly lavish party thrown by the U.S. delegation. (I was told this was expected of someone representing a country of massive wealth like the United States, and anything less would be resented.) I watched my colleagues wheel and deal, and I presume some business resulted from their activities. And then, the day before we left, we met in Jimmy Manton's hotel room, where Paul pulled from his briefcase a large envelope full of dollar-denominated Argentine bonds, which constituted part of the reserves of our Argentine company. The bonds numbered in the millions of dollars. As I later figured out, they wanted to take them back to the States and trade them for dollars. Paul or Jimmy, I don't remember which, said: "Ron, as the new kid on the block, why don't you carry these bonds back to New York? We can dispose of them there."

It totally unnerved me. I hesitated and finally declined, probably setting my career back, at least temporarily. One of the others carried the bonds to New York and I never heard anymore about it (although I never asked and never found out for sure). Later our Argentine manager was arrested for carrying $100,000. It was a stark introduction to the way AIG played in the international arena to protect its far-flung interests.

A powerful contributor to AIG's success has been its uncommon ability to get what it wants from governments here and abroad. AIG executives learn early on to approach government and regulatory problems in the same aggressive way they attack business issues in general. The company routinely tries to persuade, cajole, or, if necessary, intimidate officials at all levels anywhere in the world. A more benign description would suggest it is based on a simple strategy: harness the full force of the U.S. government into looking after vital business interests, in this case, AIG interests. This take-no-prisoners approach is one that Hank Greenberg not only endorses, but passionately practices. He monitors and often participates in the various issues the company faces with governments.

The AIG campaign to achieve majority ownership of its Mexican affiliate is a case in point. For many years, the Mexican government remained adamant in limiting foreign ownership of insurance companies to less than 50 percent, and AIG fought for years to get the policy changed. It was made worse by the fact that the Mexican government would call for capital increases and wouldn't let the foreigners participate. So the "less than 50 percent" was gradually whittled down. Greenberg and others met frequently with the Mexican ministry of finance; the company threatened trade and financial retaliation by the United States; and it pressed the U.S. State Department to take up its cause. Nothing worked. Greenberg railed to Congress and the U.S. Trade Representative's office, but to no avail.

Then Pat Foley, general counsel for domestic political issues at AIG, noticed a pending change in New York State law in 1981. The new law would allow banks and insurance companies registered in New York State to hold up to 2 percent of their reserves in risky Mexican bonds. Bingo! Just what AIG had been looking for. This was just as the Latin American debt crisis was about to begin, and the Mexican government wanted the new law so that lenders could continue buying its debt. AIG wanted to own more of its company in Mexico. All the makings of a tradeoff.

AIG had backed New York Governor Hugh Carey, so Greenberg got him on the phone, explained the situation, and asked him to sit on the reserve bill until Mexico changed its minority ownership rules. The Mexicans, dumbfounded at what had happened, appealed to the U.S. Treasury (which also wanted the reserve bill passed). Governor Carey's office called Hank more than once to ask if he was ready to pull his hold on the legislation. "Absolutely not," Hank replied each time. "When they let me own my company, I will let you know." The Mexicans, with much more at stake than AIG, ultimately caved in, passing legislation that lifted the majority ownership prohibition for AIG. With that, Hank gave Hugh Carey the go-ahead to sign the New York bill. Hank got his majority ownership of the Mexican subsidiary and New York State made it easier for financial institutions to buy Mexican bonds. Perhaps the sweetest detail about this particular horse trade is that it applied only to AIG. Mexico did not ease ownership restrictions for any other U.S. insurers.

O ne of the most difficult challenges AIG faced occurred about six months before the seizure of the American hostages at the Tehran embassy in 1979. K.C. Shabani, an Iranian emigrant who had become a naturalized U.S. citizen, had worked at a rather insignificant job in California with AIG for nearly 20 years. He turned up in an AIG computer printout in the 1970s as an Iranian who knew Farsi and would qualify for work in Iran. Greenberg picked him for a new assignment: Persuade Iranian authorities to allow AIG to be the first foreign insurer to operate there.

Shabani spent a year and a half lobbying an old friend, who was a minister in the Shah's government, to get permission for AIG to open its doors in Iran. More important, he divorced his wife and married the Shah's social secretary, whose brother was the lover of the Shah's older sister, who had real influence on the Shah. So suddenly he was in, with regular Saturday tennis games at the palace and the social whirl of Tehran. Finally, in 1975 the Iranian government passed a law permitting AIG to become the country's first foreign insurer. Shabani was made the manager, and the company did well.

When the Shah fled in 1979, AIG's vice president for the Middle East happened to be there at the time and was caught in Iran for three weeks before getting a flight out just before Ayatollah Khomeini returned. Shabani wasn't so lucky. The Ayatollah's government seized AIG's assets and threw him in jail.

Greenberg personally took charge of the effort to secure Shabani's release. "We will not only get Shabani out of jail, but we will get him safely out of Iran," Greenberg said. "First and foremost, we owe it to him and his family. But to do anything less will send a terrible message to our employees all over the world. It could happen to them as well. We will always make their security and safety our first priority."

AIG scorned formal task forces and committees; instead, Greenberg just pulled together the people needed to work on a problem, a group that was constantly expanding as he had an inspiration or hit on something new to try. I was soon on my way to Houston, where the brother of the Iranian foreign minister was a physician. Unfortunately, the doctor explained that his brother was virtually in disgrace, would soon leave the government and probably the country, and could be of no help, which is exactly what happened. Nor could AIG's usual ally, the

U.S. government, be of help. AIG's first principle of political success—
secure the power of the U.S. government to help attain objectives—was
next to useless because U.S. relations with revolutionary Iran were virtually nonexistent. So AIG executives spread around the globe looking
for another way to free Shabani.

After many weeks with no real progress, Nottingham, in charge of
the Middle East, and I and went to Washington for meetings at Foggy
Bottom. "This unfortunate situation has gotten much worse," we were
told. "The Iranians allege they have searched Mr. Shabani's office. In
his desk drawer they found a pair of woman's panties and some drugs.
Drugs and adultery are both very serious offenses, in some cases capital
offenses, in Iran. This weakens our hand tremendously and gives us virtually no basis for demanding his release."

"That is absurd," Nottingham replied. "I know Shabani does not take
drugs nor deal in drugs, and he is faithful to his wife. We would have
pulled him from Iran otherwise. Obviously, if the Iranians did find this
evidence—and that's a big if—it was planted." The official looked
incredulous but explained that even if what Nottingham said was
true, the Iranians said otherwise, and that gave them an ample excuse
to keep Shabani incarcerated. When Nottingham asked what the State
Department normally does when a citizen is jailed under false pre-
tenses, the official bristled and said it does everything in its power to
get the person out. He promised he would "actively follow this case"
and brought the interview to a close. In thinking about the situation,
we were convinced a real reason for Shabani's problems was his wife's
role as the Shah's social secretary and her connections.

On November 4, 1979, Iranian militants seized the U.S. embassy
and some 70 Americans began 444 days of captivity. Getting attention
for Shabani's situation, always difficult, became virtually impossible.
How could you argue over the seizure of one American company and
the imprisonment of its manager, apparently for dealing in drugs
and having extramarital affairs, when 70 American diplomats and soldiers were being held captive? AIG had been preparing to approach the
U.S. government to make a formal claim about the seizure of its company, but the hostage crisis made that move pointless.

Shabani's wife, Nasrin, added to the complications in this deli-
cate situation. Shabani had made a giant professional leap when he

was picked to run AIG's Iran operations, strictly because of his Iranian ancestry, from a fairly inconsequential job in California. Suddenly he was president of AIG's company in Iran, and he quickly became a minor star on the Tehran social circuit. Nasrin was a great asset to Shabani while the Shah remained in power, but became a liability after he fled the country. Nasrin was allowed to leave the country after Shabani was jailed, but she insisted on returning to petition for his release.

If her former position weren't bad enough, her manner was sure to make matters worse, and did. Typical of her actions was a visit to the judge's quarters to plead Shabani's case. She returned to Tehran and was accompanied by an AIGer of Middle Eastern descent, Henri Beidas, who came in from London to help. Nasrin came to the meeting dressed to the hilt—something like a Dior dress, Armani scarf, Prada shoes, bedecked in expensive jewelry, topped with a full-length mink coat. This, to see a revolutionary judge serving under a strict Islamic regime. Her behavior was as obnoxious as her attire was inappropriate. Beidas reported that she loudly denounced the government and the judge and demanded Shabani's immediate release. Luckily, she wasn't imprisoned herself.

About this time Ken Nottingham and I visited former Attorney General Ramsey Clark, who has an unusual law practice in Greenwich Village focusing on indigents, refugees, immigrants, and the downtrodden and whose wife, an American Indian, acts as his receptionist. We paid $25,000, and Clark said he could keep Shabani from being killed but couldn't get him out. He did just that. Meantime, Shabani's wife was working her own angles.

After many months, the authorities released Shabani from jail, but seized his passport and ordered him to remain in the country. Nasrin, by then in Paris, planned to return immediately, but AIG told her to stay put. The company planned to get him out and didn't want her seized in his place. We got in touch with a group of Kurds and paid them to smuggle Shabani out of the country to Turkey. But the Turks won't let you in without a passport. So Greenberg and Nottingham visited Secretary of State Cyrus Vance, who agreed to issue a new passport that we had delivered to the Turkish border. Greenberg gave the go-ahead after AIG's Washington contacts gave their blessing to the move.

After several days of anxious waiting, Greenberg finally got word that Shabani was safely out of Iran. The news came at one of AIG's monthly Public Policy Fora, a fancy name for dinner discussions with prominent politicians, for which the politicians are paid. A secretary walked quietly into the room and slipped Greenberg a note. He immediately interrupted the guest, the late senator Daniel Patrick Moynihan, and exclaimed, "Shabani's out." Once he had heard the full story, Moynihan quipped, "Why don't you take responsibility for getting the embassy hostages out, too?"

By the time Shabani returned to New York, his hair had turned white and he looked terrible. He said that twice while he was imprisoned, guards came to him, told him to make out a will, gave him the Qur'an to read, and took him outside to a wall, where he was blindfolded. Each time they fired over his head, had a hearty laugh, and escorted him back to his cell. The mock executions were terrifying because real executions happened in the prison regularly. Shabani says that the chief executioner was Mahmoud Ahmadinejad Khatami, the current president of Iran. A friend of Shabani's from Orange County in California, who was in prison with him, confirms this. They say they saw him daily for a year, and that he was the one who would go to the yard after someone was shot and give them the coup de grace, usually a pistol shot to the head. This has been reported to the State Department and the *Wall Street Journal*. But no action has been taken. A number of the American embassy hostages also have fingered Khatami as being one of their guards in the embassy.

Shabani's escape sounded almost as harrowing as his imprisonment. He had expected to be taken out alone, but when the smugglers picked him up outside his Tehran house early one morning, they had two other passengers in tow, both former ministers under the Shah. Shabani told us he would have rather remained in Tehran than get in the car with these two. One had many thousands of dollars strapped to his body. As they wound out of Tehran and began the 800-mile drive over the mountains to Turkey, they had to negotiate a series of armed checkpoints. Each time, the big man pulled out a wad of bills and paid off the soldiers. This happened again and again until his money was virtually gone. But by then they were in Turkey.

Nottingham recommended a nice retirement package, a year's pay, and other things. Greenberg told the manager in California to give him an office and a secretary, and that he could work as long as he wanted—in other words, a lifetime sinecure.

I discussed this incident recently with Greenberg. His memories and mine were the same, except for who got Shabani out of Iran. He said it was not the group of Kurds I remember, but he would not reveal who it was in case he needed them again. Later I confirmed my version with someone who would know. The important thing is that we got him out.

When I began this book, I discovered that Shabani, now in his 80s, had continued working for AIG until three years ago. The fact that he worked for the next quarter of a century says something about the excitement of AIG. It gets in your blood, even when your life has been threatened.

Shabani fared better than his once influential brother-in-law. When the Shah fled Iran, the brother-in-law relocated to Monaco with the Shah's sister. Driving down a winding road, his car was attacked by a machine gunner intending to kill the Shah's sister. He threw himself over her, she was not hurt, and he was shot in the leg. When he was in the hospital, the Shah sent a representative to tell him a Swiss bank account had been opened in his name and the Shah would keep replenishing it as needed. In other words, it would be topped off for the rest of his life. Eight months after that, he was driving alone on the same road, his brakes gave out, and he died. No allegations were made, although you could certainly be suspicious that the brakes were tampered with.

We received a call from our office in Managua alerting us to the fact that we were likely to be closed and ultimately put out of business because of a law passed over 50 years earlier. AFIA (American Foreign Insurance Association), which no longer exists but was our principal competitor overseas, was in the same boat. I was dispatched to Nicaragua by Greenberg with the understanding that I would coordinate with the general counsel of AFIA, who was also en route. The idea was to get the lay of the land and decide if we needed U.S. government help. I was expected to call on the U.S. embassy while in Managua.

I was met at the airport by our country manager—standard operating procedure for a senior visitor from the home office. Over dinner he explained what had happened. As I recall, when a law was passed authorizing foreign insurers to operate half a century ago, it had an expiration date that would be upon us shortly. When it came, foreign companies no longer could operate. Nobody had ever paid attention to it, and our manager hadn't known until days before that the provision existed. He said there was also considerable suspicion that local Nicaraguan companies were jubilant about it and were behind an effort to make sure the law wasn't renewed.

The next day I learned the reason AFIA had sent its lawyer for this assignment: He had gone to West Point with Nicaragua's president-cum-dictator, Anastasio Somoza, who came from a family that had produced its share of dictators. He said he could secure an appointment with Somoza and did so almost immediately. Perhaps my memory has failed me, but I remember we got to Somoza's office by crossing a moat from the main part of Managua and heading up a hill to a castle that overlooked the city. Medieval protection for the leader.

We were ushered past innumerable guards, most holding machine guns, until we entered the president's gargantuan office, but we were shown in alone with no escort. Who knows, perhaps Somoza had a magic button to press for help or perhaps he had a gun in his desk drawer. This giant of a man, in all dimensions, looked up from his desk, saw me, and said, "Who are you and what the hell are you doing here?"

It was incredible. Here is a dictator, in a heavily guarded castle above the city, with guards everywhere, and we had breezed past them all and been shown into his office unescorted. No one searched us or asked for an ID or even a business card. No one even asked who we were. And I, it turns out, didn't even have an appointment. I was just taken along by his friend. Realizing this, I quickly explained that my company was the other one about to be closed by Nicaragua's law.

Somoza quickly dispensed with the niceties, heard our complaint, and yelled outside to one of his minions, "Get me the president of the Supreme Court on the line." What followed was a royal dressing-down of the president of the court. He told him, "I want the problem fixed and fixed immediately." The president could not get in one word edgewise. I was fairly sure he was trying to say this should be fixed by the Congress since it was an expiring law, but Somoza would not listen. His view was presumably that the law could be thrown out by the highest court. Somoza ended the conversation with the justice with the warning: "I have been considering replacing the entire court. This gives me another reason." Then he hung up. As we left, President Somoza said: "That should take care of it. It's all yours now. See, in our little country, we fix problems for foreign investors."

We returned to the city, and our manager and I met with our lawyer, a son of the president of the Senate. He was very nervous about the conversation we had had with Somoza. He did not want to take the case to the Supreme Court. He also felt awkward because of his father's position. Apparently, he, too, felt the Congress should straighten out the problem. I pushed him hard, noting the president of the country had told us what to do, and he finally said he would do it. Then I returned home just in time for Thanksgiving.

The Monday after Thanksgiving weekend I was a hero in the New York office until our manager called from Nicaragua and said the whole deal had fallen apart.

Our lawyer refused to do what we had asked. The problem finally got fixed about six months later when the law was changed by the Nicaraguan Congress. I am not quite sure what lesson I learned. I guess the lesson is that even if you get to the top, uninvited, an order from the president can't necessarily fix things, even when he is a dictator. No wonder President Kennedy complained that he gave orders and nothing happened. Somoza, incidentally, later fled to Paraguay, where he was assassinated.

The late 1970s was a period when a number of AIG employees were imprisoned around the world. In 1978, one of the company's most adventuresome, some would say cavalier, and independent executives was head of our biggest operation in West Africa—Nigeria. Louie Lefevre comes from an aristocratic Huguenot family still owning property in upstate New York dating back to the eighteenth century. Wherever Louie was assigned around the world, he always took his polo ponies with him, even though some of the countries had no tradition of playing polo. Louie would get it organized.

In Nigeria, he was in the middle of a feud, per company instructions, with the Nigerian government. In effect, the country nationalized 60 percent of AIG and AIG rejected the compensation offered. After a long hassle, Lefevre was arrested. The Nigerians' timing was terrible, as we shall see. This would turn into an international incident.

Louie's incarceration was in a special jail for foreigners, many of whom were being shaken down. One of Louie's jailmates was an Italian contractor who had been there for six months over an ongoing dispute about kickbacks with a Nigerian general. He was released every Wednesday night for a conjugal visit with his mistress, his meals were catered by an Italian restaurant, and he had his contracting firm come in and build a tennis court on the grounds of the jail.

He asked Lefevre if he played tennis. Louie said, yes, he did. He then asked if Louie had whites and a racket. Louie explained he didn't expect to get to play when he came to jail. The contractor said his tailor would come and fit him and they would get him a racket. And although they needed more players, "until we have you fitted out you can't play." Sort of an all-white rule, like at Wimbledon.

At this point we had called on the State Department more than once and finally secured its agreement to send instructions to the ambassador to Nigeria, Donald Easum, to intervene. They resisted at first because they did not want to disrupt U.S.-Nigerian relations, especially with a planned visit of President Carter on the horizon. We heard that Ambassador Easum, not exactly on our side in this dispute, visited Lefevre, who conveyed in a relaxed manner that he was fine and did not want out of jail. This weakened our case considerably, although we later found that Louie, independent soul that he is, was concerned that this would be screwed up by the embassy or us and didn't want to get in a dangerous situation where he might encounter a Nigerian on a dark night or something like that.

As part of our practice of pushing all buttons, we called on Tommy "the Cork" Corcoran for help. Ken Nottingham, AIG vice president for Africa, went to Washington and joined Corcoran in his limousine to meet with the assistant secretary of state for West Africa. About seven officials were at the meeting, and Corcoran, as only Corcoran can, opened the meeting by claiming, "What is going on with these Africans is outrageous." He said he came home and four trees were cut down. He asked his servant to talk to his next-door neighbor, the Ivory Coast ambassador, who had a tree cutter take them down. Corcoran called on him and the ambassador said, "Your leaves were all over my yard and I have diplomatic immunity, so you can't do anything."

So Corcoran, who had a friend in the garbage business, asked him to dump garbage in the ambassador's yard every day. The ambassador took Corcoran to court and sued, but, as Corcoran gleefully relates, he waived his diplomatic immunity to do so. So he countersued and got compensation for his trees. His next comment was, "Now, there is this innocent American in Nigeria."

Nothing came out of this meeting. But, as I mentioned earlier, the timing was bad for Nigeria. Apparently, there was no coordination between the president of Nigeria's office and the office responsible for nationalizing AIG, for President Carter was embarking on a long-planned trip to Nigeria that coincided with this incident. Knowing this, Greenberg and Nottingham called on Secretary of State Cyrus Vance, but did not get much satisfaction.

Traveling with the president was the late Jesse Hill, an African-American, president of an Atlanta insurance company, who today has a road named for him in Atlanta. En route, President Carter gave him a report in his briefing book about the investment dispute and Louie's internment, saying: "Jesse, this is right up your alley. You handle this one."

Meantime, we talked to Charlie Brower, a White and Case attorney we retained to work on this matter, and now a member of the International Court of Justice in The Hague. Brower said he had some friends at NBC and would try to get the story on the evening news. Sure enough, on NBC's evening news, there was an interview with Louie's wife, a photo of Louie in military uniform, and his child and dog. Quite an all-American scene and a devastating piece of public relations. The cameras showed the president being greeted in Nigeria and then switched to the story of Louie.

Next day there was a church service at the Baptist church in Lagos since President Obasanjo, like Jimmy Carter, was a Baptist. Apparently, Secretary Vance had not discussed the situation with President Carter, since he did not want this incident to interfere with the success of the trip. Jesse Hill walked down the aisle of the church, without interference, as a black Baptist can do, and sat with President Carter, telling him the story and that it had been on the evening news. Carter was furious and dressed down Vance after church, and Lefevre was freed the next day.

I n the late 1970s I was in South Korea with Dick Rivers, a law partner of the legendary Robert Strauss, then U.S. trade representative
and former chairman of the Democratic National Committee. We were
trying to obtain a license to write non-life insurance, a goal that had
eluded AIG for years. Hank Greenberg had visited Korea to push
for the license on more than one occasion, and we had constantly pes-
tered the U.S. government for help. Before leaving for Korea, we
encountered a situation in Washington that taught us the stark reality of
our new legislative weapon (discussed below), imposing restrictions
against the Koreans. We called on Ambassador Strauss, who said,
"I would be delighted to pick out one or more Korean exports and
limit their entry into the U.S." Strauss was facing Jimmy Carter's reelection campaign, and halting Korean textiles, for example, could have
been helpful to the campaign.

It dawned on us that if we succeeded in blocking their exports, we
could not have the ban lifted at will. In fact, it probably would be very
hard to get lifted because so many industries would have an interest in
keeping it. And our name would be mud in Korea. We would likely
never get a license. So we had a powerful tool we were afraid to use.

During the Korean visit, Rivers and I received what we saw as a
none-too-subtle threat. Nevertheless, we were aggressive with the
Koreans and even more aggressive with the U.S. embassy. Finally, after
several days of our pressure, in exasperation, the American ambassador
complained, "You are becoming an irritant to U.S.-Korean relations."
According to Matt Nimetz, a former undersecretary of state who is
now a partner with General Atlantic Partners, a global private equity
firm, this inflammatory statement was "all too often representative of
the U.S. stance towards problems an American business has with a foreign government. The embassy takes the viewpoint of their 'client,'
which is not the American businessman but the host country."

T here are endless stories about AIG's overseas adventures that illus-
trate Greenberg's caustic humor. AIG had a joint venture in Turkey
with Turkish newspaper group Tom Ayat—the Turkish American
Insurance Company. An internal audit indicated that the partners were
stealing money. So Greenberg, John Roberts, and Ken Nottingham went
to Istanbul. On arriving, an official from the company explained that the

chairman had a serious heart condition, was in the hospital, and could have no visitors. The implication was clear: This status would continue as long as the AIG officials were there. So they went to dinner. Another official, Tyler, came and said there was something important he needed to talk to them about. Greenberg, who was in a foul mood, asked, "Why do we have to talk at dinner?" He kept saying it. Tyler explained that the company building was on fire and it looked like the building would burn down, destroying all records. So Greenberg said, "We might as well go home tomorrow—there is nothing left to salvage here."

Roberts, Greenberg, and Nottingham were flying to Egypt after a board meeting of Iran-American, the AIG company in Iran. They planned to see the joint venture company they established in the free zone in Egypt, and their partners there arranged for them to fly by the pyramids. Roberts was reading *The Green Guide* to Egypt ad nauseum, talking about dynasties, pyramids, and the like again and again. Finally, Greenberg, the only Jew on the plane, who was tired and exasperated, said: "John, will you shut up? My people built the pyramids. I know all about them."

In the mid-1970s, AIG stumbled onto an issue that would fundamentally change the rules for business operations around the world. It took hours and hours of executive time, but this serendipitous development was worth every moment. First, however, AIG executives had to understand that there was even an issue and what it was. It all began with variations of a conversation that repeated itself again and again but all had the same theme. These conversations were reminiscent of what Starr himself had said when his company was expropriated in Cuba: "Look, what is our business? It's no more than a guarantee, a piece of paper. . . ."

U.S. companies, if they are to succeed overseas, have no choice but to adapt to the customs of the countries where they operate. That means doing some things they would never do in the United States. AIG is no exception. But AIG, in typical AIG fashion, is much more aggressive than most others in its dealings abroad. When threatened with expropriation or being forced to sell a local company, as it was in Nigeria,

Egypt, Pakistan, and various other countries, AIG unleashed the fury of Washington against the country. It used its considerable political clout to threaten trade sanctions, cut off aid, and take whatever other dire actions it could find. Often they were successful, but not always.

It may be that other multinationals like Exxon or Haliburton or General Motors let forth with their firepower as well. But there are two big differences. One is that these are high-profile behemoths that are well known both in Washington and in the countries in which they operate. So when they protest, it is heard and listened to. A second, and until 25 or so years ago much more important, difference is that they are either extractive industry or engineering/construction or manufacturing companies, that is, the kind that our government would readily agree deserve compensation for expropriation. After all, they build huge facilities— facilities you can see and touch. No doubt, these have tremendous value. Not so AIG. C.V. Starr aptly described an insurance company (falling into the category of service companies) when Castro nationalized his Cuban operation ("it's no more than a guarantee, a piece of paper"), and for many years that is exactly how the U.S. government looked at it. Other companies had a prima facie case to begin with. AIG had to make a case. So AIG had to push doubly hard to persuade its own government that its overseas operations had any value. After all, what is a piece of paper worth? Then, if it won that battle, it had to battle the country that took the action against it while fighting a constant rearguard action to keep its own government from abandoning it.

Pan to a discussion with the desk officer for India at the State Department. "I understand your company was nationalized in India. So were lots of others. But what is yours worth? No buildings, no machinery, no factories. Nothing. No real value."

"But we are insuring people's lives. We're guaranteeing a future for their families. And we are investing a portion of the premiums we collect."

"But when you think of the hundreds of millions U.S. Steel spent on their plant. Or the money the auto assembly plants spent. Now, that's real money. And we have to get them compensated."

And that's the way the conversations went. How we ultimately made the jump from these discussions, investment disputes, to trade, I'm not quite sure. I suspect it came from having lots of discussions in Washington. I remember a conversation that occurred about this time (early 1970s) with an assistant secretary of commerce. The talk was about whether insurance could be traded. This, I discovered, was a totally alien concept. When I gave the one obvious example of an insurance product that I thought for sure was traded—marine insurance, which insures the transit of goods, both domestically and internationally—it was summarily rejected.

So we groped our way through this subject and gradually learned a new terminology—trade terminology. Soon, we were constantly repeating a new word—"services"—and arguing that insurance, credit card transactions, transportation (airlines, ships), banking transactions all fell into this category. More important, we argued that services were traded just like goods and commodities were traded. For those in government with an intellectual bent, and for private economists, there were plenty of arguments around to knock this notion. For one, the intellectual/theoretical basis for trade in services had never been established. They cited famous and respected economists like Adam Smith and David Ricardo, who denigrated services as unimportant, second-class economic activities that had no value and could not be traded.

We organized to deal with this challenge. We attracted other, like-minded service industries and created a new trade association, the Coalition of Service Industries (CSI), which Hank Greenberg chaired and ultimately was mimicked in a number of countries overseas. We lobbied for a private advisory committee structure that was included in the Trade Act of 1974, which was an important first step in getting services recognized in trade. Under the structure, I was appointed chairman of the government's Industry Service Advisory Committee and Greenberg was appointed to the high-level committee that advised the trade representative, the Trade Policy Advisory Committee. We started building an intellectual basis for our argument through participating in conferences in the right places—Bellagio, the Rockefeller Foundation center in Italy, Ditchley near Churchill's homes close to Oxford, and others. I wrote a book for the Council on Foreign Relations—*Beyond Industrialization*—to help make the case for services.

It was 1984 amendments to the trade law that first recognized that services are traded like goods and commodities. In that same legislation, for the first time, services were included along with goods and commodities in the Section 301 provisions. Section 301 is what gives the U.S. government the authority to retaliate against a country that takes discriminatory action against an industry. So if a country blocks the licensing of an insurance company, the United States can levy duties on that country's exports to the United States. Ultimately, services were put on the agenda for a trade round, and some rules were established to govern trade in services. Over the past few decades, there have been additions, including the adoption of trade rules governing financial services.

By the time this had run its course, which took some 30 years, AIG would reap numerous benefits. First, a whole new category of trading activities had been recognized—trade in services—and rules to govern trade in this category had been established. That meant if a country were a signatory to a particular provision, the presumption is that AIG would be able to operate without discrimination. Second, AIG had a new weapon to use in its battle for open markets and against nationalization, expropriation, and shades of expropriation—both a country's agreement with GATT rules and the Section 301 provisions. Finally, AIG's worldwide reputation had been substantially enhanced by the very visible leadership it had given to advancing this issue. An article in the *National Journal* on August 30, 1986, quoted a Washington trade expert: "[I]f Shelp hadn't thought up the idea, if Greenberg hadn't been such a pest, . . . if American Express hadn't jumped in . . . services wouldn't have flown as an issue." Clearly, AIG was known as the leader of the services issue.

Fortune magazine used to periodically identify the "Ten Toughest Bosses in America." This was a list that virtually every CEO wanted to avoid, but Hank Greenberg was disappointed if he was left off. Direct reports to the bosses on this list get all kinds of reactions—from sympathy to awe. Once I was late for the kind of lunch you wanted to be invited to, the monthly luncheon/salon hosted by the late John Diebold, the father of automation. I arrived about 10 minutes late and John said, loud enough for the rest of the table to hear, "That's all right, Ron. We know who you work for. We are glad you got here at all."

When I was recruited to be CEO of the New York City Partnership, the organization of about 200 CEOs founded by David Rockefeller, my experience with Hank Greenberg was a job-clincher.

At least three of the CEOs on the search committee said to me: "In this job you have to deal with the governor, the mayor, and every CEO in town, most of whom have gigantic egos. Anybody who can successfully work for Hank will find this job a cinch."

All of us who worked at AIG would get asked by friends, colleagues, and the chance acquaintance: "How do you work there? How do you stand it? Don't you live in daily fear of getting dressed down in front of everybody else or even fired?" Hank Greenberg's temper and sharpness with everyone—subordinates, journalists, directors, government officials—is a legend in business and political circles. At times, the legend of his temper seems to get equal billing with the breadth of his accomplishments. Which is really unfair. What he built so totally overshadows any difficulties of temperament that it really becomes a red herring used to shift focus from AIG's phenomenal growth.

The question is: How accurate are the tales of Greenberg's temper? Does he really explode at people regardless of who they are as often and as loudly as is reputed? Why does he do it? Is it possible, just possible, he uses it as a management tool?

One senior executive still at AIG in a staff position said to me that Greenberg snapped at him a couple of times when he first started at the company some 20 years ago just to make sure he knew who the boss was (as if there could be any doubt) but not since. He is convinced, based on watching Greenberg over the years, that he virtually never dresses down staff people, but shows no such restraint toward the heads of profit centers. Why would that be? Probably because he considers the latter a hell of a lot more important. After all, they make him or break him. To make his ambitious numbers, they have to succeed. If they do not, he blows up at them. That, of course, puts staff people in a secondary position, but that is true in most companies.

The biggest humiliation in getting cut to pieces by Greenberg is that it is seldom done privately. Chopping you up in front of your peers is one thing—after all, you are likely to see the same happen to them. But in front of outsiders it is another thing altogether. I hardly ever remember that happening. Another school of thought is that he is compensating for his size. While vigorous, dynamic, and slim, Hank is not tall, about 5'7", I would guess. The most noticeable characteristic is the eyes that burn right through you. So naturally, because of his height the rap is that he has a Napoleon complex. I don't believe this is true. Here is a man of great self-confidence, in his work, with distinguished citizens from all walks of life, with women. He may suffer from other complexes but not that one.

The other complex some say Greenberg has is an inferiority complex—or better said, insecurities. The argument goes that he has to be loud and overbearing to compensate for his lack of background, for not coming from the best family. It has been argued that he bought an interest in Loeb Rhodes just to have an entry into upper-class Jewish circles. That is not true—there was a real business interest, since Loeb Rhodes partners were significant owners of AIG. But I am not a psychologist and find these hard to sort through. The closest I came to thinking there might be something to this was one morning when he, Ed Matthews, our CFO, and I were checking out of a hotel. I didn't know Hank was behind me and I was holding my gold American Express card. Suddenly, I felt an arm on mine and he said, "Why is yours gold and mine green?"

I responded, a bit shaken, "Because I paid $20 more for it." He smiled and let go of my arm. From that encounter, however, I am not ready to conclude that Hank Greenberg has an inferiority complex. Maybe instead he wants whatever others have, and then some.

There is no doubt that Greenberg's success has enabled him to overcome any feelings of inadequacy he may have had when he began his career at AIG. He was not part of the establishment and had a chip on his shoulder. He was very conscious that he wasn't part of it. This was made worse by the fact that Youngman and Tweedy were the epitome of the WASP establishment. He was concerned about clubs like the Links and Brook. That has changed. Now that he is an integral part of the establishment—witness being vice chair of the Council on Foreign Relations and chair of the Asia Society and all the nice incidentals like being invited to the Bohemian Grove in California—he could care less. The past epitome of the establishment is Jim Robinson, scion of an old Atlanta banking family and chairman of American Express. Robinson was not a favorite of Greenberg's and at one point he wanted to take over his company, but was dissuaded by his board or his Starr partners. It is probably the one acquisition that did not occur that he most regrets. Greenberg is not really interested in the Jewish establishment. There was little involvement with this community except supporting the Home for the Aged in Riverdale which I suspect is the retirement home his mother moved to at some point.

Learning to survive at AIG meant learning to manage Hank Greenberg. Managing your boss is important anywhere but is presumptuous when it comes to Hank since the tendency is to think of Hank Greenberg managing you. It is really hard to manage him. But there are some lessons to be learned. Lesson No. 1 is to save the contentious issues—the issues he is likely to disagree with you on—to discuss with him in private. He does not like to be taken on in public. But one-on-one, he would almost always listen to your advice and often take it. Lesson No. 2 is more difficult: Try to deal with Greenberg's people management talents so that he does not decide that berating you is a way to get more work done. This is tricky, but I believe Hank knew that if he yelled at me it did not lead to increased work on my part but instead it just made me pout.

The point is that Greenberg is a master at managing people. It is a skill that serves him well. I remember an incident early in my career at AIG that involved a meeting in Greenberg's office on the Philippines. Cesar Zalamea, president of Philippine American Life, was there, along with eight or nine other executives. We were sitting in the anteroom to the left of Greenberg's office and he came through the door connecting the two. He had barely sat down in "his" seat (regulars knew better than to sit there, and we tried to tactfully move those who did, even VIPs, to another seat), when he exploded. Five minutes of yelling and screaming about this Philippine problem and then there was a pause to let Zalamea or others give what was taken as a feeble explanation. The meeting went on for about 30 minutes, walking orders were issued, and we quietly left, glad to be out of there. I was one who was not called on and I certainly did not volunteer.

Within five minutes, I was summoned to Greenberg's office for the next meeting. It was as if the last meeting had never occurred. Greenberg was gracious, funny, and expansive, and we had a pleasant meeting. There could be several such meetings a day. After a couple of encounters like the first two, witnessing Greenberg's seemingly Jekyll-and-Hyde personality, you either figure out what is going on or you live a very jittery life, every day in fear of an encounter with Mr. Hyde.

Humble Beginnings in Shanghai
The two-room office of American Asiatic Underwriters (AAU), started by Starr
in 1919.

Motohir Nagaska, Starr, Mrs. Rudoph Bing, Rudolph Bing, Yoshio Aoyama C.V.
Starr financed a production of *Madame Butterfly*, sparing no expense on authentic
sets and costumes designed to show the Japan that he knew.

C.V. Starr
Said by associates to always
be well attired.

Friends and Colleagues
C.V. Starr stands to
the left of C.J. Smith,
with whom he worked
for some 50 years.

Starr Partners
Second from right, William Youngman; next to him, C.V. Starr; two to the left,
Artemis Joukowsky, Hank Greenberg; behind Mr. Greenberg is Gordon Tweedy.
Just in front of Tweedy is Ernest Stempel, and K.K. Tse is in front of and to
the left of Stempel. Two over is Houghton Freeman, and E.A.G. Manton is next
to him. The taller man behind Manton is John J. Roberts.

A Powerful Pack
Left to right: Ernest Stempel, Hank Greenberg, Gordon Tweedy, Artemis
Joukowsky II.

The Importance of China
Hank Greenberg (right) with Buck Freeman (right rear), AIG vice president of Foreign General Insurance in Beijing, with Song Guohua and other officials of the People's Insurance Company of China, shortly before AIG set up a partnership with China in 1975, which marked the first alliance between China and any foreign insurance company.

October 10, 1984: Company Listed on New York Stock Exchange
Hank Greenberg, center, with AIG comptroller Peter Dalia to his left and K.K. Tse to his right.

AIG Japan Headquarters, Tokyo
The building is across from the Imperial Palace moat.

Chairman Greenberg receiving a glass replica of a *tamuli* (chieftan's horn) on behalf of the family of the late Earl Carroll, Philamlife's first president, from Philippine president Fidel V. Ramos 1997.

The Bund in
May 1998
Grand reopening of
AIA headquarters in
Shanghai, marking the
company's return to
its former location at
No.17.

Greenberg meeting with China premier Zhu Rongji in Beijing in May 1998, not long after Greenberg was named an "Honorary Citizen" of the city.

Chairman Greenberg with SunAmerica chairman Eli Broad in 1998. The following year, AIG would complete its acquisition of SunAmerica, the largest acquisition in AIG history.

South Korean president Roh Moo-hyun (center) gives a thumbs-up, along with New York Stock Exchange chairman Richard Grasso (left), and American International Group chairman and CEO Hank Greenberg (right), before ringing the opening bell at the New York Stock Exchange on May 12, 2003.

Hank Greenberg speaking in August 2005, calling for renewal of the
U.S. Terrorism Risk Insurance Act. (Corbis)

I came to realize, correctly I think, that it was at least partially if not mostly a show. Sure, Hank got mad, but he was also putting on a performance to make a point. He was careful when he put on the show. If it was somebody who would not respond but act adversely to AIG's interests, he would not do it.

That's not to say Hank doesn't have a gruffness about him. Friends who still work at AIG tell me that Hank, unlike other leaders, has not mellowed as he has gotten older. He is still just as tough as he was before, if not more so. If he is irked, he often picks up the phone and calls congressmen, ambassadors, CEOs, or whomever, and lets them know what he thinks. My AIG friends say that once they learn of these phone calls they have the unenviable task of picking up the pieces and smoothing ruffled feathers.

The final lesson for doing more than surviving and actually prospering at AIG is to learn when to deliver bad news. Any executive at times has to do that, and it is better to be the bearer of bad tidings than have the boss hear it from somebody else. We joked at AIG about when to deliver the news to Greenberg if you must and we had a solution that sounds facetious, but the joke had a big dose of seriousness in it. AIG had a full-time masseur. Those on the magic list got to visit him once a week, but Greenberg was with the masseur every afternoon at 4 P.M. I always thought he spoiled the massage by spending most of the time on the phone talking to different AIG executives. If you called him with bad news around 4 P.M., as he began his massage, it was likely to be a very unpleasant conversation. But if you called closer to 5 P.M., when he had been on the table an hour, you generally got a mellower, more reflective Greenberg.

"Hank, there was a big fire in Thailand today—our loss could hit $40 million." Hank's reply: "Well, that's life. That is why we are in the insurance business. I am sure our reinsurance will cover lots of it. Talk to you about it tomorrow."

However, all this imparted wisdom didn't work for many who dealt with Greenberg. They lived every day at AIG on edge, a bundle of nerves. They were never really comfortable for fear they would get the call, a summons to his office. I never knew what to suggest—you overcame your fear or you just lived with it. Not a great way to live. I called his new office recently and talked briefly to a friend whom I used to work with. I suggested getting together for lunch. She was enthusiastic until I told her what I was doing. Then the conversation became icy. She was tense, jittery, and said we had better not have lunch. What did we have to talk about, anyway? She obviously was terrified that Greenberg would not like me writing this book.

I honestly think the occasional encounter was the worst. Those who dealt with Hank day in and day out tended to do the best. They got used to it and understood it the same way I did. It was just Hank's way—impassioned, volatile, and totally dedicated to AIG. However, those who dealt with him only every now and then did not have the luxury of getting used to him. Many—most in fact—were very anxious or often outright agitated when they had to meet with Greenberg. For them, there was no solution. Fortunately, they were only occasional encounters. I suspect Hank rather enjoyed having his employees ill at ease. It kept them on their toes.

The bottom line is inevitably that when you are with Hank, you are on edge. Even in a room full of people where you are across the room talking to others, you can never quite forget he is there. The force of his personality and the fear people have of him is always present. Actually, it is quite remarkable. While it is mainly employees who are scared or at least tense, it can also be directors, clients, officials, or casual acquaintances. Hank is too smart and observant of other people not to be aware of it. Whether he could change his personality enough to put others more at ease, I do not know. Whether he would want to, well, that I doubt.

Leslie Gelb, president emeritus of the Council on Foreign Relations, told me about his working relationship with Greenberg, who was vice chairman of the council. He said he knew Greenberg's reputation and has observed his explosions at his people. Les said he hid nothing, put it all on the table, including bad news and his failings. And he said they had a wonderful relationship. Les's explanation: Greenberg knew he was not hiding anything. The yelling at AIG, Les surmised, was because he feared they were trying to conceal bad news.

For the meetings in Greenberg's office, one was always greeted by Mr. Wang, a Chinese gentleman who was with Greenberg when I joined the company. He left the day Greenberg resigned from AIG and is with him in his new office. He would take your coat and sit you in the conference room adjoining Greenberg's office, where most meetings were held. I believe—but am not sure—that he goes back to the Starr era. I had other kinds of conversations with Wang and I suspect others did as well. If I were going to Brazil, he would say to me: "Mr. Shelp, I have two apartment buildings in Rio. Could you check on them?" Or if I were off to Hong Kong, he would say, "Mr. Shelp, I have an office building in Hong Kong. Could you check on it?" It was like our dining room waiters with hundreds of thousands of dollars in AIG shares. The common guy did pretty well at AIG. That was part of the legend, and Greenberg reinforced it by living modestly. His apartment in New York is modest, his home in Brewster is very nice but modest. He does not spend lots of money on art or clothes or other things. I remember his once telling me Churchill Shoes was having a sale and it was a good opportunity to get some nice shoes reasonably. While Greenberg likes his limo and private jets and other perks from the Starr empire, considering the lifestyles of most billionaires, his is very modest.

There were a number of hallmarks of the AIG empire—the magnificent corporate houses and penthouses around the world, such as Morefar, Lookout, and the penthouse on top of the AIG building in Bermuda; Greenberg's office and other offices in the art deco headquarters at 70 Pine St. in lower Manhattan, which Greenberg bought from Cities Service for a mere pittance of $15 million; the company dining room with an Asian-oriented menu served by Chinese waiters; the luxurious company jets.

At the conclusion of my trip to China in 1981, the other 10 visitors and I visited Lookout, a sumptuous treat by any standards, but especially after three weeks in the China of that time. Later we hosted a Chinese dinner at my New York apartment for the same group, which was arranged by the Chinese waiters at AIG, who provided an exotic menu of many courses. They got some of their Chinatown friends to do it. Each course was served by one of the cooks or waiters in my apartment, who called the Chinatown restaurant and told them to get in a taxi and bring the next course. Like other senior AIG executives, I stayed in most of the Starr guesthouses around the world, including Bancho House, a lovely home virtually in downtown Tokyo whose cook was alleged to have been General MacArthur's cook.

Lunching or hosting a lunch in the AIG dining room always was a treat for both the host and the guest. It would start with drinks—at least before the era of the austere, healthy lunch hit us. That was at the time we had a small corporate dining room for officers. I remember Greenberg giving the order to cut back to two drinks with lunch. So many hard-drinking, old-time insurance men would go to a bar across the street, knock back a couple, then hit the executive dining room for two more. I even remember Jimmy Manton, our chairman, telling me that when he was younger they would go out and negotiate an insurance coverage all morning through lunch. Then many drinks later, he felt he had done a good day's work and would go home after lunch and sleep off the drinks.

In any case, drinks were followed with fresh carrots, celery, and peanuts. Then the order: My favorite was "scrod a la Greenberg," a piece of broiled scrod done at a very high temperature for a short time. There was always one other fish plus a regular menu, fresh vegetables like snow peas with lunch, and then fruit or ice cream topped off by crystallized ginger, which the Chinese believe is good for the digestion. Cigars were offered on special occasions—Cuban cigars, which we would bring back from overseas and charge to our expense accounts as long as they were given to the dining room.

At one point, there was an equal employment opportunity suit threatened by an Irish waitress against AIG because the dining room had exclusively Chinese waiters. To make matters worse, allegedly the Chinese weren't all legal immigrants. So a group of Irish waitresses were hired. They all quit within a relatively short time span because the Chinese made their life absolutely miserable. I don't know what they did back in the kitchen, but it worked. Today, there are still all Chinese waiters but a few Chinese waitresses as well.

Once a month we had a management meeting hosted by Greenberg over lunch in his dining room. A *Forbes* magazine article featuring me was released on August 30, 1982, the day of our monthly meeting. It was in the "As I See It" section and included a photo. This interview was based on my book on services, *Beyond Industrialization*. Since I hadn't told Greenberg about the interview and remembered the old axiom about not surprising your boss, my nerves were on edge when the meeting was convened. At these meetings, Hank would work his way around the room, asking for reports on important developments.

There were always a few laughs. Artie Joukowsky, head of our Socialist Country Division, was just back from Eastern Europe. He bubbled excitedly about his visit to Bulgaria, where, it seems, his great-grandfather (a Russian) had been a savior of the country. Artie had been grandly feted in Sofia. After talking on and on, Greenberg interrupted Artie with the comment: "Do we pay you to do this, Artie, or do you pay us?" The room rolled with laughter, and the next person was called upon. As we worked around the room to where I was sitting at the opposite end of the table, I began to feel queasy. While the article was very favorable and supported AIG's position on services, and it was a coup for an AIG executive to get this kind of exposure, Greenberg was not exactly known for wanting to share credit with others. Just before my turn came, I was getting outright indigestion and wondered whether to mention the article. Maybe he hadn't seen it yet.

Hank turned to me and said, "Ron," and before I could respond he said, "I saw that article in *Forbes*. That was great. Just what we need. Congratulations." Relieved, I proceeded to give my report. The volatile personality was on my side that day. But it should have been. It was a great story for the company, which is probably the way Hank saw it.

I was often a passenger on one of the G4s AIG owned. They were a luxurious way to travel, with the design personally supervised by Greenberg, who was always threatening to take flying lessons. But Hank, in my experience, has received a bad rap over use of the facilities on the plane. The press has reported on numerous occasions that there is the master bedroom where he, his wife (if she is with him), and his dog sleep. If you need to go to the bathroom in the middle of the night, you are under orders not to disturb him but to go to the pilot's bath. I never found this to be true. He would say to me, "Don't worry about disturbing me, just go."

Most AIG executives did their best to avoid flying on the planes with Greenberg, mainly because they liked to relax when flying, and such trips led to a ton of additional work with Hank, or, occasionally, they could get another dressing down. Once I was in Europe but had not come over on the plane, which was there also. The executives who had flown over with Hank had all scattered. I saw Hank and he asked me how I was getting back. It was the weekend and I said I had never seen Prague and was excited about visiting it.

"I'm not flying back on that plane alone. You're coming with me," he responded. No criticism of going to Prague for a little fun or spending company money for a flight back—just the idea, I think, that I could have joined him but hadn't planned to. I remember once flying with him from Europe to the United States. That trip was a good example of the doubling up of work that came out of these trips. I literally took notes all the way across the Atlantic and reached Teterboro Airport with a notebook full of assignments. Then it took me weeks to work through them. The way Hank's mind worked, if he didn't see you, he didn't think of so many things or didn't have time to. If he was with you for an extended period of time, it was another matter. "Why don't you, look into this, Ron? Did you ever think about . . . ? I'll bet we could do this, don't you think? Give a call to . . ." Having said that, Hank did seem to relax on planes. He was always talking to the pilots and comparing notes about schedules, routes, and the like. Another time we were on a short trip to Washington. As the plane banked to land, there was a gorgeous view of Washington with all its memorials lit up at night. Hank said, "There is only one job I would take in this town." I didn't need to ask, "Which one?" It wasn't Deputy CIA director, a job I heard he had turned down.

One of the great delights in Washington was working with Tommy Corcoran, who Mike Murphy lived with when he was a student. He tutored the children of Corcoran academically and athletically. I remember well my first meeting with him. Corcoran, Youngman, and Rowe had an office that filled nearly a block in downtown Washington. By the time I came to know Corcoran, most of the offices were empty and he was past his prime. On my first visit, I was kept waiting in the reception area for about half an hour and then was shown to a huge office with photos of Tommy with every dignitary in Washington. About 45 minutes later Corcoran walked by and said, "Come with me, Bub," and showed me to another giant office with a similar photo display. About 10 minutes later, he looked in and said, "Be with you in a minute, Bub." Finally, about 20 minutes later he took me to a third office like the earlier ones.

"Now, what can I do for you?" he asked.

Before I could formulate a question, his secretary looked in and said he had a phone call. He picked it up and started referring to the person as "Mr. Vice President." A few minutes later she looked in again and said, "Other line." He picked up that line and listened with his left ear. He placed both phones down on his chest and said to me, "It's Mike Mansfield, the Senate majority leader." That was my first encounter with the legend. I was young but somewhat calloused coming from New York. Just think what a potential client with less experience would have thought. Very impressed, indeed. Having said that, I recently saw another colleague from AIG who spent more time with Corcoran than I did, and he said he would never underestimate "the Cork" and bet he was indeed talking to the veep and Senate majority leader.

Corcoran was involved with Opus Dei, the Catholic lay organization made famous in the recent bestseller *The Da Vinci Code*. On more than one occasion he said, don't pay me for this assignment, just give it to Opus Dei. Corcoran was absolutely paranoid about having his conversations taped. This probably came from the vast variety of his lobbying and other activities, involving everything from pure company representation to government deal making to his controversial effort to try to influence the Supreme Court. As I say, he was getting old when I dealt with him and I saw examples of this that were humorous and a bit sad. He would call me from what I assumed was a pay phone, bark, "Call me back, Bub," and hang up but leave no number. Then a few minutes later, he would do the same thing again. Because I hadn't called back, he would complain to Greenberg, "That new kid you have working for you doesn't call me back." Greenberg would complain to me, I would explain, and the cycle would start again.

Matt Nimitz suggests there is more to this story than meets the eye. When Matt was running Governor Carey's transition operation, he received a call from Corcoran: "Matt, I am calling on behalf of AIG and we are very interested in talking to you and the Governor-Elect about who the next State Insurance Commissioner will be." I said I was busy just then. He said, "no problem, take this telephone number down and call me when you are free. It is a pay phone in Times Square and I will stay here till I hear from you!" He was an old man and it was winter, so I made time for him at the office and in fact we chose an excellent insurance commissioner whom Hank and others felt comfortable with.

I actually doubt now that he was really at a Times Square phone booth, but his ploy had the effect of getting me to offer him an appointment."

On the last day it was permitted to give cash contributions to political parties, one of our political operatives—or, better said, government relations people—got in a limousine with Corcoran and drove through New York's garment district. They made various stops, where they were handed bags of money. Then they drove to Washington to deliver about $300,000 in cash to some very prominent senators. There is a strong sentiment that the money went no further. In other words, it did not get to the Democratic National Committee.

Pat Foley, our state government relations lawyer, loves to tell the story of observing Corcoran in representing the aspirin manufacturers. "A kid had died from taking an overdose of aspirin and Congress decided to limit what you could sell to 25 aspirin per bottle. The manufacturers say it is uneconomical unless they can make it 60 per bottle. Corcoran calls to the Hill and gets it changed, then sends his bill to the companies and one, St. Joseph's, I believe, said they would not pay their share of the bill. That night, the Congressional bill was back to 25 a bottle and stayed that way until Corcoran's bill was paid. Then it was raised back to 60 per bottle and passed."

Many lobbyists predicted Corcoran was finished when Nixon was elected, but at the first big presidential dinner, Corcoran was there as Anna Chennault's date. He was irrepressible and stayed so until he died.

There were other lobbyists and consultants involved with AIG, at home and abroad. One was a true Southern gentleman, Henry Dudley, known to everyone as "Cousin Henry." His son, also a lawyer, was named Spottswood. Henry's forte was dealings with the military. Thanks to Cousin Henry, I was elected to the Georgetown Club, which was, at the time, an exclusive membership sought after but tarnished a bit by the scandal over Tongsun Park, the Korean businessman who stood at the center of an influence-peddling scandal. Park frequented the Club. Henry Dudley's fortune was made when he was named an executor of the estate of Marjorie Meriwether Post, the E.F. Hutton and cereal heiress.

Another charming consultant was Richard Helms, a man many have called the best head of Central Intelligence ever. He was sacked by

President Nixon. He was available to us for advice and, I am confident, for other, more confidential matters as well.

An embarrassment of riches came my way about five years after I joined AIG—I was elected to the prestigious Council on Foreign Relations. Jack Howell, chairman of Schroeder's, who had requested that I speak in Asia, nominated me. At the time I did not realize how difficult it was to be elected. I waited to be called, and I was. Later I came to realize what it was really like. Mayor John Lindsay nominated my wife but asked that she promise she would not join the long list of distinguished New Yorkers angry at him because they weren't elected.

I sought out Hank in private and told him about my election. He was clearly miffed. He had waited to be elected for some time, but hadn't yet been let in. After all, how could someone of his extraordinary accomplishments be overlooked and I get in? His only comment: "Why do we want to be involved with organizations like that?" I asked if I could look into why he wasn't elected, and he nodded. I soon found out there was nothing I could do. The election process was a bit mysterious, with the board generally electing whomever the nominating committee put forth, and Greenberg had been passed over by the nominating committee several times. A big hunk of serendipity came into play just at the right time. Just about the time I inquired about Hank, David Rockefeller, chairman of the council, broke the rule stating that a board member would never get involved in the election of members, and wrote a letter to the nominating committee praising Greenberg and his qualifications. So they nominated him, and the board duly elected him.

I did not take credit, but when Hank thanked me for getting involved, I didn't say I did not deserve due credit. I kept silent. After all, I tried. Then he went on to be elected a director and vice chairman, and had a room, a program, and a chair named after him.

The most unnerving experience I had at AIG occurred on the day that my wife, June, and I returned from a very pleasant vacation in Europe. "My God," I yelled out. "This letter says I owe AIG one and a half million dollars." It was a cash call for partners in one of the C.V. Starr tax shelters. I broke into a sweat and fretted and called around for the next eight hours to get an opinion. Jet lag was ignored as I tried to work my way out of this jam.

The letter was from a fairly low-level functionary and explained that one of the real estate investments had gone awry and all the partners were expected to contribute. Naturally, it invoked Greenberg's name, part of standard operating procedure to get something accomplished. Finally, late that night, I reached Angelo Mariani, who prepared my tax returns and handled shelters for AIG. He had a much bigger relationship with AIG than with me, but quietly said: "You are not a general partner so you are not liable." Ironically, I never was called about the call for funds even though I understand others more intimately involved with C.V. Starr were. Whether anybody ever anted up, I never found out.

AIG's original logo had been a companywide joke for years. I was especially embarrassed, since the advertising department reported to me. Some even gave me responsibility for the logo but it had been picked in a companywide contest early in AIG's history before I worked there. Submissions were sent in from all over the world, and the winner, which many of us joked looked like two elephants screwing, was drawn by a fairly low-level employee in the Philippines. The winner was selected by the man who made all the important decisions—Hank Greenberg.

The change in the logo finally came in 1988 when AIG sponsored a yearlong series, "The Next President," which consisted of interviews by David Frost with all the Democratic and Republican candidates running for president. Because no one could figure out what the elephant logo was, the ad agency, Bozell, redesigned it for use both on TV and in print ads. The new logo simply said "AIG" in white letters, with a blue background in a rectangular box—not earthshaking, but clear and a giant improvement over the first logo. Greenberg went along, so the new design was used and the old one was quietly forgotten.

I left AIG in the mid-1980s for another position, but kept up with the company. Hank offered me a share in C.V. Starr if I would not leave. When I declined, he said that he would like me as a consultant. He added: "You will be back." None of this happened. Hank resented it when his senior people left the company. He gave you a great opportunity, compensated you well in the long term, and expected loyalty. I don't think he could understand how you would want to work anywhere else. Besides the new opportunity I had, I felt there was a fundamental flaw in the compensation program that would, over the long term, deter attracting and keeping young people—the program whereby if you left before retirement age, you would lose your SICO and your C.V. Starr shareholdings. My viewpoint was confirmed when Hank found it necessary to hold a meeting of all SICO shareholders (expanded to about 700) in Florida in 2001. The idea was to get them to appreciate SICO and also to stop the defections to other companies.

After stepping down as president of the New York City Partnership, I visited with Hank. He felt (correctly so) that after having that job, no position he could offer me at AIG would be big enough for me.

Over the next 15 years, Greenberg continued to build AIG into an even greater financial powerhouse. He aggressively expanded overseas and grew in most markets, and he made gigantic acquisitions in the U.S. market so that for the first time the company earned at least half its revenue from within the United States. In fact, for those AIG old-timers and new-timers who wanted to work for an international company, it was disappointing. Many were distressed at the drive to develop the domestic market. By this time I had left AIG, and as a significant stockholder (by my terms), I remembered Greenberg's lectures about sticking to what you know and worried that AIG was getting overextended in areas where it had little experience. I also wondered if some of this expansion and these acquisitions were being made because Hank Greenberg was getting bored with the standard fare. After all, he was a builder—one with an expansionary vision—and a risk taker.

Obviously, I was wrong. The expansion, domestically and internationally, has been a huge success. Companies have been acquired, new licenses issued, new lines of insurance undertaken. For example, in India, in 1999, AIG's joint-venture general insurance company, Tata AIG General Insurance, received a license to market both commercial and personal line products and Tata AIG Life Insurance Co. received its life license. AIA received a license to sell life insurance in Vietnam, the first license granted to a U.S.-based company. Clearly, AIG has not lost its touch in penetrating difficult foreign markets.

After many trips and much negotiating, the company finally struck a deal in the principal Eastern European countries. I traveled to some of these countries once with Artie Joukowsky as we worked at hammering out understandings. Joukowsky argued that these countries resented being called Eastern European and came up with "Socialist Countries." The company that controlled these joint ventures was in Bermuda (which the heads of the socialist companies loved because it gave them an excuse to travel) and was called the European American Insurance Company.

There were two companies in the former Yugoslavia—one in Hungary, and one in Poland. The local counterparts handled insurance within their respective countries, and these joint ventures handled international business—worldwide business ventures, ships, and so on. Since the fall of the Soviet Union, these companies disappeared, and now AIG companies and other foreign-owned companies compete against national companies within these countries.

After many fruitless efforts, AIG finally worked out a satisfactory business arrangement with Russia. Always thinking ahead, Greenberg and Roberts visited Ingosstrakh, the large Russian insurance company, in 1969. They initiated a cooperative effort whereby they reinsure each other. For example, AIG does the bonding on Airflot, the Russian state airline, and reinsures back 50 percent to Ingosstrahk, which does the same for contractors that are AIG clients that go into Russia.

But the current initiative was launched when Gerry Corrigan, head of the New York Federal Reserve Bank, asked Hank Greenberg, a director and later chairman of the New York Fed, to join a meeting with Boris Yeltsin to explain our financial system. Hank asked John to go, and at a three-day seminar in Moscow, he and other financial experts spoke. The chair of the meeting was a former high-level KGB person.

When John returned, Corrigan called Greenberg again and said that he read the speech that attracted the chairman's attention. "They want the two of you to come back." Roberts believes it was a phrase that he used—"nation building"—that did it. They met with him, and he said insurance is fine but all our wealth is in the ground and we need you to get investors for us. They were given a Kremlin tour, including a pass to get by all the guards in the Kremlin. They visited Stalin's home and were entertained lavishly. In return, the former KGB person came to the United States, visited Morefar and received the bells-and-whistles tour.

AIG made an application—which was approved—to establish the AIG Russia Insurance Company, insuring in local currency. It success-fully operates today.

Pursuant to the AIG philosophy of ingratiating itself with govern-ments when it can, the company helped organize a tripartite state bank with the Rothschilds and an American bank. But it was not very suc-cessful. AIG was the last to drop out. ALICO also has a wholly owned company in Russia that can only do domestic business in rubles.

On the domestic side, in 1990 AIG bought the International Lease Finance Corporation (ILFC), the world's premier commercial aircraft leasing company, which has grown to be the world's largest aircraft leas-ing company. This was done in a stock swap deal, as was the purchase of SunAmerica Inc. in 1999. This huge company, founded and chaired by the celebrated Los Angeles entrepreneur Eli Broad, who built a new pavilion at the Los Angeles County Museum to house his extraordi-nary contemporary art collection, is a leading company in retirement savings. It sells annuities and manages a family of mutual funds, among other things. The other gigantic acquisition was made in 2001 with the purchase of American General, which provided domestic life insurance and annuities and related products.

I heard some mumblings that these had been difficult acquisitions. Greenberg said no. The American General acquisition went on for years because American General was talking with Prudential, but they finally came around. There was apparently some dispute with the American General people because their long-term compensation program vested at age 55 and Greenberg wanted them in the SICO program, which you couldn't get until you were 65. It was resolved.

How did this expansion, especially the domestic expansion, change AIG? For one thing, no matter how good a manager Greenberg was and how determined he is to be on top of everything, this becomes harder and harder. AIG inevitably became more bureaucratic. There are many more layers of management to penetrate with a new idea. People who reported to Greenberg before—especially staff functions—report to Tom Tizzio, the former president and vice chairman, or to Howard Smith, who resigned as CFO over the accounting scandal. Having said that, if you needed to see Greenberg, you could—and fairly promptly, unless he was out of town. That would be true in very few companies this size.

Jeff Greenberg, Hank Greenberg's son, was working at AIG during this period. He would later leave and become chairman of Marsh & McLennan before his board forced him out at Attorney General Spitzer's insistence. Jeff is very proud of his father's accomplishments and tells about him "building a magnificent enterprise on a global scale, enriching thousands of people, helping shareholders, customers, economies, creating jobs. It also allowed the Starr Foundation to do what it does: doing good by doing well."

Jeff explained he was taught a great deal by his father, since the environment fostered achievement and encouraged high standards. This has helped in the balance of his career so far.

Also, the new size of the company—almost $100 billion in assets—dramatically elevated AIG's profile in the United States. Before these acquisitions, AIG was known only to those in the insurance industry and to professional investors. Now AIG is a target for media and competitors and is more of a target for those who don't like Greenberg. After all, it is one of the largest consumer finance companies, the first or second life insurer in the United States, the largest property and casualty insurer, the largest in variable annuities. Today, more than ever before, the company cannot afford to be questioned about its ethics or honesty. It should operate as if it is in the proverbial fishbowl. It has to be more professional, more careful, and recognize it is looked at as a leadership company.

Domestic political insurance issues that would have been of little interest before—redlining, credit life insurance, tort reform, Superfund—are now big issues. But AIG doesn't expect to get its way as much as to just realize some damage control—make an issue less onerous than if the company were not involved. And AIG continues down the iconoclastic road it has always followed. It was never a joiner, including the major trade associations. Today, it is a member of neither the American Insurance Association nor the American Council for Life Insurance, the premier trade associations for the industry. Even so the company is often looked upon to take the lead on issues. At the same time, overseas, it is no longer basically going it alone. MetLife, New York Life, Ace—they are competitors that are involved extensively overseas. The company continues to play a big role in the key international issues such as the financial services agreement that was finally reached in the World Trade Organization in 1997.

One quote will not satisfactorily sum up the excitement, challenge, and intrigue of working at AIG with Hank Greenberg, but something he has said on a number of occasions suggests the outlook he brought to his work as he untiringly searched for opportunities for AIG. That quote represents a philosophy that drives everyone who works with him: "All I want in life is an unfair advantage."

Chapter 10

Morefar

O ne of the special prerequisites of working for AIG was staying at the company's spectacular guesthouses around the world. Often, these had been homes of C.V. Starr, AIG's founder. Sometimes ownership rested with Starr himself, other times with one of the Starr companies. Two of Starr's guesthouses were unforgettable: Morefar in Brewster, New York, and Lookout in Hong Kong.

Even if you dislike golf, which is one of many characteristics shared by C.V. Starr and M.R. Greenberg (and me), the course at Morefar is so dramatic, so challenging, with beautiful vistas, special landscaping, and striking sculpture especially designed for the course strategically placed around the 18 holes, that if you are fortunate enough to be invited to play Morefar you should put aside your distaste for the game, accept and play with zest. While I never have been to Morefar just to play golf (which is in stark contrast to the very reason many go), I have played around the course with guests like Michael Harrington, head of the Irish Insurance Association, whom I had retained to help AIG overcome opposition to foreign insurers and get licensed as the first American insurer in Ireland. Greenberg asked me why we invited Harrington there. When I told him he was key in getting the Irish license, Greenberg nodded, but my guess is he was thinking, "If we have it, why do we need him now?"

Back in Dublin, Harrington had heard of this private course (probably because I described it to him). A lover of golf, he and his wife made their only trip to America just to play the course at Morefar. Michael saw a round of golf at Morefar as the best payment possible for fixing government "meddling" (although he did take his cash pay as well) and said to me, "'Tis extraordinary. Only in America would you ever find such a place."

Starr originally built a nine-hole course, not to use himself, but for his friends. A man with fine taste in art, he placed sculptures by an Italian artist he liked around the first nine holes. The course proved so popular that he built a back nine and commissioned additional sculpture. He did not live to see that course completed. While many of us used this course as a draw to develop business, by the time he built it, Starr's career was too advanced for him to think that way. Most of the friends he invited to Morefar were employees and business colleagues, since his business life was the center of his social circle, anyway. Most of the others he invited he would have known through business also. Other than having as a guest the occasional student he supported, he preferred surrounding himself with those he saw every day.

The sculpture is exquisite, works executed for Morefar that could sit anywhere. One, for example, is a boy fishing, casting a long line over a pond. About the only relationship this piece has to golfing is that a frustrated golfer might see this and wish he were fishing instead of banging a little white ball around the course. On the ninth green is a whimsical piece that very nearly relates to golf. Near the hole stands a large, tall lady with a bemused look on her face that suggests as she looks at you, "Why do you play this silly game? Isn't this an exercise in frustration?"

But while Morefar is indeed much more than an artistic private home with a world-class golf course, it is not at all what you would expect a rich man's weekend estate to be. The name came from Starr's years in China. When Starr, obviously American looking, would ask where something was, he explained, the Chinese would point and say "more far." When he looked for a weekend house, he found what he wanted in Brewster in Putnam County—an old stable house and hundreds of acres of land. He remodeled the main house, put in some guest cottages, and over time put in a pool, tennis courts, and the golf course. The house is not at all spectacular and is unnoticeable from the road.

Cocktails were served every evening on metal chairs near the pool, with the same chair reserved for Starr, much like the chair reserved for Greenberg in his office sitting room. Morefar was a comfortable home, a modest home, where an accomplished but modest, or if not modest, shy, man could entertain his many guests.

Those who have visited Morefar since Starr's death over 30 years ago have found the routine continues, but without a host. First, one needs to receive a weekend invitation. T.C. Hsu, for many years president of the Starr Foundation, gave Greenberg the names to invite for many years. Then apparently Greenberg complained about the names, to which T.C. responded, "Do it yourself or find someone else," which is normally not the way one responds to Greenberg. (This says something about T.C.'s influence and Greenberg's pledge to live up to his promise to Starr to guarantee T.C. a meaningful job.) For a while, reportedly, Gladys Thomas, the former head of communications who moved to the Starr Foundation, did it, but that did not work out, either. Until Greenberg's departure, company presidents responded to the question from Greenberg's office of who among their people were Morefar candidates.

An invitation to Morefar is a way to reward AIG executives and their families and the occasional outsider—only, generally, guests are left to their own devices, except when one proclaims himself the senior AIGer there for the weekend and therefore the self-appointed host. Occasionally Greenberg, whose house is down the road (as are homes of a number of old-timers, including less accomplished members of Starr's business family, such as his driver), would drop by, but more likely he would invite you to his house for a mean game of tennis on Saturday or Sunday morning. His personal physician and the company doctor, Jack Harness, lived next door to Greenberg for many years and was regularly accused of stacking the tennis games in favor of Greenberg and himself, since he determined who played with whom.

All the properties that abut Morefar were made available by Starr directly or indirectly through being a citizen in good standing of the Starr community—Greenberg, the late Gordon Tweedy, K.K. Tse, Youngman, T.C. Hsu, Helen Graham Park. The Starr family not only worked together but played and socialized together. The homes are maintained by Land O'Beyond, a company created to take care of the estate and properties adjoining it. While Greenberg took over Starr's house at Stowe, the ski resort he developed, and seems to be treated with the affection Starr had at St. Anton, Austria (another resort Starr helped develop), he never took Starr's own house at Morefar. It could be that it is not his style. Certainly, AIG needs a place to entertain, and it would interfere with his privacy if he lived at the Starr house. He must be aware that he would be criticized in the company for doing so, since this was the center of Starr's life and so many people use it, unlike the Stowe place, a house at the ski mountain without the social life swirling around it as it does at Morefar. The point is that while in many ways he is following in Starr's shoes, in other ways Greenberg has kept his distance.

To cover the exorbitant costs, as Greenberg puts it, Morefar was turned into a profit center or, more elegantly said, a club. There was considerable grumbling among AIG executives about this. Insurance brokers and others AIG do business with can join. They can use Morefar to play golf, and lunch is served in a clubhouse away from the main house. If an executive from AIG invites a client to play at Morefar, there is a charge back to his profit center. I do not know if the course at Morefar has been rented for a day to other companies.

Morefar has always been representative of the empire Starr built, but it is one part of the empire that will be denied to AIG executives and their guests going forth, unless they are permitted to become golf club members. Under the final disposition of Starr's estate, owner-ship of Morefar passed to C.V. Starr & Co., as did Lookout, although most of the rest of the estate is with the Starr Foundation. Greenberg is chairman of C.V. Starr, and in his pique at what happened to him at AIG, Greenberg has denied AIG the use of Morefar (except for some golf memberships). Rumor has it—and it is only rumor—that he plans to move into Morefar.

There are Morefars in other cities in other countries. In Hong Kong, Starr's home, Lookout, is a magnificent structure overlooking the sea. I stayed there after returning from a trip to China in 1981 and entertained the nine others who had made the trip with me as part of a Chinese affinity invitation (everyone has a similar profession or similar interests), which was common then. Banjo, his house in Tokyo (which was torn down and sold to take advantage of exorbitant land values—it reputedly brought a billion dollars) was a wonderful place to stay. What I most remember about my visits is the remarkable food, prepared by a chef who was allegedly General MacArthur's cook, and later became Starr's cook. About the only thing he could not match was a Morefar specialty—a soft-boiled egg served with shells removed. (The AIG president in Japan tells a wonderful story about when Greenberg made the decision to sell Banjo House. The Japanese bank they used came to the office, and they discussed the proposed sale. Then about three hours later, a vice president of the bank, very senior, called him and asked him to come to the bank. When they met, he said AIG was a very important client and they were obviously in trouble or they wouldn't sell this property. Therefore, the bank would do whatever possible, including advancing large sums of money, to get them over their financial difficulties. This had to be handled very carefully because if word got around Japan that a company was in difficulty, their business would suffer.)

There are a number of other properties, generally penthouses atop the AIG office buildings in Bangkok, Bermuda, and so on. Starr clearly did not like hotels. He preferred to stay in one of his homes, with servants and cooks who suited his taste around. He was more comfortable, and that is the way he did business when he traveled, which was constantly.

These houses are one more example of what a remarkable man C.V. Starr was. He had many interests and built an extraordinary business. He did not make the one mistake entrepreneurs often make. He did well in choosing a successor—Maurice (Hank) Greenberg, who took what Starr left and turned it into a gigantic company. At Morefar, when you visit Starr's grave and look at the shoulder-high bust of him on a knoll between the 13th and 14th holes, where he seems to be looking out over his domain, you are saddened by the damage that has been done to this great company. Starr too would be distressed at his company's troubles and the damage to its impeccable reputation. Marion Breen, Starr's first cousin and one of his secretaries, says it tarnishes his memory. He would also be distraught and saddened about Hank Greenberg, his successor, who, as longtime employee Marion Fajen puts it, "was like the son he never had."

Chapter 11

The Mystery of What Happened at AIG

W hen Starr chose Greenberg to be his successor shortly before he died, he bet that his business and personal instincts would be as right as they had been so many times in the past. He passed over William Youngman and Gordon Tweedy, Harvard College and Harvard Law, Yale and Yale Law, respectively, aristocrats he had brought in to succeed him. Time has proven Starr right. The achievements of Hank Greenberg in making AIG the world's largest insurance company and much more—a large airplane leasing firm, a company with significant activities in asset management, retirement funds, equity investments—suggest that Starr could not have made a better choice. Greenberg had a reign that approaches Starr's. Starr founded the company in 1919 and was in charge until he died in 1968. Greenberg joined C.V. Starr & Co. in 1960 and ran it from 1968 until 2005—37 years.

Greenberg proved as formidable in building AIG in the last third of the twentieth century as Starr had in the years since he founded it. He shares many characteristics with Starr and had a few Starr did not possess. He is driven, creative, brilliant, more ruthless, and equally internationally oriented, sharing Starr's special fascination with China. Both Starr and Greenberg had involvement with and connections to the intelligence community. Starr was deeply interested in the arts; Greenberg only viscerally. Starr even underwrote a production of *Madame Butterfly* at the Metropolitan Opera and was intimately involved in virtually every aspect of the show, down to choosing a Japanese designer (Motohiro Nagasaka) and director (Yoshio Aoyama) and bringing them from Japan. Greenberg is more directly involved in the political world, with connections in Washington, Albany, and capitals around the world. Starr had connections but worked primarily through surrogates like Youngman. Greenberg is a leader in the non-profit community, including chairing the Asia Society and serving as vice chair of the Council on Foreign Relations. He speaks frequently on public policy issues, very unlike Starr, but that is at least partially explained by the fact that Greenberg was CEO of a prominent public company. The rest is explained by Starr's alleged shyness (something I have come to question as I have researched this book and talked to those who knew him) and the different role a CEO plays today as compared to 40 years ago.

In the years immediately before the winter of 2004–2005, Hank Greenberg was at the peak of his power. He had finally overcome his oft-expressed frustration that his achievements at AIG were not recognized outside insurance circles. The company was riding high in earnings and return on equity, although it had never returned to the stock price high of over $100 it reached in 2000, a price that many, including at least one director, said it should never have attained, anyway. AIG was ranked No. 9 on the Fortune 500 list. Greenberg was recognized as the industry spokesman and opined on subjects from terrorism to the madness of the insurance cycle. He personally knew the premier of China, George W. Bush and a succession of presidents before him, and various other political leaders around the world. He was chairman of one of the nation's largest foundations, the Starr Foundation, and was a leader in the nonprofit world. His activities and generosity at the Council on

Foreign Relations led to a room being named after him, and he was honored at a dinner I attended after the naming ceremony. He chaired council task forces and general meetings and served as vice chairman. A wing of New York Hospital was named after him, as were other buildings. And he was one of the wealthiest men in the country.

On March 14, 2005, Hank Greenberg fell from this aerie of leadership in business, politics, nonprofits. Ironically, he was suddenly elevated to national, even international, prominence—a prominence that had long eluded him and been a real frustration, probably because he led an insurance company instead of a big industrial company, an entertainment conglomerate, or a bank. But this newfound prominence was of a kind that he, or anyone, would gladly do without. It was on that day that Hank Greenberg was fired (euphemistically, permitted to resign), after a 37-year reign as CEO of American International Group.

What has happened since then has turned into one of the most bizarre and seemingly inexplicable corporate scandals in memory. While it is packed with drama and peopled with a long roster of A-list characters, it should have never happened.

It leads to a series of questions, the answers to which are not so obvious:

- Why would Hank Greenberg, one of the most successful CEOs ever, nearly 80 years old and already a billionaire several times over, allegedly risk his reputation and potentially even his freedom over what turns out to be fairly modest "fiddling" with AIG's reported earnings?
- Why did AIG's outside directors, each of them flattered to be hand-picked by Greenberg to serve on one of the most illustrious boards ever, turn on him so quickly and force him out in such a humiliating way? What happened behind those boardroom doors? Was this a coup led by one or more directors?
- Why did Eliot Spitzer go after Greenberg with such incredible zeal, labeling him a criminal on national TV before he had been charged with anything—and then never charge him with a crime? Would this be the ultimate victory on which he would launch his gubernatorial campaign, bringing down what Spitzer has called the "world's most powerful businessman"? Did he believe, as he

alleged, that Greenberg was generating a negative publicity cam-
paign against him? Was he?
- How did the unique corporate culture at AIG contribute to
  Greenberg's incredible success and, now, his potential disgrace?

The controversy has plenty of drama—the Spitzer, SEC, and insurance regulatory investigations that for many months seemed to com-
pound exponentially, with new investigations and lawsuits on almost
a daily basis. Two weeks after Greenberg resigned as CEO, files were
removed from the AIG office in Bermuda and Spitzer threatened
criminal action against AIG. The board then felt compelled to force
Greenberg to step down as chairman as well. This was barely four
months after Spitzer forced Greenberg's son, Jeffrey, to resign as chairman and CEO of Marsh & McLennan over the awarding of insurance
contracts on the basis of which insurer offered Marsh the most generous kickbacks. One wonders when Spitzer stops or if he was after
all the Greenbergs. Was the remaining son, Evan, CEO of Ace, the
Bermuda-based insurance company, next?

To many, the nature of Greenberg's character would seem to
explain both the phenomenal growth of AIG and his ultimate downfall. His aggressive, ambitious, pecuniary personality shaped a corporate culture that was incredibly driven and that led directly to the kinds
of arrangements to maximize reported earnings that Spitzer exposed.
If it had not been the finite insurance arrangement with Berkshire
Hathaway's General Re that Spitzer went after, and the placing of reinsurance with offshore companies AIG secretly controlled (all charges
Greenberg's successors at AIG admitted), it would have been something
else, especially given the regulatory climate companies find themselves
in today. That is because the AIG culture is entrepreneurial to the nth
degree, and puts profitable growth above all else. The standard AIG
executives were held to when I was at the company was 15 percent
growth in revenue, 15 percent growth in profit, and 15 percent return
on equity year in and year out. It still is.

The capstone of this culture is the golden enticement of being
invited to become a shareholder of C.V. Starr, a private partnership
of AIG's star performers. For those who "made their numbers," the

rewards topped any in corporate America. Many Starr shareholders are centi-millionaires and several are billionaires.

To understand AIG, one has to understand its origins in the Shanghai of the 1920s and 1930s, the world, literally, of *Terry and the Pirates*. By the time founder Cornelius Vander Starr moved his headquarters to New York in 1939, AIG had become a unique anomaly—an American company that had its beginnings overseas—and has kept much of this international focus to the present day. Ninety years later the company earns one-third of its revenue from activities outside the United States. On the one hand, it has given AIG a giant leg up against other American companies that ventured abroad much later. On the other, the international habits acquired from operating around the world long before it operated in the States were certainly a contributory reason why AIG got in trouble. Overseas business practices and ethics are simply different, and AIG may have imported some of those practices to a home market that takes a dim view of many of these habits.

From its beginnings in China, AIG has always played a heavy (some would say heavy-handed) role around the world. Protecting its interests meant going way beyond the business realm and playing in the political arena. These acquired habits stayed with the company and with Hank Greenberg as AIG moved to become a major player on the domestic front. In recent years a series of domestic acquisitions propelled AIG into a giant that matched Greenberg's expectation and exceeded Starr's wildest dreams. As it became a more prominent public company and Greenberg a commanding figure, its profile rose. Greenberg gradually replaced the old AIG board with a hand-picked assortment of high-flyers (e.g., U.N. ambassador Richard Holbrooke, former Nasdaq president Frank Zarb, former senator and U.S. Defense Secretary William S. Cohen). They gave the company prestige, opened doors, helped solve problems, and never questioned Greenberg's authoritarian rule, at least until the serious troubles started.

The expectation of the investment community that AIG would continue to outperform everyone else required finding ways to do so. In an ever tougher environment and over a period of years, AIG devised a number of innovative solutions. Many were, in essence, bringing home the habits of a rambunctious overseas style and applying them here. One was to set up offshore insurance companies that on paper were independent but in reality AIG controlled. An example is the previously mentioned Inter-Hemispheric Insurance Company, a Bermuda company established as a joint venture with Munich Re. The company was subsequently renamed Richmond Insurance Co. and in 2005, after Greenberg left, AIG had to admit to regulators it controlled the company, since AIG not only managed it but guaranteed its outside investors like Munich Re against loss.

To calm insurance analysts who feared AIG had assumed too much risk, excess business was placed with (reinsured by) one of these off-shore entities like Richmond Insurance and thereby some of the exposure was transferred to them. These entities were really controlled by AIG, so the true exposure remained with AIG. So AIG's risk had not been lessened one iota. Of course, no one knew that but AIG.

Another solution involved establishing the controversial arrangements involving finite insurance with General Re. This is the specific deal that probably cost Greenberg his job and led several officials at General Re to plead guilty to the charges. The allegation was that the transactions, occurring in 2000 and 2001, involved two $250 million loans dressed up on the books as premium revenue. AIG, post-Greenberg, said the transactions should not have been recorded as insurance, and financial statements would therefore have to be adjusted to record the transactions as deposits rather than as consolidated net premiums. This means the company's reserves for losses will be reduced by $250 million, something Greenberg was apparently trying to boost at a time when investors thought they were too low.

To outsiders, these two examples—placing insurance with independent reinsurers you actually control and utilizing a seemingly bogus finite insurance transaction to boost reserves—epitomize AIG's culture, personified by Greenberg, a culture that suggested you had to make your numbers whatever the cost and that led to the excesses and made its downfall virtually inevitable in the post–Enron environment. If Eliot Spitzer had not been the agent of Greenberg's departure, they argue, another regulator or an enterprising plaintiff's attorney would likely have played that role.

That conclusion is premature. It is true that the General Re transaction occurred five years ago, suggesting this sort of action could have been a one-time event. And the creation of offshore insurance companies, many of which were controlled by AIG, had gone on for much longer. There are some other AIG abuses as well, but not very many that weren't practiced by others in the insurance industry. Abusive use of finite insurance, for one, is a very tough call to make. The ultimate question is simple: Did the transaction involve transfer of risk or didn't it? There were undoubtedly many times when it did not and they did not involve AIG. It was only when Eliot Spitzer dogged the situation in a high-profile way that it became an issue. Having said that, there has definitely been a culture change. Sarbanes-Oxley, Enron, WorldCom—all have come together to create a very different regulatory climate. It has made boards very gun-shy and most CEOs and CFOs very, very careful. But like many trends, these, too, wax and wane. Today's extreme regulatory climate will in another day be supplanted by a softer one. At a later time, some of today's excesses will seem excessive not in action but in regulatory attitude.

Even before AIG was taken over by the government in September of 2008, one had to question the future of the company. While the scandals seemed to have had little effect on AIG's earnings, one has to be pessimistic about its prospects for attaining anything close to its past growth and profitability. First, it is a company that has matured. To continue to grow at the same rate would go against what has happened with other businesses. Since the incentives it had developed to reward stars, SICO and C.V. Starr, can no longer be used (although a plan to virtually replicate the SICO plan, except administered onshore by AIG, has been initiated), it is difficult to find a way to motivate—and reward—key producers the way Greenberg did for so many decades. One of the reasons is that these two incentives had a mystique about them—a mystique that often exceeded what an executive might actually earn. That cannot be replaced.

Chapter 12

Greenberg's Fall from Grace

"The seeds of destruction were sown when Hank started adding high-powered directors to his board," according to a former employee and longtime observer of AIG. A current AIG director, not necessarily agreeing with this assessment, said: "They were all good directors and they made a contribution. But they were not directors who brought to the company what we needed. They were for Hank, no other reason. Just to add prestige to his board."

Ambassador to the United Nations and secretary of state aspirant Richard Holbrooke; Carla Hills, former U.S. trade representative; former senator from Maine and secretary of defense William Cohen; Martin S. Feldstein, chief economic adviser to Ronald Reagan and president of the National Bureau of Economic Research; and Frank Zarb, former chairman of Nasdaq. That is quite a lineup, and it is not the entire board.

Could the old public board, consisting of more insiders, have fore-stalled or even prevented Greenberg from losing his job? The old board, many of whom were employees of Greenberg, working at his pleasure and often living in fear of him, would certainly not have rolled like the current board. The outcome would have been the same. They too would have felt the pressure generated by Attorney General Spitzer and the daily headlines about malfeasance and wrongdoing. Concern and threats from investors would have added to the pressure. Spitzer might have threatened to bring criminal charges—charges no financial service firm has ever survived. Hank Greenberg eventually would have to resign. Besides, the insiders would have had to excuse themselves from the deliberation.

But the way it happened might not be the same. Greenberg says he got a phone call from Frank Zarb telling him the board wanted him to step down. No in-depth person-to-person conversations (except a reported visit from Pete Peterson, then chairman of the Council on Foreign Relations, and Zarb asking him to resign). Just a phone call from someone he considered a very good friend. Under an earlier board, that would not have happened. Directors, many of whom were his employees and friends, would have sat down with him and talked it through, but with the same result.

His ouster was the end result of problems that started many months earlier. In the fall of 2004, Spitzer brought bid rigging charges against Marsh & McLennan and several insurance companies, including AIG. Spitzer said Marsh solicited fake bids from companies like AIG to make sure certain insurers won business. For example, AIG would bid high on a piece of business offered by Marsh, as insurance broker, and another insurer who had bid lower would get the business. Then another time, the opposite would happen and AIG would get the business.

The rigging was unquestionable and it was illegal and unethical. According to an AON executive, Marsh was the only broker doing it. First, before any bids were submitted, Marsh determined which company would win the business. Second, they set a target for the winner to submit for its bid. Finally, they obtained losing bids, which they called "B quotes," from other participating insurance companies. At least 17 executives, including four AIG employees, have pleaded guilty. (A senior executive of another insurance brokerage firm asserts that Marsh was the only broker participating in the bid rigging.)

This bid rigging was not carried on at a very high level within AIG. So none of it touched Greenberg or his senior officers, although it probably put him on Spitzer's radar screen. The other issue that came to a head at approximately the same time involved Brightpoint and PNC Financial Services, two AIG clients, and directly involved Greenberg, at least in settlements with the SEC and the Justice Department.

In the first, Brightpoint, a cell phone distributor in Plainfield, Indiana, was charged, along with AIG, with committing accounting fraud. It was described by the SEC as a round-trip of cash—a mechanism for Brightpoint to deposit money with AIG in the form of monthly premiums, which AIG was then to return to Brightpoint as purported insurance claims payments. The purpose was to build up a reserve, in this case $11 million, to use when earnings otherwise would drop or come in below analyst expectations.

AIG paid a $10 million fine to settle the case, which was doubled because of its failure to cooperate with the investigation and for its delay in turning over subpoenaed documents, including a paper on how to market these policies. This document was produced by the Loss Mitigation Unit of AIG. Brightpoint's fine was only $450,000. The case was settled in September 2003.

In the PNC Financial Services case, AIG had formed special-purpose entities to let PNC clean up its financial statements by moving $762 million in nonperforming assets to off-balance-sheet entities. The SEC states that these did not meet accounting requirements. AIG reached a tentative settlement with the Justice Department and SEC in the summer of 2004. At the 11th hour Greenberg rejected it and decided to fight the settlement. Then in October 2004, AIG issued press releases disclosing that both the SEC and the Justice Department were considering legal action that was unwarranted. The SEC and Justice Department formally warned the company it was facing civil action. Finally, on October 25, Greenberg gave in and issued a statement that the company would seek a prompt settlement of all outstanding issues.

Except the price had risen since Greenberg rejected the first deal. The total penalty was up $20 million to $126 million. The settlement was signed by the end of November. Justice agreed to defer prosecution of criminal fraud against the AIG subsidiary (AIG Financial Products) that had designed the transaction and to drop the matter at the end of 2005 if there were no further problems.

Fortune magazine reported in the summer of 2005 that these two incidents, especially the PNC one, shocked the board. The directors were not so upset about the charges themselves, but that Greenberg blew up the first settlement. They saw this as the typical Greenberg ployof pushing around regulators—only you couldn't treat the feds like AIG habitually treated, or mistreated, state insurance regulators. As one director put it to me, without Brightpoint and PNC, the subsequent matter with General Re would not have seemed as important. Having said this, nevertheless, my sources suggest the alleged director concern was exaggerated. While they thought Greenberg mishandled this and it cost the company more than it should, he did not mishandle very much. So he was 80. He was as sharp and incisive as 30 years ago. Might as well keep a good thing as long as you can. In short, nobody was ready to dismiss Greenberg at that time.

Nevertheless, at this time, Bernie Aidinoff, retired from Sullivan and Cromwell and a longtime director, and Frank Zarb former head of the Nadsaq, both members of the audit committee, approached Simpson Thacher & Bartlett, to advise the committee.

By February the climate seemed to have calmed down. On February 9, Greenberg could announce revenue of $100 billion with $11 billion in profit, compared to about $14 million in 1967, the year he took over, an incredible record of growth. Ironically, on the day before, February 8, Berkshire Hathaway lawyers had arrived at Spitzer's office with evidence incriminating Greenberg. According to *Fortune*, federal prosecutors were quietly looking for other companies that General Re had helped to dress up financial statements. To keep the investigation quiet and because they were in competition with Spitzer and did not want his office to know, they sent an informal information request to Berkshire. But on December 30, Berkshire made a public disclosure of the investigation of General Re, prompting Spitzer to send Berkshire a subpoena demanding information on General Re's finite insurance business. On February 8, Berkshire's lawyers arrived to tell them about the finite insurance transaction between General Re and AIG. The lawyers said Greenberg had initiated it and gave them a bundle of documents about it. Another story, according to the *Times*, is that during their investigation of insurance industry practices, prosecutors had stumbled across details of the transaction.

Spitzer confirmed to me that both stories were basically accurate. He said that "the larger insurance bid rigging investigations and the finite insurance inquiry converged to ultimately lead to the AIG–Gen Re finding." In any case, on February 9, Spitzer's office issued a very detailed subpoena and followed it up two days later with a subpoena for Greenberg's deposition. The basic charge was that in two distinct transactions AIG had paid General Re a $5 million fee that would allow it to increase its reserves by $500 million.

Spin forward over the next month as matters come to a head. Greenberg hires a prominent criminal lawyer and a famous litigator. The AIG board has no choice but to start an internal investigation. This is the board that, after Brightpoint, said any employee who didn't coop- erate with regulators would be fired. Reportedly—and I was unable to confirm this—Pete Peterson, chairman of Blackstone and the Council on Foreign Relations along with Frank Zarb, the board's lead director, went as emissaries from the board to ask Greenberg to resign. If this meeting did occur, Greenberg did not accept their proposal.

D-day was Sunday, March 13, when AIG's independent directors gathered at the offices of their law firm, Simpson Thacher, for eight hours. Greenberg called in periodically from a yacht, *Serendipity II*, off the Florida coast. Some report he was invited to the meeting and declined; others say he was not invited. My understanding is that he was welcome at the board meeting but chose not to go. If it was a meeting of independent directors, it would make sense that he was absent. In any case, Greenberg reportedly was quite abusive with the directors that day, with statements like "You're going to destroy the company," and "If I have to go, the stock is going to tank."

At some point during the meeting, a director, probably Zarb, asked Greenberg if he was going to take the Fifth Amendment when he met with investigators to give his deposition, which was scheduled at that point for March 17, just four days later. He said he wasn't sure but that his lawyers were advising him to. (Ultimately, he did.) That was the turning point, and, since at that time no delay was thought possible for the deposition with Spitzer, this left directors no choice but to ask for his resignation.

There were some directors, including former U.S. trade repre- sentative Carla Hills, who were invited to Morefar every Labor Day with Henry Kissinger and others, who pleaded to keep Greenberg, but eventually the board unanimously agreed to ask for his resignation as CEO while letting him remain as chairman. On Thursday, March 23, a group from Greenberg's attorney, David Boies, arrived in Bermuda. The next day was Good Friday and the AIG office was closed. With no one around, they used an employee's electronic passkey to gain entry and, with the help of movers, hauled more than 80 boxes of SICO documents out of the building. This was interpreted in the Attorney General's office as evidence of an attempt to move documents beyond the reach of U.S. regulators or to destroy them.

Spitzer, who received news of what had happened while on a ski vacation in Colorado, was enraged. He said this "document caper" was unacceptable and the company could face indictment for obstruction of justice. Martin Sullivan, the new AIG CEO, fired Mike Murphy for his part in the document caper and for refusing to answer questions from the outside AIG lawyers. Until Spitzer's charges were dropped, Murphy could not leave Bermuda and return to the states. He continued to work for SICO until Greenberg got angry and dismissed him. Boies faxed Hank Greenberg's resignation to the board before they convened on Monday after Easter.

Right after he was ousted as CEO, Greenberg left for China to accept the Chinese government's prestigious Marco Polo Award. By the time he returned to New York, he had been forced to give up his role as chairman as well. It is remarkable that Greenberg would leave to accept this award in the middle of his AIG troubles, though it is a great honor in China. You would expect a feisty street fighter like Greenberg to stay and battle for what he believed was rightly his. Going to China instead speaks of a fervent dedication to China and how proud he is of his accomplishments there. Maybe it suggests he had concluded there was nothing he could do about the situation at AIG, anyway. It also suggests he was not giving up and retiring but already looking ahead to his post-AIG career, where China could play a big role.

When directors are asked what was the decisive factor that drove them to seek Greenberg's resignation, they point to the possibility he would take the Fifth Amendment in his deposition with Spitzer. Many also were uneasy about their own liabilities, although none admit this.

They had followed the recent developments with WorldCom, where directors had been asked to ante up out of their own pockets.

Succession had been a huge topic at AIG board meetings intermittently for many months. Would things have turned out differently for Greenberg if one of his sons succeeded him? Jeff, the oldest, who insiders described as jealous of Evan's promotion at AIG as the reason he left first, told me that while he enjoyed working with Greenberg, found it challenging and stimulating, he left because he wanted to be more on his own to try what he had learned at AIG in a different environment. Whereas Evan, who later became president of AIG, reportedly went to his father and asked to be made CEO as he had been promised. Greenberg might have granted that, but Evan also wanted to be CEO of SICO, and that request led to an explosive argument that led Evan to leave the company. If either had become CEO, Greenberg would have stayed on as chairman and that would be very tough sledding. Jeff argued it would be equally tough to work for the "architect and builder" of the company even if you were not his son. But Greenberg was known for always pushing his sons harder than anyone else, so that is a debatable proposition. He subsequently has changed his mind about them working for him. In the interview with *New York Post* gossip columnist Cindy Adams, he said that he should have never had his kids work for him and that Sandy Weill, former CEO of Citigroup "should have put his kids in my business and mine should have gone to work for him."

Succession was a favorite theme of Richard Holbrooke's, the former U.N. ambassador. Greenberg had finally named some potential successors after much pushing. He initially named Edmund Tse, who heads international life operations but is 64 years old, and Martin Sullivan, who ran the foreign general insurance business, as co–chief operating officers. He named Zarb chairman of the executive committee at the same time. He subsequently changed his successors to Sullivan and Donald P. Kanak, a star Asia hand at the company.

Succession planning at AIG, which many argued was forced on Greenberg, has nevertheless been managed by Greenberg and not by the board, the opposite of the way it should be. Greenberg and Zarb periodically had lunch where the succession subject played a weighty role. Greenberg put his recommendation for a successor in an envelope to be opened if something happens to him. But he changed his mind, often month to month. In any case, if something were to happen to him, Zarb would open the envelope and read Greenberg's recommendations to the board. One source said it was just a matter of a year or so when the board would have named a new CEO anyway. Discussions about succession had gone on for several years and the time had come. But Greenberg would have remained chairman.

When Greenberg was forced to resign, the board chose Martin Sullivan as his successor, which apparently was Greenberg's recommendation. Greenberg and those board members involved had gone back and forth in making this choice. Kanak is extremely well educated, with degrees from Oxford and Harvard, fluent in Japanese, and married to a Japanese woman who is head of her own company. His grandfather-in-law was speaker of the Japanese Parliament. Kanak would seem to fit the bill for AIG's international operations. Sullivan, on the other hand, started with the company in his teens. He has no college education but worked his way up. One director said to me, "You know Hank. You don't really expect him to like Kanak, do you?" Clearly, he could empathize more with Sullivan and where he came from, although you have to honestly ask if he thought Sullivan could do the job, or better said, do the job he had done. There are many others who would ask that same question.

Ten months later, effective January 31, 2006, Donald Kanak resigned as vice chairman and COO, collecting a $10 million severance package. Under a noncompete clause, he cannot work in the insurance industry for 18 months. There are no plans to fill the position he is vacating. He is walking away from AIG's lucrative deferred-compensation plan that pays out to executives who run the course of their careers at AIG. This plan was in Starr International (SICO) before and is now funded by AIG instead, but it includes basically the same terms.

A casualty of the Greenberg ouster was the close friendship between Hank and Frank Zarb. This situation shattered a nearly 30-year friendship of two financial stars who had even traveled jointly with their wives. They first met in the 1970s when they were introduced by Felix Rohatyn when Zarb was at Lazard Freres. Zarb was later at Smith Barney and the bank had a minority interest in the Russian American Investment Bank in which AIG was the principal investor. Greenberg invited Zarb and his wife to join him on a trip to Russia and a meeting with Boris Yeltsin in the early 1990s.

Later Greenberg gave insurance broker Alexander & Alexander a $200 million cash infusion and recommended they hire Frank Zarb as CEO, which they did. The company was sold to AON Corp., another big insurance broker, and AIG made a 50 percent return on its investment while Zarb received a generous severance package. Then Greenberg had the Starr Foundation give $3.5 million to construct a building for the Zarb Business School at Hofstra University and give an additional $500,000 to endow a chair. Greenberg and Zarb and their wives attended the dedication of the building. In 2001, after Zarb left Nasdaq, Greenberg asked him to join the AIG board.

It is not surprising, given this background, that Greenberg expected loyalty from a friend he had helped often. But, as Charles Elson, a corporate governance professor at the University of Delaware, has said, "Professional responsibility as a director trumps personal relationships." Zarb agrees with this. At the meeting where Greenberg was ousted, Zarb, who was known by other directors as Greenberg's confidant, said, "I'm here to represent the shareholders, not Hank." Ed Matthews, former AIG CFO, summed it up when he said: "Hank's very upset with Frank. After all Hank's done for him, he thought at least Frank would give him the chance to present his side to the board."

Greenberg apparently feels Zarb's actions were a power grab. There are others at AIG, including a very senior executive, who agree. This executive argues that Zarb has a long-term agenda for AIG. Sullivan, the new CEO, is very open, friendly, and low key, and he follows orders. So if Zarb, or other board members, ask him to do something, he does it. But long term, Zarb wanted different leadership, such as the new AIG director from Citibank, Robert Willumstad, who replaced Zarb as chairman. He may want to change the direction of the company. None of this is clear, but there is suspicion of Zarb.

To close the circle, I requested an appointment with the new CEO, Martin Sullivan, which several executives at AIG suggested. Hank Greenberg is down on Sullivan and now I am too for very petty reasons. I was told by e-mail from his PR department that he couldn't see me because AIG was writing a book on itself. I was flabbergasted—not because he wouldn't see me but because of the reason. He might give secrets away to me? Are they afraid to let him speak to me? This is a total non sequitur. I would hope it was a decision Sullivan was not involved in.

This interview and others with AIGers were blocked early on
by John Wooster, their retired PR guy, who has what I would consider a real sinecure—a nice office and travel around the world to get
this book written. This has gone on for a long time and if they have
a writer yet, I am not aware of it. God help us. For the same reason, because of this new AIG book, Wooster would not let me see
any photos of Starr, Greenberg, and so on, or any of the oral memories written by old-timers. As a shareholder, I would hope AIG has
better things to do right now than write a book, which already has been
written at least once before, anyway. The last one was by a distinguished
Fortune writer, the late Walter Guzzardi, but Greenberg would not let
it be published, allegedly because it gave more credit to Starr than him.
I persuaded friends at AIG that an outside writer who is a former
employee friendly with AIG would give the book more credibility than
an insider. They all agreed and apologize that Wooster is handling this.

I talked to Frank Zarb, AIG chairman, and he suggested I write Sullivan
directly and spell the issues out to see if he really meant what the e-mail
said. First, it took six weeks to get an answer. Every week I would call and
they would say he still had it. Finally, in the sixth week, I was told he had
sent it to John Wooster, my kiss of death. I never heard from Wooster, con-
sistent with his refusal to talk to me for the past seven months. He must be
afraid of something or embarrassed by what he is doing or have such juicy
material he does not want me near. Not likely for a corporate book. Believe
it or not, Wooster is still at AIG with the same assignment, which obviously
is going nowhere unless it is to be a history of a company that was.

From March until May 2005, Spitzer uncovered other abuses and dis-
crepancies so that by the time he filed a civil suit against AIG and
Greenberg and Howard Smith, the deposed CFO, there were numerous
charges in addition to the General Re finite insurance allegation. In the
course of three months, as Reuters noted, there were an amazing number
of allegations and developments to cope with:

Feb. 14:
—AIG says it has received subpoenas from Spitzer and the SEC
regarding products that might help companies smooth earnings
or hide losses.

Feb. 15:
—Two executives who worked at AIG plead guilt to fraud charges.

March 14:
—Greenberg steps down as chief executive.

March 15:
—AIG loses its triple credit rating from Fitch ratings.

March 22:
—AIG says it has fired two executives after they signaled they would invoke their Fifth Amendment right against self-incrimination.

March 29:
—AIG says Greenberg will step down as chairman. Former Nasdaq chairman and AIG board member Frank Zarb will assume his duties.

March 30:
—AIG acknowledges accounting errors stretching back 14 years, including its treatment of a transaction with Berkshire Hathaway Inc.'s General Re Corp. unit. AIG loses it triple-A credit rating with Standard & Poor's.

March 31:
—AIG loses its triple-A debt rating from Moody's Investors Service.

April 3:
—AIG says it has learned of unauthorized efforts to remove documents and information from an office in Bermuda.

April 12:
—Greenberg refuses to answer regulators' questions. His lawyer, David Boies, says his client needs more time to prepare for his testimony. Greenberg invokes his Fifth Amendment right against self-incrimination. Separately, Greenberg gives his wife $2 billion of AIG shares three days before he steps down as chief executive.

April 26:

—New York regulators say they are investigating whether AIG wrongly pocketed tens of millions of dollars that should have gone into a state workers' compensation fund.

May 2:

—AIG says it will restate its financial results for 2000 through 2003 and the first three quarters of 2004, resulting in a $2.7 billion reduction in net worth.

May 18:

—Florida orders AIG to turn over information about previously disclosed accounting misrepresentations, or else perhaps be suspended from doing business in the state.

May 20:

—A New York grand jury weighs possible criminal conduct by individuals at AIG, according to newspaper reports. Senior Vice President Joseph Umansky testifies in exchange for immunity.

May 26:

—New York Attorney General Eliot Spitzer and Insurance Superintendent Howard Mills file a civil lawsuit against AIG, former AIG Chairman Maurice Greenberg, and former AIG Chief Financial Officer Howard Smith. The regulators charge that the company manipulated its books to deceive regulators and the investing public. They also say former top management engaged in many fraudulent business transactions that exaggerated the strength of AIG's core underwriting business to prop up its stock price.

—Ohio authorities file suit against AIG's former CEO to put a hold on the transfer of more than 41 million shares worth over $2.6 billion to his wife.

Spitzer, in explaining why he brought civil charges and not criminal charges said to me: "There was a determination to bring as civil cases because a greater sense of proportionality in terms of what we put in the document, greater likelihood in getting remedies we cared about, that would get the company and industry reformed we cared about. There was simply a better fit between a civil case and allegations."

When I asked what are the possibilities for criminal charges with another government agency, Spitzer replied, "I am pleased a number of agencies have lined up seeing the facts in a similar way." That obscure comment could mean there will be no criminal charges since we brought none or it could mean there could be criminal charges since, for one, the district attorney in Virginia is bringing them against certain defendants.

Martin Sullivan spent his first months as CEO troubleshooting and handling a wave of regulatory problems. The board met often, if not in person, by phone. There were difficulties with the stock, as you would expect. It peaked at $74 on February 13, 2006, and went down to $50 by early April, a 32.5 percent decline. It was back up to $67 at the time this book first went to press, in May of 2006. After AIG's near bankruptcy in September 2008, the stock has lingered between $1.00 and $1.50 during 2009.

Finally, on February 9, 2006, AIG announced a $1.6 billion settlement with state and federal authorities, the biggest paid to regulators by any financial services company in U.S. history. This is almost twice the $850 million insurance broker Marsh & McLennan paid and tops the $750 million WorldCom, the telecom giant, paid the SEC. It also exceeds the $1.4 billion that 10 leading investment banks paid Spitzer and the SEC in 2003 to settle claims that they produced misleading and self-serving analyst research.

Basically, while AIG did not admit or deny charges, it de facto admitted everything it was charged with and apologized for it. The company negotiated the best it could to get the fine down, but did not do well. Its approach was typical of a financial services company—put regulatory problems behind it. After all, no financial company facing criminal charges has ever survived. But it is not a strategy Greenberg would have agreed to unless his board absolutely insisted. After the settlement was announced, Greenberg issued a statement questioning this expenditure of shareholder money. He said the size of the settlement was disproportionate to the impact of AIG's alleged misconduct and a political trophy for Spitzer as he campaigns for governor of New York.

The money is to be used as follows: one fund, totaling $800 million, is available to investors who lost money in AIG stock after its accounting irregularities were disclosed. By early April AIG had lost $40 billion in market value. So that is not much recompense. Another $375 million fund will repay former customers who may have paid too much to buy AIG insurance policies (the bid rigging scandal). A third fund, for $343 million, goes to the states that AIG cheated by underpayment of taxes related to workers' compensation premiums earned in those states. New York gets $100 million and AIG also paid $25 million to the U.S. government to resolve criminal liability arising from its accounting missteps. Ironically, as Spitzer told me, New York got nothing for his efforts on the worker's compensation funds because in New York it is based on losses rather than premiums paid. So if losses are minimum, you receive minimum. AIG's biggest legal problem is behind it, although it will face a number of lawsuits brought by officials from other states, investors, and others, which will probably take years to settle.

In April 2005, barely a month after Greenberg's resignation, Spitzer appeared on the Sunday morning show *This Week with George Stephanopoulos* on ABC. Speaking about the AIG case, he said: "The evidence is overwhelming that these were transactions created for the purpose of deceiving the market. We call that fraud. It is deceptive. It is wrong. It is illegal." He went on to say that "AIG was a black box, run with an iron fist by a CEO who did not tell the public the truth."

This sparked a strong reaction among those in the business community and business journalists. Even those without an opinion on Greenberg's guilt or innocence were incensed that the attorney general would condemn him on national television before he had even been charged with a crime. I asked the attorney general about this and said it was widely interpreted as saying Greenberg was subject to criminal charges. He said if you look at the transcript what he said was "responding to a statement David Boies made in his effort to characterize facts he was aware of and if you understand the statement in that context, the presumption of the statement that I intended criminal charges may be suspect."

That translates into saying that he was not necessarily accusing Greenberg of criminal charges. But since it was widely perceived that he was, an apology or at least a clarification was in order. In April, the

Wall Street Journal published an op-ed by John C. Whitehead, former head of Goldman Sachs and deputy secretary of state and a friend of Hank Greenberg's. He said, "Something has gone seriously awry when a state attorney general can go on television and charge one of America's best CEOs and most generous philanthropists with fraud before any charges have been brought, before the possible defendant has even had a chance to know what he personally is alleged to have done, and while the investigation is still under way."

On December 22, 2005, Whitehead published a second op-ed in which he said, "After reading my op-ed piece, Mr. Spitzer tried to phone me. I was traveling in Texas but he reached me early in the afternoon. After asking me one or two questions about where I got my facts, he came right to the point. I was so shocked that I wrote it all down right away so I would be sure to remember it exactly as he said it. This is what he said:

" 'Mr. Whitehead, it's now a war between us and you've fired the first shot. I will be coming after you. You will pay the price. This is only the beginning and you will pay dearly for what you have done. You will wish you had never written the letter.'

"He went on in the same vein for several more sentences and then abruptly hung up. I was astounded. No one had ever talked to me like that before. It was a little scary."

A spokesman for Spitzer denied Whitehead's account of the conversation. I asked Spitzer about his disagreement with Whitehead, explaining I was surprised he would get into a disagreement with an "icon of the business community." He said, "We disagree," referring to Whitehead. And that was all he said.

One has to wonder what was behind the fervent zeal with which Eliot Spitzer went after Hank Greenberg. Surely, it is more than moralistic indignation about an alleged violator of Wall Street practices. Maybe the attorney general really believed these accusations were an outrage and was determined to pull down Greenberg and other offenders he went after. His gubernatorial ambitions must have played a role since the "sheriff of Wall Street" became a New York State hero.

And there was pure pettiness. A former AIG executive who is close to top management told me that Greenberg bought a parking lot near the AIG headquarters that Spitzer's father wanted badly, and Spitzer's view was Greenberg had harmed his father. So this made him more determined to get Greenberg.

Now that AIG has settled with Spitzer and the other agencies, the road is clear for a court battle between Spitzer's successor and Greenberg and Howard Smith, former AIG CFO. It could begin in the next few months but will probably be long after Spitzer leaves office. Both men have denied all charges and indicated they will fight these allegations tooth and nail, although Howard Smith is below the radar with all the attention centered on Greenberg. It actually came to a head with a hearing in Attorney General Cuomo's office in September 2008.

There are a number of charges in the suit brought by Spitzer and New York Insurance Commissioner Howard Mills.

First, there was the overarching accusation that from the 1980s (if not earlier) until Greenberg's departure from AIG in 2005, the defendants routinely engaged in misleading accounting and financial reporting. This reporting gave an unduly positive picture of AIG's underwriting performance for the investing public. Specifically, it:

- Engaged in two sham insurance transactions to give the investing public the impression that AIG had a larger cushion of reserves to pay claims than it actually did—transactions that Greenberg personally proposed and negotiated in phone calls with the then CEO of General Reinsurance Corporation. A long time AIG executive says he saw written instructions from Greenberg making sure risk was to be transferred.
- Hid losses from its insurance underwriting business by converting underwriting losses to capital losses.
- Created false investment income–a scheme personally approved by Greenberg and Smith that involved falsely reporting the income from the purchase of life insurance policies as investment income. As a result, there were investment losses rather than the more embarrassing underwriting losses.

The suit discusses Greenberg's active involvement in monitoring the price of AIG stock and in urging the AIG traders to buy the stock. But it makes no specific charges.

It also charges AIG with deliberately booking workers' compensation insurance premiums as regular liability insurance revenue, which had the potential to reduce AIG's contributions to state workers' compensation systems and avoid paying state taxes on those premiums.

Finally, beginning in the mid-1980s, AIG set up several offshore entities for the purpose of reinsuring AIG and its subsidiaries. The charge is that AIG repeatedly misled regulators about the nature of its relationship with these entities. For one thing, they were controlled by AIG and should not have been used for AIG or AIG-related reinsurance. The three companies—Coral Re, Richmond Reinsurance Company, and Union Excess Reinsurance Company—had several common characteristics:

1. They were created by AIG.
2. AIG found the investors and drafted all documents related to the initial capitalization.
3. They were undercapitalized.
4. They had passive investors backed by AIG or its affiliates.
5. The management and administrative functions of each were performed by the same AIG affiliate.
6. Officers of the three offshore entities had numerous relationships with AIG and with each other.

One of the charges was in the area of responsibility of a senior executive of AIG. He told me, "It was dead wrong, maybe an error on the attorney general's part but dead wrong." He predicted Greenberg would be exonerated on all charges.

But it was the first transaction, the one to increase reserves, that drew the most attention and cost Greenberg his job. The highlights of what happened are discussed in the suit against AIG and Greenberg/Smith. It alleges that on October 31, 2000, Greenberg called Ronald Ferguson, president of GenRe suggesting that GenRe purchase up to $500 million in reinsurance from AIG because he wanted AIG to show increased reserves. But, in the same conversation, Greenberg also said that he wanted the deal to be risk free. The suit describes a riskless transaction that creates reserves as nonsensical. An insurer can properly generate and record reserves only if it is taking on genuine risk that there will be claims that would require future payment. Greenberg allegedly wanted AIG to be able to book hundreds of millions of dollars in reserves from GenRe, but he did not want there to be any risk that AIG would actually have to pay any claims.

Ultimately, AIG's subsidiary, National Union, and GenRe's subsidiary, Cologne Resp of Dublin, entered into two contracts. In form, GenRe was to pay a total of $500 million to AIG and AIG was to provide $600 million of reinsurance coverage. AIG would be able to show reserves of $500 million in accordance with Greenberg's original design. The first of the sham contracts would allow AIG to book $250 million of reserves in the fourth quarter of 2000, and the second sham contract would allow AIG to book another $250 million of reserves in the first quarter of 2001. In fact, GenRe did not pay and the only genuine service performed by either party was that GenRe created false and misleading documentation to satisfy Greenberg's illicit goals.

Finally, to supplement this effort, AIG made fictitious "adjustments" on a quarterly basis to create additional reserves in late 2000 and early 2001.

D avid Boies is a perfect lawyer for Hank Greenberg. He is as much of a risk taker as Greenberg. In fact, he is a passionate gambler who ranks craps as his favorite game. And he has played right on the edge from the beginning. Boies's fame comes from arguing Vice President Gore's case to be president before the Supreme Court, a case he lost. He met his first wife, Caryl, on the high school debating team and married the 16-year-old in a Mexican ceremony they kept secret from their parents for two months. He studied law at Northwestern University, where he was forced to leave after an affair with a professor's wife (who later became his second of three wives). Then he talked his way into Yale Law School, where he graduated second in his class (1966).

After law school, Boies joined Cravath, Swaine, and Moore and early on won a big case in which the client was IBM. Eventually, he had to leave in a dispute over representing George Steinbrenner in his suit against Major League Baseball. Time Warner, which owned the Atlanta Braves, was one of Cravath's biggest clients. His departure was accelerated by Boies's habit of blabbing to the press and taking on high-stakes contingency cases, something many Cravath partners did not appreciate.

So Boies opened a small, six-man firm, and today the firm, Boies, Schiller, and Flexner, has 197 lawyers in offices in 11 cities and revenue of over $150 million. His cases share similarities with Spitzer's.

According to *Forbes*, both men tend to try their cases in the press, to push until they overreach, and to rely on questionable tactics that sometimes backfire.

Boies defeated Vietnam-era General William Westmoreland in a 1982 libel suit against CBS by quoting the commander's own words back at him. Acting for the U.S. government, he destroyed the credibility of Bill Gates in the 2000 antitrust case by goading the Microsoft chairman into making broad statements that were contradicted by internal e-mails.

Boies, who needed a waiver from AIG to take Greenberg as a client because AIG had been a previous client, indicated his strategic prowess early on by persuading Greenberg to reverse the $2 billion transfer of AIG stock to his wife a few days before he resigned. It was reported that this was distracting from the case at hand.

"We know each other, we like each other, we respect each other," says Boies of his relationship with Spitzer. "I am a political supporter."

Spitzer's strategy in his cases has been one of intimidation. Since becoming attorney general in 1999, he has terrorized Wall Street, bloodied Merrill Lynch, mutual fund companies, and Marsh & McLennan. He has a strategy he has used often: find a long-established but shady-sounding practice in an industry, expose it as a scandal, single out a villain and threaten criminal prosecution, flush out the scapegoat, and extract a sizeable settlement. He relies on the Martin Act, a vaguely worded state law that enables the attorney general to file civil or criminal charges in a broad range of securities cases. This is where intimidation comes in. When chasing Merrill Lynch, they dug in their heels. He went on the *CBS Evening News* and warned that if the firm continued to maintain that what happened was inappropriate but wasn't illegal, there will be no settlement, but "there could be criminal charges." Merrill quickly agreed to pay a $100 million fine.

Boies himself is a brilliant practitioner of Spitzer's divide-and-conquer strategy. In a dizzying pirouette, acting for shareholders, he played Christie's against Sotheby's in the 2001 price-fixing scandal. First he negotiated with Christie's, which was cooperating in a government investigation; then he offered to settle with Sotheby's if it incriminated its rival. Boies further split Sotheby's from Alfred Taubman, its former chairman and largest shareholder, by invoking the directors' fiduciary duty to sue Taubman for the scheme. As a result, plaintiffs collected $512 million in the settlement, including $115 million from Taubman, who later went to jail.

Boies has had his share of over-the-top cases—and has repeatedly landed in hot water. He and his clients have been sanctioned at least three times. In one 1998 case, Boies tried to get New York Supreme Court Judge Edward Greenfield removed from a lawsuit—three years after his client, New York landlord Sheldon Solow, had settled the underlying complaint. Boies cited flimsy allegations of corruption dug up by Solow's investigators involving the judge's clerk, which raised at least "the appearance of impropriety" by the jurist. But in a testy courtroom exchange Greenfield accused the litigator of ignoring "basic law that everyone knows after the first year of law school." Still another judge fined Boies and his client $46,000 for filing the "barely sensible" motion. "It was startlingly unusual," says Greenfield of the incident, which occurred as he was retiring at the mandatory age of 76. "I'd never seen anything like it in 35 years on the bench."

Boies was fined again in 2003. This was after filing a federal Racketeer Influenced & Corrupt Organizations suit against a doctor who had sold an East Hampton, New York, waterfront mansion to Hard Rock Cafe founder Peter Morton. Solow, who owns a house nearby, had already lost a state-court suit seeking to overturn the sale. "Boies was brought in to have more artillery," says Morton's lawyer, Errol Margolin. The Second Circuit Court of Appeals called the suit "frivolous," however, and ordered Boies, Schiller, and another firm to pay double costs.

In a high-profile price-fixing case against the Click modeling agency last year, New York defense attorney Aaron Richard Golub convinced a federal judge to fine Boies, Schiller $30,000 for failing to respond to discovery requests—even though the court insisted it do so. "No attorney can expect an exemption from court rules simply because that attorney chooses to take on more work than he or she can handle," said U.S. District Judge Henry Pitman in a May 2004 opinion. "We nailed them left and right," Golub says. Boies explains that despite the sanctions, all the modeling agencies, including Click, settled for undisclosed amounts.

B oies narrowly escaped sanctions in a Florida lawsuit over the estate of celebrity jeweler Harry Winston. He and partner Robert Silver agreed to pay a former Winston employee a bonus of up to $1 million for help with the case. The Florida Supreme Court called it paying a witness and suspended for 90 days the license of a Florida lawyer who worked with Boies. Boies and Silver, who are licensed to practice in New York, were exonerated last year by the New York State Bar Association.

David Boies plays close to the edge and so does Hank Greenberg. They will make a formidable team. And they began in earnest. They sought testimony and internal documents from Spitzer, something that is usually done only the other way around. Greenberg's lawyers say they looked for evidence that the attorney general improperly pressured witnesses into admitting wrongdoing and implicating them. Nevertheless, it is very unusual to depose a prosecutor.

Chapter 13

The Great Survivor Vows to Bounce Back

The past four years have probably been the toughest years of Hank Greenberg's life, even tougher than landing on Omaha Beach. He has been ejected from the top job in a company, AIG, that he had built into the world's largest insurance company. Only two weeks later he had to resign as nonexecutive chairman of the company. His integrity has been questioned, with allegations of fraud levied against him. The New York attorney general called him a criminal on national television. He is no longer on speaking terms with prominent people he thought were among his best friends. And his reputation probably has been damaged beyond repair.

By 2006, AIG had settled civil suits against it by the attorney general's office and the New York superintendent of insurance. If Greenberg can prove in court the charges therein were fallacious, especially the one involving the finite insurance arrangement with GenRe, it will be a big step forward toward vindication.

Greenberg continues to be as aggressive legally as he is in business. He wants vindication and it's his very nature. In late June 2006, SICO sought a court order to force AIG to hand over notes and minutes of AIG board meetings from February 9, 2005 on. Greenberg said he needed records of board actions that led to a $1.6 billion settlement between AIG and regulators announced in February, according to the *Wall Street Journal*. The suit invoked a special Delaware law that allows shareholders to see corporate records if they suspect wrongdoing. Ostensibly, this allows shareholders like SICO some redress for the settlement AIG made with the regulators. But more important, it had a direct bearing on the case Spitzer and Mills brought against Greenberg and former CFO Howard Smith. If there was a basis for eliminating or reducing these charges, then the charges against Greenberg would have to be reduced. Greenberg finally did receive copies of the board minutes. But the suit was far enough along toward settlement, that it was not clear they had an effect on the charges.

The downside is that the parade of lawsuits nettles investors and could affect the stock. There have been stockholder settlements but the price of the stock today is so low, since the government takeover, that the point is not relevant. And there will be a plethora of other legal actions that will go on for years. One brought in 2002, before Greenberg resigned, was by the Teachers Retirement Systems of Lousiana that sued in the name of AIG to recover millions of fees AIG paid to Starr. In late June 2006, a judge blocked a bid by Greenberg and others to block the lawsuit. According to the Associated Press, this means Greenberg may face trial on allegations he reaped excessive pay through fees AIG paid to Starr.

But the biggest risk he faces is the outcome of a case in Alexandria, Virginia, where a federal grand jury brought criminal charges against former GenRe CEO Ronald Ferguson, former finance chief Elizabeth Monrad, and former general counsel Robert D. Graham. They also charged AIG vice president of reinsurance Christian Milton with the same offenses. Together they face a total of 12 criminal charges, including conspiracy, securities fraud, wire fraud, mail fraud, and making false statements to the Securities and Exchange Commission. The legal charges refer on several occasions to unindicted co-conspirator No.1, who is widely believed to be Hank Greenberg. There is a difference of opinion in the legal progression on what this means. One is that it is a legal technique you use to make your case. You want to prove there was a conspiracy and you draw in the unindicted conspirator as part of the case without a specific intent to indict the unindicted conspirator. Another view is that the federal prosecutors dug through thousands of pages of documents and listened to hours of recorded conversations and didn't find any hard evidence that Greenberg knew his company might have been committing a crime. He does not use e-mail extensively and was not captured on audiotape discussing the deal. Therefore, it is unlikely he will face criminal charges. A third view is that the indictments suggested that prosecutors are homing in on Greenberg. Jacob Frenkel, a former SEC enforcement attorney who now works as a defense lawyer, said: "There's no question that the prosecutors' sights are beyond those four. Whether they will be able to climb further is the open question."

If a jury was to acquit Chris Milton, then the likelihood of criminal charges being brought against Greenberg is minuscule. But Milton was convicted and this puts Greenberg at some risk.

Very few people are as resilient as Hank Greenberg—or as fortunate. In recent years, lots of CEOs have been ousted. But to be ousted from a job you have held for 37 years, accused of fraud, and threatened with criminal charges is much rarer. Many would have called it quits in the business world, or they would have dedicated their time to defending themselves, or they would have enjoyed a much deserved retirement, especially at Greenberg's age. But Greenberg has bounced back. He is as feisty as ever and almost acts as if nothing happened. He has built a new life, one that takes advantage of extremely unique circumstances he inherited. He has opened large, swank new offices on Park Avenue. The offices are divided by a bank of elevators. Along the left side coming out of the elevator is the Starr Foundation, which Greenberg chairs. Across the hall and along the other side is the office of Greenberg, some of the New York offices of his business ventures

along with some of his key people who came with him from AIG such
as Ed Matthews, former vice chairman and chief financial officer of
AIG, now president of C.V. Starr & Company.

His post-AIG days left Greenberg with a triumvirate of prestige,
power, and money. He is chairman of Starr International (SICO),
AIG's largest shareholder; chairman of C.V. Starr & Company, a group
of insurance agencies who place a great deal of business with AIG (or
did until recently); and chairman of the Starr Foundation, which was
one of the nation's largest foundations. So Hank Greenberg has something no other ousted CEO ever had—three powerful jobs, all related
to but independent of his former company. He is not trying to find
something to do besides defend himself against a variety of charges.
He has a surfeit of riches. He could not have planned it better if he
had planned it.

During the period when AIG was going public, SICO acquired
a large block of AIRCO stock, which owned a substantial portion of
AIG, in payment for the sale of its primary asset, AIUO. The SICO
shareholders made what Greenberg always has termed, correctly, an
extraordinarily generous decision to reserve a number of those AIG
shares for selected AIG employees. So the amount the AIG shares
were worth above book value of the assets being traded—about $110
million—was set aside to compensate existing and future AIG employees. In other words, AIG shares worth $110 million were set aside
in a special account. Greenberg and other existing SICO shareholders would keep only the book value of the AIG shares they received
from selling SICO's primary asset. SICO has approximately 311 million
shares worth about $20 billion (before any sales SICO has made). So it
was indeed a monumentally generous decision. The fact that $110 million
has grown to $20 billion within 35 years is incredible, absolutely remark-
able. It is a testimony to Greenberg's leadership of AIG. SICO owns about
12 percent of AIG and is by far the largest share holder, as a result of this
initial decision and the subsequent growth.

C.V. Starr & Co., named for the founder of the Starr companies,
owns a group of insurance agencies that places considerable business with
AIG. While not all of Starr's income comes from AIG, the preponderance
does, or did until recently. It started as a small business and is very
lucrative today. Recently, Starr bought out the interest of existing AIG

executives like CEO Martin Sullivan, so it is completely independent of AIG. It owns over $1 billion in AIG shares and provides another corporate affiliation for Greenberg.

Finally, the Starr Foundation, created in 1955, owns about 2 percent of AIG. Its assets were all AIG shares but there has been some diversification. Its directors all are former AIG executives. Because C.V. Starr & Co. owns Morefar and Lookout, Greenberg still has use of these properties. And because Starr owns Starr's old house, Brook House, at Mt. Mansfield in Stowe, Vermont, he can continue to use it. While AIG owns the corporate jets, he can always lease a jet, and I would be surprised if he hasn't. Flying commercial does not seem to be something Greenberg wants to do.

Greenberg has an investment vehicle, SICO, with many investments aimed at China, where he is still highly respected and welcome and has extraordinary contacts; a company that makes an excellent cash return in the insurance business; and a charitable foundation that not only does good work but serves as a powerful tool to spread his influence by giving to certain charitable organizations. He has use of many of the comforts of his old corporate life at AIG.

SICO is clearly planning some significant investments, probably in China. He visited China in March 2006 with Edward Matthews, president of C.V. Starr, looking at potential investments, attending a government-backed conference, and holding meetings with finance industry officials. He breakfasted with Xu Kwangdi, the former mayor of Shanghai, the kind of meeting other Western business leaders would value. Greenberg was visibly irritated that his name had been removed by AIG from the presidential suite of the Ritz-Carlton, part of a residential and commercial block he built in the 1980s. Not only that but they removed a photo of him with Zhu Rongi, the city's mayor and later the premier, from a check-in area for the apartments. Traveling with Greenberg in China, he is such a minor celebrity and so welcome with top officials, he can forget he has any problems back home.

If someone foresaw the eruption at AIG or cleverly planned a post-corporate life, he could not have done better than create these entities separate from but related to AIG. They were ready-made for Greenberg. Unlike other ousted CEOs who try to find something to do or just adjust to retirement, he has three meaningful organizations

to run, one which had $20 billion in assets to invest. It is almost as
if Greenberg planned for this, but this is a scurrilous charge that carries anti-Greenberg rhetoric too far. He did not. He did not see his
fall at AIG coming, and the structure and nature of these organizations
evolved over time.

In early 2006, while preparing to fight out Spitzer's civil charges in
court, and assuming no criminal charges will be forthcoming, Greenberg
began planning to build and expand his new empire. I asked him if the
quote attributed to him was correct: "He wanted to build a larger company than AIG."

He laughed and denied saying it. He indicated that "if they buy a
company he would not be involved in the day-to-day operation of it."
He mentioned merchant banking and other transactions his company is
looking at. We talked about AIG. He said: "It's a great company. But you
can't have a company run by outside directors and lawyers," a statement
he had made to numerous others and made publicly. He obviously does
not want to harm AIG, if for no other reason than he personally has
several billion dollars worth of AIG stock, and Starr International is the
largest shareholder. There are other reasons as well. He is rightfully
proud of what he created and wants it to prosper and grow. But what
began as a difficult working relationship has deteriorated into an all-
out war. Lawsuits are flying from both sides—lawsuits that, depending
on their outcome, dramatically affect his plans, especially for SICO.

Signaling the kind of risk takers David Boies and Hank Greenberg
are, on July 8, 2005, Starr International sued AIG to return art and
other items of Starr's that are in AIG's possession. The big risk this
brings is that it puts an offshore corporation onshore for legal purposes
and makes it subject to lawsuits as well. SICO is a Panamanian corporation domiciled in Bermuda with principal offices in Dublin but once
it sues in U.S. courts, it opens itself to U.S. lawsuits. And it received a
zinger—an AIG lawsuit alleging AIG was entitled to the SICO shares
set aside for AIG employees for the purpose of providing compensation
to AIG employees.

It is true that ways could be found to sue SICO even if it were not
an onshore company, but it would have been more difficult. An AIG
lawsuit against SICO would have likely resulted in a fight over jurisdiction. In any case, while the SICO lawsuit mentions financial instruments,

stock certificates, and keys to safe deposit boxes, the most valuable item mentioned is artwork valued in excess of $15 million located in New York, Vermont, Washington, D.C., Pennsylvania, and the Philippines. A Van Gogh painting is included.

Whether David Boies anticipated what came next I do not know. AIG fired back on September 27. The counterclaim glazed over SICO's original claim regarding the $15 million of property that AIG had refused to return; in fact, it basically did not mention it. Instead, it focused on the 311 million shares of AIG owned by SICO, which it claimed was committed to compensating AIG employees for outstanding contributions to the company's growth.

It discussed the Deferred Compensation Profit Participation Plan (DCPPP), which was established in 1970 by SICO. This plan is in two-year increments and gives participants (some 700 of them) an allocated number of AIG shares based on the amount of growth in AIG earnings per share for those two years compared to the previous two-year period. The plan subsequently was amended to allocate additional shares to participants if they remain at the company eight years from the beginning of participation in the two-year plans. Until the 1990s, participants received annual bonuses from SICO as well.

AIG noted that 33 million shares have been awarded, but 22 million have not yet been received. SICO has indicated its intention of using the remaining 270 million shares for its own benefit. The suit notes that since the beginning the SICO board has consisted almost exclusively of current AIG executives who administered the plan, but that in March of 2005 current AIG directors were removed by SICO, breaking a SICO–AIG relationship that has lasted for over 30 years.

AIG alleges that the intent was to give these shares away until they were depleted, which it is estimated could be hundreds of years. A Greenberg speech to all DCPPP participants in Florida in 2001 said participants were expected to stay until retirement or forfeit their accumulation of AIG shares, especially since the founders gave up ownership to benefit them. One intent was to keep them from being hired away by competing firms.

In essence, the suit said SICO has indicated it plans to use the shares for its own purposes (investments) and a contract had been broken

when AIG executives were removed from the SICO board. It asked
for a declaratory judgment keeping the shares for employees, a rein-
statement of AIG executives to constitute the majority of the SICO
board, and the creation of a constructive trust on behalf of AIG for
the shares.

SICO filed its own counterclaim against AIG three weeks later. The
focus had shifted fundamentally from the initial suit against AIG on
September 27, when SICO asked to recover artwork and other items
worth $15 million. This was mentioned only once near the end of the
brief. A much more important battle had come to the fore: retaining
ownership and control of the $20 billion in AIG shares. Life or death
for SICO and very important for AIG.

Now, who actually owns SICO? Greenberg and other directors, 12
voting shareholders, each of whom has basically 10 percent control of
the company but no equity interest. Common stock was at one point
owned by a Bermuda foundation, but today all shares of nonvoting
stock are owned by the Starr International Charitable Trust (Ireland),
which, according to one of the lawsuits "represents virtually all of Starr
International's (SICO) residual economic value upon a liquidation of
Starr International." So it appears that if SICO were liquidated, most
of its value (i.e., the AIG shares) would go to the Irish charitable trust.
I talked to a SICO attorney to clarify ownership and he told me it was
confidential. There are apparently some provisions whereby, if dissolved,
the shares could go to the Starr Foundation.

First, this lawsuit asserts that SICO is an independent company
formed 25 years before AIG. Second, it argues that there is not an
agreement and never has been that would require SICO to use the AIG
shares for the exclusive benefit of AIG employees. Finally, it makes it
clear that SICO is an independent private company that owns shares in
AIG, not vice versa. This is supported by quoting Martin Sullivan, AIG
chief executive, who said on a June 29 earnings call with securities analysts and investors: "The (AIG) shares owned by SICO are owned by
SICO." Greenberg, of course, has been quoted numerous times about
the close relationship between AIG and SICO.

SICO argues that its real purpose in setting up a deferred compensation program was neither to benefit the employees who gain
nor to benefit AIG. Its purpose was to strengthen AIG, enhance its

moneymaking opportunities, and thereby to benefit SICO, its largest shareholder. In other words, there was nothing eleemosynary about the DCPPP. Its sole purpose was to enhance the value of AIG shares and thereby benefit SICO.

This argument is amplified by noting that only 4 percent of the AIG shares owned by SICO have been distributed to AIG employees, and that it has never agreed to use any portion of its AIG shares for future compensation for AIG employees. SICO does pledge that all the shares set aside for employees until now will be paid. It also argues that the bonus payments SICO used to pay to participants in the compensation plan were cancelled in about 1992, without objection from AIG. Regarding control of SICO by the board, the brief argues that on March 28, 2005, four existing AIG executives on the SICO board voted to remove nine current AIG executives from that board. Subsequently, on April 14, AIG ordered three AIG executives still on the board to resign or lose their employment with AIG. This is foolish on AIG's part—to be removing AIG directors from the board when they claim they rightfully are entitled to the shares. A very distinguished attorney whom Greenberg had tried to recruit as general counsel told me he considered this an exceedingly imprudent move.

The brief argues that SICO has meaningful functions other than holding AIG stock and administering the DCPPP. It has substantial investment portfolios as well as ownership and management of real estate. In March 2005, the *Wall Street Journal* reported that the AIG board was considering abolishing the role of a private holding company, Starr International, as a payer of deferred compensation to AIG employees. Subsequently, the AIG board did abolish the participation of AIG employees in the planned 2005–2006 DCPPP of Starr International. AIG subsequently created its own plan very similar to the SICO plan. This too is contradictory—AIG claims they have a right to the shares, then forbids their executives from participating in the plan, and finally abolishes it altogether.

If AIG were right that it had certain ownership rights in SICO's AIG stock, then it would have to consolidate Starr International into its financial statements or reflect the appropriate liabilities of the DCPPP's on its books and records and include such shares as a contra-equity account on its consolidated balance sheet. It did not do so, even in its recent massive restatement of prior years. So, SICO argues, AIG has undermined its own position.

AIG benefited by having the compensation program in SICO, since it was nondilutive to AIG. The brief notes that "if the expenses of the SICO plan had been reflected by AIG, the pretax amounts accrued would have been $129.6 million, $49.4 million, and $55.7 million for 2003, 2002, and 2001, respectively." It also notes that its Form 10-K filed with the SEC in May 2005 reported a reduction of $905 million in retained earnings on its 1999 consolidated balance sheet and an additional corresponding increase to be paid in capital to reflect "expense amounts attributable to deferred compensation granted to certain AIG employees by SICO." The 2004 AIG proxy statement noted that payments under the SICO plan are not paid by AIG and will be nondilutive to AIG shareholders. In short, SICO, not an AIG affiliate, pays the deferred compensation so there is no cost to AIG or its shareholders.

The SICO countersuit has one additional purpose: It wants AIG to make it clear SICO is not an affiliate of AIG. There are probably a number of reasons, but the one named in the lawsuit is that under the Securities Laws, until AIG registers the SICO-held shares, SICO cannot pay out to those participants in the deferred compensation program the AIG shares they are due. AIG has played games in this regard again and again. It simply will not give clear clarification on this issue. One could presume this is because of the lawsuit under which they hope to gain control of the 311 million AIG shares. If they registered with the SEC that Starr is not controlled by them, it weakens their case for gaining control of the AIG shares held by SICO. But that is pure speculation. In any case, AIG announced on June 19 that it had registered with regulators for Starr International to issue SICO-controlled AIG shares to AIG executives. This left clear that the great majority of shares were still in contention. To indicate AIG is still on the SEC watchdog list, it issued a statement saying one reason it had been able to do this was because it had filed amendments to the 2005 annual report, which provide increased financial disclosure.

The attorney whom Greenberg tried to recruit as general counsel said to me he thought AIG had handled the SICO lawsuit badly and that he thought Greenberg would win and be cleared on all the other charges, although he probably would have to pay a fine.

So the battle continues and will likely continue for some time.

The stakes are such that AIG is closely watching what SICO does with the contested shares. In February 2006, AIG challenged SICO in court to give it details of its sales of AIG shares and its plans for future stock sales as the companies continue their messy divorce. This was in reaction to the fact that Starr had sold about 2 million of the 311 million shares it holds. Starr indicated it is willing to turn over information about its sales and the disposition of these shares. In a letter to the presiding judge, Starr International said it intends to continue selling AIG shares and will use those proceeds for general corporate purposes, including reinvestment. It apparently sold another 3 million shares in March.

Whichever company wins the court battle—AIG or SICO—there will almost certainly be an appeal. So it could go on for a long time. It is a complex issue that is shaped by the long relationship between the two companies.

Commenting on the lawsuit, several AIG directors feel the suit had to be filed yet do not expect to win it. Apparently, they feel it had to be filed because of the cost to AIG of having a separate long-term compensation program. They worry they are liable as directors if they don't try to regain the shares.

One respected and very creative lawyer who was with the company for over 30 years said to me back in the 1980s: "How is it that an AIG executive can also work for one or two private companies (C.V. Starr and Starr International) that do business with AIG where he gets paid by both or all three and there is not a conflict of interest? And how come we report all this to the SEC in our 10K and no questions are asked?" That never changed until the crisis that led to Greenberg's ouster. While the authorities have looked at these private companies and some lawsuits have been filed about the conflict of interest, there has not been a big issue made out of it. But the lawyer asked a very poignant question.

My opinion on this case is a nonlegal one since I am not an attorney. It is based on the merits of the case and what strikes me as fair. First, it is clear SICO legally owns the stock. It is a private company and has unquestionable ownership. The original $110 million set aside has grown to a staggering $20 billion in a little over 30 years.

But on a de facto basis, AIG and SICO were treated as one entity when Greenberg was head of both. One AIG director commented: "Hank saw it all as one big pot—AIG, C.V. Starr, SICO." In other words, star performers got the benefits of all three. He used each as he saw fit. One has to wonder if Greenberg had not been at SICO when he retired from AIG, what would have happened. Would there have been a current or former AIG executive who was a SICO director who would have organized SICO to make investments and would have broken off with AIG? Highly unlikely. More likely, the new AIG CEO would have become chair of SICO and the compensation program would have continued. AIG executives would have remained on the SICO board since, first and foremost, they are needed to determine who should be the beneficiaries of the DCPPP.

It doesn't seem fair that SICO suddenly has $20 billion to do with as it likes when that clearly was not the original intention. Yet, on the other hand, why should AIG have $20 billion handed over after it cancelled participation by its own employees in the SICO compensation plan? Since the SICO shares would not be exhausted for several centuries if ever, an appealing compromise would be for SICO to give AIG sufficient shares to fund the compensation program and to keep the rest for itself. Clearly, my idea of a compromise will never happen. The swords are drawn in the sand and the intensity of feeling is too high.

The tangled divorce between Hank Greenberg and AIG has produced a lawyer's paradise—a ton of litigation. Starr Wars, some call it. C.V. Starr & Co., the other company Greenberg headed when he was at AIG and still does, and AIG are involved in a second set of lawsuits. (Starr was the company with which the poorly performing agencies were placed before the public offering of AIG so as to keep the price of AIG up.) These lawsuits are not nearly as significant and involve a minuscule amount of money compared to the SICO vs. AIG suit. But they indicate the hostility that has developed between Greenberg and AIG.

Partners before are now direct competitors or trying to be. Starr was the managing general agent for about $2 billion in premiums on policies underwritten solely by AIG. These agencies often had executives who had similar functions inside AIG itself. C.V. Starr owns four specialized agencies—among them, American International Marine Agency,

American International Aviation Agency, and Starr Tech, which focus on energy and chemical industries. C.V. Starr itself handles excess casualty insurance in trucking, and so on. Greenberg was willing to sell it all to AIG, but the offer was some $600 million short, from Greenberg's view.

AIG brought suit against Starr in January 2006 to stop it from selling insurance for other companies, including a unit of billionaire businessman Warren Buffett. Starr and its subsidiaries traditionally sell AIG policies to big manufacturers and now have deals to sell policies written by another unit of Berkshire Hathaway and Ace Ltd., an insurer run by Evan Greenberg, Hank's son. The AIG suit accuses the Starr agencies of "flagrant misconduct and self-dealing contrary to the best interests of AIG," by diverting one-third of the portfolio intended for AIG to National Indemnity, a Berkshire unit. The most interesting part of the suit is that one of Greenberg's new insurers is one of the very groups of companies that got him in trouble over his accounting scandal.

So Greenberg, or C.V. Starr & Co., started the feud by lining up other insurers to do business with instead of exclusively working with AIG as had been the case in the past. Maybe he was dissatisfied with the compensation from AIG. Or maybe he preferred to diversify. In any case, it is one more sign of the enmity.

New York State Supreme Court Justice Herman Cahn temporarily blocked C.V. Starr from selling the insurance, but a couple of days later Starr filed suit accusing the insurance giant of trying to prevent it from competing with AIG. The suit contends AIG undertook a series of acts designed solely to inflict irreparable damage upon the Starr agencies and their subsidiaries. AIG is charged with trying to take business from the Starr agencies.

Finally, on February 17, AIG terminated its relationship with Starr Tech and its subsidiaries and said AIG Global Energy will manage future business of accounts formerly written on its behalf by Starr. A few weeks later AIG announced creation of a new unit to handle several lines of business previously handled by C.V. Starr & Co. When the dust clears, the bottom line is that Greenberg walked away with the bulk of the talent that staffed these various agencies. Customers comment that until the brouhaha started they did not even know C.V. Starr was a private company but thought they were dealing with AIG.

Of the three pegs in Greenberg's power base, the Starr Foundation should be the one that offers the least aggravation and in some ways should be the most rewarding, for it provides the opportunity to draw from a $4 billion pool and support numerous good causes, especially those in education. But it too has become a problem—only a different kind of problem. SICO and C.V. Starr were battles over business, battles that were initiated by Greenberg. The Starr Foundation is a battle of a different kind—a high-profile battle over reputation and honor.

It came after Greenberg and friends had launched an aggressive public relations campaign to restore and enhance his reputation. It has the trademarks of a campaign by the legendary New York publicist, Howard Rubenstein, although it is not. The public relations team was first led by Howard Opinsky, former campaign press secretary for U.S. Senator John McCain's candidacy for president and now with the PR firm Weber Shandwick, based in Washington. Turnover in the public relations function has been frequent. Greenberg's patience is on a short leash.

It included an article under Greenberg's byline in the *Financial Times* in July 2005 arguing that the United States is shortsighted in denying China the purchase of the oil company Unocal. It was followed in August by an op-ed in the *Wall Street Journal* explaining that it took him 17 years to secure the license for AIG to operate in China and that patience is required in dealing with the Chinese. These pieces reflect Greenberg's strong interest in and knowledge about China but also position him for further involvement since they reflect a point of view the Chinese will sympathize with. (Greenberg considered writing a book on business in China but demurred for the time being.)

A story in the October 25, 2005, *New York Post* by gossip columnist Cindy Adams discusses a visit Greenberg made to her home for an interview. He talked about wanting to write a book, *Seeing the World through Snowball's Eyes*, which would tell Greenberg's story from the perspective of his Maltese. Remember that the lawsuit against AIG for SICO belongings included files on the dog's medical records.

Snowball should have quite a story to tell. At a private dinner in Moscow, the guests didn't know the dog was hidden under the table in a duffel bag until she started barking at some gypsies singing. It scared the hell out of everyone. "I take her everywhere. In China, she never left my sight. I even took her to a state dinner." AIG executives confirmed that Greenberg and the dog were inseparable, saying that the bathroom on Greenberg's jet was reserved for Greenberg, his wife, and Snowball, while everyone else used the pilot's bathroom. (That was not my experience at AIG but if Greenberg had a dog then, he never traveled with it or it was well hidden.) Art Joukowsky confirms that when Greenberg visited Brown, the dog was wrapped around his neck.

The article also talks about his family. Some have argued that this travail has brought the family closer together. Jeff Greenberg denied this to me and said that the family has always been close and there for each other. He said he was there for his brothers and they were there for him when terrible things happened.

In the *Post* interview Greenberg talked about only losing American friends. No one international. One personal letter from an Asian head of state (China) said, "We had our cultural revolution. You're now having yours." From a public relations point of view, this interview is clearly meant to humanize Greenberg, the terrorizing executive. To me, it is demeaning to have a man of Greenberg's distinction go to the apartment of the *Post* gossip writer for an interview. Commenting on the situation his father is charged with, Jeff said that while he was not up to date on the details, his father was always ethical and didn't cut any corners. He does not think he did anything wrong.

That same month he was the honoree at the Hebrew Home for the Aged in Riverdale annual dinner on October 16. Greenberg has been a long-time supporter of this charity, the only significant Jewish organizational involvement he had over the years in New York.

In late October, Vincent Tese, an outside director of Bear Stearns & Co. and a New York director of economic development under Governor Cuomo, sent a letter to a group of powerful figures asking permission to use their name to bolster Greenberg's image. Recipients included former secretary of state Henry Kissinger, chair of the Executive Committee at Citigroup and former treasury secretary Robert Rubin, and PBS talk-show host Charlie Rose. Because the letter was apparently inadvertently sent to *Wall Street Journal* publisher Peter Kann, it was released to the press. None of the recipients would say if they would join the effort. According to the *Journal*, the list of recipients was compiled by Greenberg. Governor Cuomo did state that he wanted to be helpful and suggested he would work at getting

Greenberg honorary educational degrees where his career and contributions could be discussed. This obviously would take time. The overall
effort to sign up supporters has not been mentioned again, so presumably it has died. Greenberg or whoever conceived of this plan received
bad advice because the likelihood of many of these very distinguished
Americans responding positively is remote, especially when Attorney
General Spitzer was playing such a high-profile role. Apparently, this
PR effort has been put on the back burner.

Cornelius Vander Starr spawned a group of philanthropists inspired
by his own philanthropy and made possible by their participation
in the growth of his company. Those with Starr from the early days
have substantial fortunes in their own right and several have established foundations. The Freeman Foundation, established by Buck
Freeman in honor of his father, is the largest foundation in Vermont. It
is focused on East Asia and makes grants of about $50 million a year,
including bringing up to 50 Asian students to school at Wesleyan. Buck
Freeman works full-time at the foundation as do members of his family. The Joukowsky Family Foundation, established by Artemis
Joukowsky, makes about $5 million a year in grants with nearly half
going to Brown University. In addition, Artemis Joukowsky has given
Brown a great deal of his private funds, as he has worked on a volunteer basis as chancellor and vice chancellor. The Manton foundation,
established by Jimmy Manton, focuses on art. Recently, the foundation gave a number of English landscapes to the Sterling and Francine
Clark Art Institute in Williamstown, Massachusetts. Finally, the Maurice
R. and Corinne P. Greenberg Family Foundation tends to make grants
to medical institutions that often are matched by grants from the Starr
Foundation, which Mr. Greenberg chairs.

But the granddaddy of them all is the Starr Foundation. It was
established in 1955 but endowed by Starr's estate. It was worth
approximately $4 billion, much of it in AIG stock, and, for a large foun-
dation, has a small staff directed by its president, Florence Davis (who was
general counsel of AIG until Greenberg moved her to this job).
While the foundation gives grants totaling approximately $200 million
annually in the areas of medicine, healthcare, human needs, public policy, culture, and the environment, the focus, reflecting Starr's interest, is

on education. It has given to over 100 universities and numerous secondary schools.

Attorney General Spitzer shot across Greenberg's bow once again on December 15, 2005—this time with public implications that are very difficult to deal with. He charges Greenberg and his fellow executors of the Starr Foundation, all directors of C.V. Starr & Co., of defrauding the foundation over 35 years ago by selling foundation assets at fire-sale prices to private companies he and the other executors controlled. Spitzer said they then resold these assets and related assets they controlled for a much higher price to AIG.

No formal charges were brought. Instead, Spitzer filed a report and sent a letter to Florence Davis, president of the Starr Foundation, asking her to appoint an independent committee to look at remedies to recover assets and also to consider a reconstitution of the foundation's structure so as to guarantee it has the independence to advance its charitable mission. While there are no charges or even threatened charges against Greenberg or his co-executors, the attorney general released his report and letter to Ms. Davis to the press.

This in some ways is more damning than a lawsuit, for it leads to headlines like that in the December 15, 2005, *New York Times*: "Report says Ex-AIG Chief Defrauded Foundation 35 Years Ago." How do you respond to that? No private individual has the power to get the kind of headlines the attorney general does. Greenberg, after having been quiet for many months, lashed out at Spitzer in frustration. "For the attorney general to use his office to prosecute, and persecute, people in the press for political gain is wholly against our legal principals," Greenberg said in an interview. "It's outrageous."

Greenberg said Spitzer made public the Starr Foundation report in part because late last month he had been forced to concede that he will not bring criminal charges against Greenberg. "It's simple: He's running for another office," Greenberg said. "It has nothing to do with right or wrong."

Compounding the frustration of Greenberg and others is that the Starr settlement was approved by the New York attorney general's office and the surrogate court over 30 years ago.

In his report and letter, Spitzer points out that he discovered this information by having access to Bermuda files that were in dispute when Greenberg resigned after what Spitzer called the "document caper." He said they revealed information not previously known. So the attorney general at the time and other officials that approved the transaction involving the Starr Foundation could not have known about them.

The report alleges that assets worth more than $30 million were sold for $2 million. Most damaging is the allegation that SICO paid only $3,000 to the Starr Foundation for 20 percent of SICO, which that year was worth $20 million in AIG stock. Furthermore, Spitzer alleges, if the Starr Foundation had received the $30 million it was due in AIG stock it would be worth $6 billion today. No mention is made of the fact that the increase from $30 million to $6 billion was because of the extraordinary increase in AIG stock, an increase driven by Hank Greenberg as CEO of AIG.

Starr put the executors of his estate and the shareholders of his two private companies in an impossible situation. On the one hand, they were expected to get the estate and the foundation the highest possible price for his interests in these companies—SICO and C.V. Starr. But as principals themselves in these same companies, they had a stake in paying the lowest possible price for his interests. This was all brought on by the fact that Starr's only family were his colleagues in the company. While these were his closest friends, surely he could have found less self-interested executors.

He apparently had concluded the same thing. A recently discovered memorandum written by Gordon Tweedy states that shortly before his death Starr "was planning to change drastically the nature of the Foundation, including its personnel, and to divorce it entirely from (CVSCO) affairs." This memo was dated February 18, 1969, and in apparent compliance with Starr's wishes, certain directors of the foundation tendered their resignations in September 1968, three months before Starr's death. After his death, however, the CVSCO board, exercising its control over the foundation, agreed the resignation letters should be returned to those who resigned, except for one member who was leaving CVSCO. The fact Tweedy wrote the memo in February 1969, after Starr's death, suggests he was concerned about fulfilling Starr's wishes.

Depending on the response of the Starr Foundation board— Greenberg has recused himself on this issue—the attorney general, as the state officer overseeing charitable groups, can intervene. Spitzer explained to me he "had sent a letter to the head of the foundation. If they agree, they can remedy. And if they don't, a shareholders' derivative suit is the best analogy." In other words, bringing derivative action on the part of a nonprofit. He said this was akin to what his office has done with other foundations—put a new board in place, for example.

One AIG director believes this is exactly what Spitzer had in mind: to create a Rockefeller-type foundation out of the Starr Foundation. Appoint a distinguished board, separate it from the existing board. Ironically, this would be a greater honor to Starr than what has happened. The AIG connection would be severed once and for all. The foundation would have greater recognition. Ultimately, even if that does not happen, something has to give. The successor directors to the current board of ex-AIGers will have to be their children and friends, or they can evolve into a board of distinguished directors. As an additional possible remedy, Spitzer suggested it may be necessary to intervene in the lawsuit between AIG and SICO over AIG shares held by SICO to get the AIG shares necessary to make the foundation whole, since, Spitzer argues, some of these shares came from asset sales by the estate to SICO. (Today, those shares would not be worth much.)

Of special irritation to Greenberg and others on the receiving end of this allegation is that over 35 years have passed since the Starr estate was adjudicated. An uninvolved attorney who is a supporter of and friends with Spitzer said to me that the charges regarding the foundation were outrageous and absurd. But the statute of limitations has not run out. Spitzer, in his letter to Florence Davis, notes that the statute of limitations for actions against a fiduciary does not begin to run until a fiduciary leaves his position of trust. So the six years' limitation would not start until an executor(s) resigns from the Starr Foundation board. Spitzer also points out there is no time bar on a decree to reopen a decree of the surrogate's court. So the decree approving the dispensation of the Starr estate could be challenged.

Spitzer asked for a response from Florence Davis by January 31, 2006. The Starr Foundation subsequently advised him they had appointed an independent committee that includes two retired judges. It would take many months before the special committee reported results.

Chapter 14

Fighting for Honor and Managing from Afar

T he theme of the past three years has been Hank Greenberg's irrepressible determination to restore his honor. He may be angry, he definitely is bitter, and he is unquestionably frustrated and very irritable. For the first time since he landed on top at AIG some 40 years ago, he faces a situation he cannot control nor impact: how the press, and to a lesser extent the government, treat him.

This explains the public relations (PR) turnover in his office. The first PR counsel was Howard Opinsky, former press secretary to Senator John McCain when he ran for president in 2004 and now based in Washington with the PR firm Weber Shandwick. After Opinsky came several others, with so much turnover that it was noticed by the press covering stories about Greenberg. They would grumble: "who is it now?" and were especially frustrated since finding out something about Greenberg or C.V. Starr or securing an interview depended on your relationship with the current PR person. But it kept changing.

Opinsky may have been in charge when Greenberg went to the home of *New York Post* gossip columnist Cindy Adams, for an interview. Clearly, this was meant to humanize Greenberg. The story talked about his dog, Snowball, his sons and relationships around the world. But as I stated earlier, it was demeaning for a man of his distinction. Why should the CEO of a major international corporation go to a gossip writer's home? The answer: a PR firm told him this would get him good press. So he was taking "expert" cues from one of the few areas of expertise he does not know a lot about—public relations. Cindy Adams clearly was an easy touch for a public relations firm. But did this story reach his target audience? Do they even read the *Post*?

But this incident was the exception anyway. During the first year after he left AIG, Greenberg avoided the press. From my meeting with him, where Ed Matthews sat in and occasionally said: "Hank, not that one," suggesting a subject to be avoided, the reason for this quietude is clear: concern about legal matters. The only time I remember Hank publicly exploding and talking to the press during the first year was his response to Attorney General Spitzer publicly castigating him and the Starr directors for virtually "stealing" assets from the Starr Foundation.

Needless to say, Greenberg fired back, disputing the allegations and accusing Spitzer of trying to "demonize" him.

Mr. Greenberg, in an interview with the *New York Sun*, said he was angry that Mr. Spitzer had made the allegations in a publicly released report rather than in court.

> "The proper place to make allegations is in a courtroom," Mr. Greenberg said. "To choose this forum to do it is simply inappropriate."
>
> "To suggest that we did something improper not only is an outrage, it's an insult," Mr. Greenberg said. "Everybody should be outraged by it."
>
> He said Mr. Spitzer, who is running for governor as a Democrat, "wants political headlines."
>
> He said he viewed Mr. Spitzer's assault on him as an assault on the rule of law, and "How do people like Hitler come to power? People are afraid to speak out," Mr. Greenberg said.

Mr. Greenberg recalled the eight years he worked with C.V. Starr, who was the founder of what became AIG. Mr. Greenberg described it as "a tiny company" with revenues of $1.2 million a year, offices on Maiden Lane in downtown Manhattan, and a few hundred employees. "We were his family," Mr. Greenberg said. "I think he'd have been proud of what we accomplished. I think if he could speak, he'd say, 'Well done.'"

I think that incident gave Hank Greenberg the courage to ignore his lawyers' advice and freely speak his mind. Later, he criticized the settlement that AIG made with the Attorney General's Office, a payment of one and one-half billion dollars, for the charges made against AIG and separately against Greenberg and Howard Smith, his chief financial officer (CFO) at AIG. Greenberg, nevertheless, was careful throughout the first year after he left AIG. He kept uncharacteristically quiet, showing the kind of discipline his lawyers probably warned him was absolutely necessary. Then, about a year into his post-AIG period, either some of the lawsuits were settled or he concluded there were no longer legal risks to keep him from expressing his opinions (or possibly he just could not stand keeping quiet anymore).

The public relations front was relaunched, this time with some positive outcome. Greenberg began writing op-ed pieces for both the *Financial Times* and the *Wall Street Journal*, both, unlike Cindy Adams and the *New York Post*, solid business-oriented press outlets. Equally important, his constituency avidly reads these publications. In the September 2008 *Financial Times*, he argued that AIG needs temporary help. In the *Wall Street Journal*, he talked in one piece about China and in another about the inequity of Citibank getting all their CDCs covered by the Fed while AIG only had them partially covered.

But a well written, thoughtful piece on some important international issue about which Greenberg feels deeply is simply never as satisfying as a favorable piece about the author himself, especially when the author is trying to restore his reputation. That probably explains some of the turnover in public relations personnel, some eight different publicists, and certainly explains the biggest public relations faux pas of all. This shows how a talented CEO and his lawyers can get snookered in a field they nothing little about.

Fortune Magazine, in a Greenberg cover story, told the incident well:

In April 2006, Greenberg's team was joined by Karen Webster, managing director of eSapience, a little-known media and research firm based in Cambridge, Mass. She proposed launching a massive rehabilitation effort. Greenberg's people were interested. They had been confounded by their inability to get most business journalists to even consider the possibility that he was innocent.

Rather than go directly to the media to make Greenberg's case, Webster suggested a subtler strategy, one that would target "influentials"—public intellectuals, policymakers, and advisors who affect debate. The goal, as outlined in a business plan, would be to "change the public conversation about Maurice Greenberg" by highlighting his accomplishments and positioning him "as a visible and highly credible voice about public issues" on a small set of issues that are completely unrelated to his legal situation.

Greenberg and his lawyers agreed to pay $100,000 for the plan.

The eSapience team included Richard Schmalensee, then the dean of MIT's Sloan School, and Webster's husband, David Evans, a law professor. Those academics, the plan said, were highly regarded by the public and their peers as independent-minded. "Because they are not 'hired guns,' they are influential and listened to," the plan continued.

But academics who aren't "hired guns" still need to be paid. They billed Greenberg's team between $400 and $1,000 an hour for their services. Not everyone liked the arrangement. Howard Opinsky, Greenberg's main media strategist, objected "quite strenuously" to the eSapience plan. "I didn't think it was appropriate," he said. "The way it was explained to me and from what I saw, they had a stable of people they paid to write positive things. Which wasn't ethical."

The eSapience team created two scholarly sounding think tanks out of whole cloth: the Barbon Institute, named after Nicholas Barbon, the seventeenth-century father of fire insurance; and the eSapience Center for Law and Business. They organized a big conference at New York City's St. Regis Hotel, where Greenberg spoke about the need for government and insurance industry cooperation to prepare for terrorist attacks.

When eSapience's bills—nearly $500,000 a month—started coming in, Greenberg threw a fit and stopped paying. Then eSapience sued, and much to the embarrassment of everyone, the lawsuit became a subject for the *Boston Globe*. Their bill was about $3 million.

Greenberg dispatched his toughest trial lawyer, Boies, Schiller partner Nicholas Gravante Jr., to Boston to settle the matter. In a meeting in eSapience lawyers' office, Gravante warned that he'd go to the U.S. Attorney's office in Boston with billing-fraud accusations. Gravante returned to New York with a settlement number that was considerably below Greenberg's ceiling price. "They nearly [wet their pants]," he later told a member of the Greenberg team.

From this period forward, Hank Greenberg again became a public figure, be it at speaking engagements to industry groups, the University Club, and many more, or taking leadership roles in places like the Council on Foreign Relations, where he not only chaired general meetings but also led task forces. He publicly criticized Martin Sullivan and Sullivan's successor as well as board members, by letter, directly to reporters, and as a frequent participant in virtually all the television business programs. In the last few years, Greenberg has become a real player on television, much more than when he was chief executive officer (CEO) of AIG, be it with Maria Bartiromo on CNBC, Neil Cavuto on Fox and others, even twice on *Charlie Rose* on PBS. He never did this when he was AIG's boss either because he was not asked or did not have time. Now he has time, busy as he is, and while he is mainly asked to discuss AIG, he also comments on everything from the presidential election to various public policy issues.

This is the kind of press Greenberg dreamed of in his halcyon days at AIG. I remember an incident where his frustration at lack of coverage of himself and AIG spilled over to the point that he called Steve Forbes, CEO and editor-in-chief of *Forbes*, and summoned him to the AIG office to write a story. Not many CEOs would demand the owner and editor-in-chief, but Hank did. Steve came, and it produced a good story. He never said anything to me, but since communications reported to me, the implication was there. What a contrast—from days where only certain CEOs and insurance community types knew of Hank Greenberg and AIG, to a situation were he is flush with invitations.

As the business situation worsened at AIG, the level of Greenberg's criticism only got louder. While there should be no one who is indispensible, Greenberg seems to be one who is. Sullivan, Willmustad, and Liddy have all failed at the job he was so successful at.

All in all, Greenberg's press to date is favorable if you consider the limits of what he could achieve. It might not be what he wants, but under the circumstances it was very favorable. He has had major speaking engagements, many of which he would have been invited to deliver on the merits of his formidable reputation without any public relations help. Others were easy for a PR firm to line up, again because of who he was. He seemed to have an easier time than most getting his op/eds printed, especially in major business journals. But the hardest news to get is favorable stories about Hank Greenberg the man. Many stories have commented on his incredible record of building AIG to be the world's largest insurance company by market value. But they did not address his philanthropy, his foreign policy connections and expertise, or his dedication to family. So he regularly flashed through public relations firms trying to find a fix. But there is no easy fix.

Air time demands for Greenberg seemed to have increased exponentially with the growing problems at AIG. Greenberg's willingness to criticize the company before things went downhill made him a broadcaster's dream, especially because he is criticizing his successors. And when things turned sour, he was on the business networks as much as he wanted.

The successor he had designated, Martin Sullivan, proved he was not up to the job, although it took nearly three years before he was ousted. Sullivan started working at AIG in London when he was 18 years old with only a secondary school education. Over 30 years, he worked his way to the near-top, becoming Greenberg's chief operating officer. An AIG executive who is an old friend described Sullivan as very likable, charming, and a thousand times easier to work for than Greenberg (not necessarily traits for leading the company, much less leading it to new heights). What Sullivan knew very well was insurance. But that turned out to be only one of the skills a company as complex as AIG required.

On the one hand, Sullivan is credited with doing a good job in resolving the regulatory mess. He reached an agreement with Attorney

General Spitzer and other regulators and paid a fine of $1.5 billion. Greenberg blasted this, the largest settlement ever paid for corporate abuse, as outrageous and harmful to shareholders. But given the alternative, which could have been a criminal suit bought by the Attorney General's Office, Sullivan and the AIG board had little choice. If the past is prologue for the future, the outcome of such action likely would have been closing the company.

Arthur Levitt, former SEC chairman, helped AIG put into place an exemplary corporate governance program. This led to praise from the attorney general and the superintendent of insurance as AIG having turned the corner from the Greenberg years. But when it came to running the business, Sullivan had constant legal distractions—lawsuits against Greenberg and a countersuit against AIG by Greenberg, shareholder suits and more. It was obvious he either did not have time or did not find time to focus enough on business.

The company stock started a downward slide and ended over a year later as a penny stock. But, as early as the first few months of 2007, it had become clear that AIG was not the star it had almost always been. The core business of AIG—insurance, which Sullivan knew cold, was not doing as well as it should. The firm no longer had sterling loss/expense ratios that no other company could touch. But the first real setback that attracted considerable attention was what AIG reported for its fourth quarter earnings for 2007: a $5.29 billion loss, almost all from derivative credit swaps.

Sullivan made a public statement that may lead to his indictment for not telling the whole truth to investors. In December 2007 he said that AIG did not expect material losses from its investments linked to subprime mortgages. But then, only three months later, the first-quarter earnings for 2008 were a $7.81 billion loss, which was AIG's largest ever quarterly loss. The firm announced it would raise $12.5 billion in capital, and ultimately raised $20 billion. (I was on a European book tour and talked to traders as they scooped up the AIG offering. It had very generous terms and there was great confidence in AIG.)

When he released the earnings, Sullivan basically made a mistake that a CEO should never make. He essentially said to the world that this was the last write-off, that the problems coming from London-based AIG Financial Products were at an end. Later, he summed up his rosy view that all was great: "Excluding these external market issues, the underlying fundamental of our core businesses remain solid."

Throughout this period, Greenberg was taking potshots at both Sullivan and the board. After the $7.81 billion write-off, there was talk in the marketplace and around AIG that Sullivan's days were numbered. AIG's board issued the usual reassurance about Sullivan continuing as CEO. On May 21, I predicted Martin Sullivan had a maximum of six months to turn the giant AIG around, assuming no more write-offs and an increase in the stock. I was five months too generous, but my short-sightedness was only half my fault. One half was because I focused only on Greenberg and did not realize there were other threatening share-holders. Until early June 2008, Hank Greenberg was the only major shareholder loudly complaining about Sullivan, complaints which the company tended to brush aside as more of the same. But I should have guessed that others would soon join the chorus.

A group led by Eli Broad (a much admired collector of modern art), whose company, Sun America, Greenberg bought, and two other large shareholders, Shelby Davis of Davis Selected Advisors, a firm based on fortunes made in insurance-related investments, and Bill Miller of Legg Mason sent a scathing letter to the AIG board demanding a change in the CEO and in the board itself. The next day, the three came calling. They met with Robert Willumstad, nonexecutive board chairman, and Morris Offit, a fairly new and widely respected board member with a strong financial background.

Willumstad and Offit got an earful, not only about Sullivan but about the board itself. They made no commitments, but in a short time Sullivan was out with a $47 million settlement that became an issue with Attorney General Cuomo and members of Congress. It took this event to bring out of the closet Robert Willumstad's not very secret ambitions: he had long held aspirations to be a CEO. This was his moment and it was what some callous AIG executives predicted when he was elected to the board. One executive called this all part of Frank Zarb's plan (see Chapter 12). In any case, Willumstad lobbied for the AIG job when the board was considering hiring a headhunter to find a replacement for Sullivan. An insider known to the board serving as chairman easily carried the day, and Willumstad was named CEO on June 15, 2008.

One has to wonder if Willumstad recognized the swamp he was wading into. Unfortunately, his long sought-after CEOship would be very short lived, the shortest in the history of AIG. By the time Willumstad had taken the helm, AIG had suffered two quarters of large losses and within just one year the stock had declined more than 50 percent. He promptly announced that he would study the company closely, travel far and wide, and have a plan to restructure AIG by Labor Day. Shortly thereafter, with pressure building as the company deteriorated, but realizing it would take more time to develop a plan, he made September 25 his D-day. But he was ousted from AIG by Treasury Secretary Henry Paulson on September 17, just a few days before he could present his plan. So his tenure was slightly more than three months.

The market's lukewarm response to his appointment suggested it was not persuaded. Only Broad responded positively, even though his original letter to the board said he did not want a CEO from the board. His bigger concern was for the appointment of Bollenbach, former CEO of Hilton Hotels, as lead director.

AIG's newest CEO began his role with good intentions. It was one of his early initiatives to repair the growing rift with Greenberg.

Ah, to be a fly on the wall when Robert Willumstad made his conciliatory visit to Hank Greenberg. Did sparks fly? Or was this the beginning of a thaw in the icy relationship between Greenberg and AIG? Time would tell. The important thing was that Willumstad reached out to AIG's long-time CEO. He called him on the evening he was elected the third CEO of AIG. It was exactly the right thing to do. And it could not have happened as long as Martin Sullivan was in charge. The hostility between the two was simply too intense. And it demonstrated how Greenberg's persistence and public criticism paid off. He made key AIG executives and the board a constant pin cushion, and one had the good sense to respond.

Willumstad had at least one big plus going for him: he was not on the AIG board when it asked for Greenberg's resignation. And maybe he could begin to point the company in a new direction, the kind of direction Greenberg thought the company should go in. Hank Greenberg read the first edition of my book, *Fallen Giant*, and even if he hadn't, he must have had his suspicions of what was going on behind closed doors. On page 169 of the first edition, published in 2006, after Willumstad's election to the AIG board, I say: "Greenberg apparently feels [Frank] Zarb's actions were a power grab. There are others at AIG, including a very senior executive, who agree. This executive argues that Zarb has a long-term agenda for AIG. . . . Zarb wants different leadership [than Sullivan], perhaps even the new AIG director from Citibank, Robert Willumstad, who is expected to replace Zarb as chairman."

But Greenberg is a practical, hard-nosed businessman and if Willumstad could improve results, he would listen. Or more than likely, Willumstad asked for suggestions and Greenberg offered plenty.

During his tenure, I wondered if Willumstad could really deliver on what I bet were the two most important items Greenberg wanted from AIG: 1) one or more board seats and 2) for AIG to abandon the lawsuit to gain Starr International's AIG stock (some 12 percent all told). Greenberg made it clear that he would like some say at AIG through board participation. More so given the stock had fallen nearly 50 percent in the past year.

It did not necessarily have to be him but it did have to be directors he approved of. Even if he wanted a seat it was debatable that AIG could elect him with two pending legal matters he faced: the pending state civil suit over what happened at AIG when he was there and the possible SEC Wells notice over the same issue plus one other similar issue where AIG was involved with finite insurance.

Greenberg's second demand was that the AIG lawsuit be dropped over the $20 billion (the price before AIG plummeted) in stock. That suit was probably bought by AIG to keep stockholders happy since transferring the stock back to AIG would be a real bonanza for shareholders. But the board would have had to approve dropping the suit and that could have been contentious. Perhaps the meeting of a former and a new AIG CEO would only result in some transitory good will. But it would have benefited AIG shareholders and the organization itself if it yields something more substantive.

In any case, the Willumstad-Greenberg meeting went well. Both made public comments to that regard. Greenberg, never timid, must have laid out to Willumstad his anger and distaste for Richard Holbrooke, a director who was also a distinguished diplomat given credit for negotiating the Bosnia crisis. And Greenberg's request was indeed heard. Shortly after their conversation, Richard Holbrooke, who Greenberg considered his nemesis for something mysterious that happened regarding his leaving the company, abruptly resigned. Holbrooke issued a statement saying the problems were too big at AIG and he did not have time to do them justice. (The hostility was so great that a request to the Starr Foundation from the Asia Society, which Greenberg previously chaired and Holbrooke currently chairs, for a major gift was deferred until Holbrooke stepped down as Chairman. Of course, now that AIG has imploded, whether the Starr Foundation still has the funds is another question.)

My speculation would be that Willumstad must have explained the situation to Holbrooke and suggested that for the good of the company, he should leave. And on July 17, 2008, he did on one day's notice. What I don't understand is a similar resignation from Ellen V. Futter, president of the American Museum of Natural History, a few days later. It is hard to imagine that she collided with Greenberg. The Starr Foundation had given the museum $35.6 million and Greenberg only resigned from her board after leaving AIG. But it was the same, sudden, one-day notice resignation.

Not too long after these events Willumstad was ousted as CEO. He was unable to enact his plan to resurrect AIG, and as a result of his inability to carry out this plan he declined his $22 million severance package. To his credit, he felt that he could not justify the severance when AIG employees who spent their lives at AIG and lost everything were so damaged.

So why were Willumstad's credentials for the AIG job considered less than as successful as his career at Citigroup has been? First, as chairman of AIG, he had walked hand in hand with Sullivan much of the way. So it was unavoidable: some of Sullivan's failings rub off on him. Secondly, a mantra of Hank Greenberg, which his devotees firmly believe, has always been that at AIG you have to know insurance. Willumstad's statement that the insurance divisions reported to him at Citigroup was not sufficient. Third, the notion that he would have a plan for the company by Labor Day was not reassuring to shareholders or anyone else. It bespoke of how complicated the company was and why another insider as CEO could do better. Surely a seasoned insider at AIG could move quicker and with more confidence. Finally, the company had taken a step back in its much praised reform in corporate governance. Willumstad would not only become CEO, he would remain as chairman.

Looking back at Greenberg's press during Willumstad's short reign, both Greenberg and Willumstad publicly mentioned the second Greenberg demand: settling or, better yet, dropping the mutual lawsuits over SICO's ownership of, by now, some 10 percent of AIG stock. But while the initial change in directors happened quickly, this one dragged on. One of the demands of Greenberg to Willumstad was to end the lawsuit and then he would help—but not before. Willumstad said he consulted Greenberg regularly, and he probably did in the early weeks, but that faded with the increasing pressure of AIG business. At one point, I saw Greenberg, being interviewed over a New York business station from China. In answer to a question about Willumstad, he brushed it off with: "I have heard nothing."

Yet Hank Greenberg has spent $250 million on public relations and legal fees to clear his name and regain his honor. The legal fees were worth it when you consider the legal matters he confronted. The public relations fees are debatable, but he considered these fees worth the cost.

Greenberg went through so many publicists that a senior partner at one global media firm likened the job to that of the drummers in the movie *This Is Spinal Tap*, who continually die off mysteriously. Greenberg is now working with his eighth public relations firm. "It is sad," says one fired advisor. "He has all these people who are feeding off his desire for revenge. He wants his reputation back."

All the efforts by Greenberg to improve his reputation pale besides the national public relations disaster that struck AIG starting the week of March 15, 2009. It neither began quietly nor ended quietly. The lead story in the *New York Times* on March 15 focused on the bonuses. And the story of the bonuses and what accompanied the bonus story only got louder all week.

AIG had announced only a day or so before it would pay bonuses, some up to $6 million dollars, to executives who had worked in the financial products unit. In others words, as it was put by many, those who sunk the company and forced the U.S. government to lend it billions of dollars were going to be rewarded for it. And this was because their skills were apparently needed to unwind the derivatives and related deals.

All week, the "bonuses" dominated talk on the talk shows. Because I had written a *Wall Street Journal* op-ed early in the week about the bonuses, even I was invited on a number of the shows.

Liddy could try to dodge the outrage since this bonus package was negotiated by his predecessor two back, Martin Sullivan. But he was scheduled to testify before Congress and went into a maelstrom where he tried to win some support by saying he asked the recipients of the bonuses to return half. Although some returned their entire bonus, this was not really well received. Crowds gathered around AIG offices across the country and the employees were warned of steps to take to avoid identification as an AIG employee. Buses took those opposed to the bonuses to employees' homes where they demonstrated. Even Greenberg spoke out noting that bonuses were preceded by contracts with the bonus as the payoff at the end and that in his 45 years with the company, there had never been contracts including one for him.

Finally, the House of Representatives passed a bill to tax the bonuses with a 90 percent tax, even though there were warnings it might be unconstitutional. The president discussed the bonuses on the lawn of the White House and the treasury secretary's job was threatened.

But by the weekend the president was leading a calm response and his advisors indicated they might not sign the congressional bill. Meantime, AIG as a brand name was severely damaged and probably never can be repaired. So ended the worst public relations fiasco in the company's long history.

Chapter 15

The Battle of the Lawyers

Greenberg's adversaries at AIG and enemies like former Attorney General Eliot Spitzer have found out he is very litigious. If they were surprised, they shouldn't have been. He believes he was wronged in being removed as chief executive officer (CEO) and is persuaded he has been mistreated on numerous other matters. And as a lawyer, he believes creative use of the law can be a winning strategy. Equally important, he has the money to pursue this belief.

Thus, throughout the four years since he left AIG, Greenberg has battled in the courts and either won or come to a draw more times than he has lost. By far the two most important cases are the lawsuits between AIG and SICO over possession of 12 percent of AIG's shares and the state suit against him for the finite insurance case. This is the issue that led to his resignation. What could be equally as important is the criminal trial in Connecticut involving four officials of General Reinsurance Corporation and Chris Milton, formerly of AIG but now with C.V. Starr.

AIG wants the SICO shares because a portion of them could be used to reward employees and it would not be charged against AIG earnings. There also is a sense that the shareholders expect them to obtain the shares, which is why they filed suit against Starr International (SICO) to begin with. Perhaps most important, if AIG obtained the shares giving 12 percent ownership of the company, a vigilant pest would be out of their hair once and for all. The belief among AIG experts is that they will not win the suit but had to file it.

On the other hand, SICO's primary objective is to use the shares they hold for investment purposes. Before the AIG crash they were worth $20 billion, a nice investment fund. And Greenberg's aspiration is to develop interest in a spectrum of businesses, not only in China but around the world. But only a few months after he left AIG and established offices for SICO, C.V. Starr and the Starr Foundation on Park Avenue, AIG filed to get possession of the AIG shares held by SICO.

This was accounted for in Chapter 13, "The Great Survivor Vows to Bounce Back." It started in the summer of 2005 and has continued ever since. There was a time when there was a promise made by Willumstad that the suit by AIG would be dropped. Greenberg made it clear he would not help out AIG until it was dropped. But it never happened. Since Willumstad clearly wanted Greenberg's help, he would have made every effort to persuade the board to drop the suit. But that would have been a hard sell. And then as AIG's problems got even more serious in the summer of 2008, and the company moved along to near bankruptcy, I am sure that Willumstad put it on the back burner.

So the lawsuit—AIG versus SICO and SICO versus AIG—continues. One could argue that with the dramatic drop in AIG shares, it is a suit of much less importance monetarily. But it involves 12 percent of the company, which even at $1.40 a share in March 2009, is a significant figure. And it gives considerable power to Greenberg over AIG. It was in March of this year that a judge ruled against SICO's motion to drop the AIG claims. The case will finally go to trial in June, four years after it was filed.

The other lawsuit is New York State (Attorney General Andrew Cuomo) versus Maurice (Hank) Greenberg and former AIG CEO Howard Smith. This is the same civil suit brought by Attorney General

Spitzer and Superintendent of Insurance Howard Mills against AIG in 2005 and settled in early 2006 for $1.6 billion. Greenberg and Smith are accused of sham reinsurance transactions, manipulating the company's financials, and fraudulent business transactions. Greenberg's attorney's managed to stretch out the case for some three additional years. For example, one maneuver argued that Greenberg and Smith should have legal documents from AIG that would enable them to defend themselves. That was argued in court and eventually in February 2008, Greenberg was granted the information.

Bloomberg reported in June 2008 the following:

> Maurice "Hank" Greenberg, American International Group Inc.'s former chief, appealed a judge's decision ordering him to sit for a deposition in a 2005 civil case in which New York's attorney general accuses him of fraud.
>
> Greenberg filed a motion in an appeals court in Manhattan to delay the deposition, rescheduled several times, and now set to begin in July. Attorney General Andrew Cuomo filed papers yesterday to oppose any delay.
>
> Greenberg wants the appeals court to throw out the ruling by New York State Supreme Court Justice Charles Ramos. Greenberg argued he needs access to more documents to prepare himself for the sworn testimony, according to court papers.
>
> "It will never end, there will always be another document, always another appeal," Ramos is quoted as saying in Cuomo's opposition papers. "This is a 2005 case. Mr. Greenberg could have been deposed while the criminal case was proceeding, but I decided not to do it. I exercised my discretion, and now I regret it because this case is never going to proceed."

The statement by Judge Ramos in the last paragraph says it all—constant maneuvers to delay the testimony. Clearly, Greenberg's lawyers would prefer he never get deposed. Preferably, they would have a settlement that avoids any testimony.

His attorneys and Cuomo's came very close to reaching a settlement. According to media reports, the talks first broke down because those working with New York Attorney General Andrew Cuomo had wanted the agreement to include language that could have indicated Greenberg had some part in the fraud. The *Wall Street Journal*, citing a person familiar with the matter, reported in its September 6 edition that Greenberg could be fined at least $100 million.

As part of the settlement, Greenberg would give money to a New York charity. It was important to Greenberg to specify the charity he would pay his fine to, and that wording stipulated that if he gave $100 million he was not going to admit he did anything wrong. This was a sticking point and reported as follows: Greenberg and the New York State AG also seemed to be nearing a settlement. Greenberg was prepared to pay New York State as much as $100 million to subsidize home heating costs for the poor. But Greenberg would not agree to have the settlement include language describing the payments as a penalty or fine. He wouldn't even agree to the usual boilerplate language in which the defendant "neither admits nor denies wrongdoing." That nondenial was too much of an admission for Greenberg.

But this agreement fell apart, one reason being AIG's derailment because of its near collapse in mid-September. At a court hearing Monday, David Ellenhorn, a lawyer from New York Attorney General Andrew Cuomo's office, said the sides were preparing to put the settlement on the record "the week AIG crashed."

"Mr. [David] Boies; Mr. Ellenhorn; Mr. [Eric] Corngold, my boss; we reached a settlement," Ellenhorn said. "It was leaked to the press that weekend." This meant Greenberg didn't have the money to pay the fine because he had lost billions with the AIG crash.

This left the option of testifying instead of a settlement. His civil defense lawyers, led by Boies, Schiller & Flexner's David Boies and Nicholas Gravante, had supported their client's desire to testify, arguing that a refusal to talk would hurt his chances in ongoing civil litigation, including the pending possibility of a Wells notice from the SEC. Robert Morvillo, his criminal lawyer, argued that testifying increased Greenberg's chance of indictment.

Greenberg, until recently, seemed inclined to follow Boies' and Gravante's advice. In three and a half days of depositions over the month of September 2008, Greenberg testified at length about other accounting matters at AIG that are also part of New York's civil complaint. But he and his lawyers kept postponing the interrogation on the

Gen Re matter until Saturday, citing AIG's collapse and a sudden illness which had left Greenberg bedridden.

In a statement to *Fortune*, Morvillo said: "The continued investment of resources for the last three and a half years by the U.S. Department of Justice in a reinsurance transaction between AIG and Gen Re, which had no impact on the earnings or revenues of either company, and which took place eight years ago, in the current atmosphere of huge corporate defalcations and misdeeds threatening the economic security of the United States indicates a troubling lack of perspective."

He added, "As a result, I have advised Mr. Greenberg that he should decline to testify on this subject matter until such time as a semblance of fairness is injected into this process."

At the hearing, Greenberg asked, but was unsuccessful, that his testimony be kept confidential. Obviously, he was concerned about taking the Fifth Amendment over the issue of finite insurance with General Reinsurance Company, a Berkshire Hathway company. This was the principal allegation that led the board of AIG to dismiss him. But he did take the fifth on this issue.

But he testified fairly freely on other matters. After the hearing his lawyers swore this case would never go to trial. If that is true their client will have to be more willing to settle and the AG will have to lower the fine. Otherwise, it is only lawyering, putting on a front that supports your point of view and hopefully gets you what you want.

Directly related to the New York charges is the Wells notice that Greenberg received the week of May 12, 2008. The charges are the same as New York's charge and the Connecticut criminal charges I will discuss next. The fact this came forth some three years after the event was first highlighted tells you a lot about the criminal system. And it suggests it can hit you at any time.

"It is a stark reminder that after years of silence from the commission doesn't mean an enforcement action is unlikely," said Jacob Frenkel, a former SEC enforcement lawyer now at Shulman Rogers Gandal Pordy & Ecker in Rockville, Maryland. "A much anticipated case becomes closer to reality."

Greenberg hasn't been charged and says he has done nothing wrong. He said shortly after receiving the Wells notice that the defendants turned to fraud "to get the deal done" after they were unable to complete the legitimate transaction he sought. Since Chris Milton still works for him, that was an incredible statement unless he is excluding Milton from that statement. The Securities and Exchange Commission (SEC) sued the five defendants as well as AIG in 2006. Ultimately the insurer agreed to pay more than $1.6 billion to settle state and federal claims of improper accounting and bid rigging. The individuals themselves have not dealt with the SEC.

Greenberg's attorneys have the opportunity to persuade the SEC that there is no basis for a Wells action. If he loses there will be a civil trial. Wells notices do get dropped but this is a rare occurrence. Almost always they go forward. So this is one more issue, like the New York charges, Greenberg would like to get behind him.

The only criminal charges in the entire AIG-Greenberg case involve a scheme of using reinsurance deals to inflate AIG's loss reserves by roughly $500 million between 2000 and 2001. The trial was in Hartford, Connecticut, and four defendants from General Reinsurance Corporation, including former CEO Ronald E. Ferguson and Chris Milton, vice president from AIG, were convicted in February 2008. The appeal of the convicted defendants was denied. Greenberg was an unindicted alleged co-conspirator.

The judge presiding at the trial, Judge Droney, said in his denial of conviction appeal, that starting with Greenberg's Oct. 31, 2000, phone call to Ferguson, there was an agreement to carry out a transaction to artificially inflate AIG's loss reserves and deceive AIG's investors about the amount of the company's loss reserves and the quality of its earnings. Droney said there was "an adequate basis for a rational jury to conclude" the conspiracy began with Greenberg's phone call.

Earlier in this book as well as in talking with others, there was a sense that if Chris Milton were acquitted, Greenberg would have no concerns for a criminal trial, but if he were found guilty—it could be a treacherous situation. Milton was convicted and subsequently sentenced to four years in prison, a $200,000 fine and supervised release of two years. As a British citizen, he is likely to be deported after he serves his sentence. It is far below the guidelines of federal sentencing guidelines and is considered lenient. One attorney at the trial thought it was a victory for Milton and his attorneys considering what they were up against.

Because this sentence is "light," it is unlikely that Greenberg will be subject to a criminal trial. The apparent logic is that Milton will not move to reduce his sentence by turning state's evidence against Greenberg. This is something that does not seem to be in his nature anyway but it is argued a very long sentence might change his mind. Any way you look at it, four years in prison is a long time. To me it would not have been a short sentence.

Of the myriad of legal matters Greenberg has faced, one that came out satisfactory over time is the accusation by Attorney General Spitzer against Greenberg and other trustees of the Starr Foundation. Spitzer basically charged the directors with defrauding the foundation. There will always be a bad taste in the mouth of those directors who were accused by Spitzer in a high-profile way through an article in the *New York Times*. The Special Committee appointed by the foundation, which Greenberg recused himself from, spent many months studying the history and developments of the Starr Foundation.

In March of 2007, in an exhaustive 179-page report on the foundation, the special committee of the Starr Foundation exonerated Hank Greenberg and other directors. The attorney general's response was quick: a spokesman for Attorney General Andrew Cuomo said, "This office is not surprised that a foundation controlled by Mr. Greenberg issued a report exonerating him of wrongdoing."

But nothing more has been said in the past two years. It appears the charges against the foundation will be dropped. If this had been pursued, it could have led to a list of new directors of distinction with existing directors removed and it would have been more like a Rockefeller Foundation. But it did not happen.

There were other law suits that were costly but peacefully settled. A Louisiana pension fund reached a $115 million settlement in a shareholder lawsuit against former executives of American International Group.

The lawsuit challenged hundreds of millions of dollars in commissions paid by AIG to C.V. Starr & Co., a privately held affiliate controlled by former AIG Chairman Maurice "Hank" Greenberg and other AIG directors.

The Teachers Retirement System of Louisiana alleged that that New York–based AIG could have done the work for which it paid Starr, and that the commissions were simply a mechanism for Greenberg and other Starr directors to line their pockets.

Attorneys for the plaintiffs said the settlement includes a $29.5 million payment from Greenberg and three other individual defendants, with the remaining $85.5 million covered by liability insurance. Greenberg himself paid out nothing.

In early March of 2009, Greenberg sued his former company for fraud, saying AIG misled investors about its exposure to subprime mortgages.

> Greenberg, 83, claimed in papers filed in federal court in Manhattan that the company, once the world's largest insurer, has ruined his fortune by lying about its financial health. Mr. Greenberg claimed misrepresentations by the defendants— which include former Chief Executive Martin Sullivan, former Chief Financial Officer Steven Bensinger, the former head of AIG's financial products division, Joseph Cassano, and four directors—led him to acquire stock in AIG at an artificially inflated price as part of his deferred compensation plan.
>
> Mr. Greenberg is seeking a jury trial and a recovery of the difference in value between the price he paid for the shares and the "true and fair" value.
>
> He said AIG's "material misrepresentations and omissions" caused him to acquire shares as part of various deferred compensation plans at an inflated price, and later to lose nearly his entire investment after AIG's losses became known.
>
> Remember that on December 5, 2007, Martin Sullivan told investors: "we are confident in our marks and the reasonableness of our valuation methods . . . [W]e have a high degree of certainty in what we have booked to date." But what Sullivan didn't tell investors was that on November 29—one week earlier— PricewaterhouseCoopers had "raised their concerns with Mr. Sullivan . . . informing [him] that PWC believed that AIG could have a material weakness relating to the risk management of these areas."
>
> AIG shares closed at $54.37 on January 30, 2008, the date that Greenberg said he acquired AIG shares through the deferred

compensation plans. The shares closed Monday, March 2 at 42 cents on the New York Stock Exchange.

Greenberg is seeking the difference not only for what he paid for the shares and what he says the shares were worth, but a reimbursement of more than $70 million of taxes.

But the highest profile legal matters in the whole AIG-Greenberg saga did not directly involve him but his nemesis—Eliot Spitzer, the man who damned Greenberg on national television, caused the AIG board to conclude they needed his resignation, and then a few days later, because of the "document caper" involving Starr files being removed from AIG offices in Bermuda, led Greenberg to have to give up his chairmanship of AIG. This started Greenberg on a multiyear saga of redeeming his reputation and ultimately watching AIG nearly collapse, saved only by the government. So this man, Spitzer, cost Hank Greenberg his job, ruined his reputation, may have cost him much of his fortune, and could be blamed for the destruction of AIG since I doubt AIG would have collapsed if Greenberg was still CEO.

Consequently, Greenberg has every reason to be angry with Eliot Spitzer. In fact, his feelings should be much stronger than anger, and that is a very weak understatement.

In Hank Greenberg's office on Park Avenue, as in offices up and down Wall Street, there should have been considerable satisfaction, if not outright elation, on the day Eliot Spitzer resigned on March 12, 2008 (effective March 17) for participating in a prostitution ring. Spitzer apparently partook of this vice not just once but eight or nine times. And this was only a little more than a year after being sworn in as governor of New York, having been elected by the largest margin ever.

But Greenberg did not step out into the halls and cheer along with others who has suffered the wrath of Spitzer or lived in fear of it. Instead, according to *Fortune* magazine, he went home and shared a bottle of wine with his family that evening. Considering how much the man (Spitzer) changed his life for the worse, it is probably hard to let elation sweep you away.

Many on Wall Street believe Spitzer was set up to pay him back for his unethical behavior. Hard to believe but not inconceivable. Nobody ever accused Hank Greenberg of being part of this scheme, however.

The "Sheriff of Wall Street," as Spitzer was dubbed, was out of his life at last or so he thought. But he wasn't. Nearly a year after seeming to recluse into oblivion, Spitzer emerged as a columnist for *Slate* magazine. On March 19, he came forward again in full force to comment on the AIG bonuses as a sign of what he investigated about AIG when he was New York's attorney general. Spitzer's thoughts on the AIG bonus scandal could be summed up as such: I told you so.

Long before the March 2008 bonus debacle, Spitzer battered AIG with a deluge of accusations. During his tenure as New York attorney general, he pursued AIG for deceptive accounting practices that he believed misinformed investors. The company eventually declared that they would pay to squelch the allegations, leading to Greenberg stepping down in 2005.

Spitzer saw the 2008 scandal as vindication for his previous crusade against AIG's policies, a symbol of his prescience. For all those jumping on the bandwagon of Wall Street greed and deception, Spitzer seemed to say been there, done that.

In a March 2008 interview with WNYC radio, Spitzer asserted that "We pursued AIG and Wall Street's structural failures in a way that others shied away from because it was politically unpalatable for them to address those issues. Now it is the flavor of the month." Spitzer's political exile obviously did not dampen his hunger for a fight.

Spitzer's posturing begs the question: is this the beginning of a political comeback? It could be a long shot. Spitzer was known as righteous and unforgiving during his 30-year political career, and the public often had a critical viewpoint of him. From Main Street to Wall Street, reaction to his downfall after the prostitution scandal ranged from silence to glee. The journey upward for a politician, married and caught soliciting a prostitute, is essentially a vertical one.

The likelihood of Spitzer's return remains to be seen, but one thing is certain, Spitzer believes he is in the moral right in the battle against Greenberg and AIG. As criticism ramped up against AIG bonus payments in March of 2008, he continued his crusade. In a *Slate* article on the company, he wrote "it all appears, once again, to be the same insiders protecting themselves against sharing the pain and risk of their own bad adventure."

Spitzer is clearly unchanged. He is the moralizing, crusading private citizen he was as attorney general and governor. And he will undoubtedly take other pot shots at AIG and Hank Greenberg.

Chapter 16

A Losing Struggle to Save a Lifetime's Work

The summer of 2008 was the beginning of the end for AIG, as least to Hank Greenberg and other old-timers who gave the better part of their lives to building the company.

Things could have been different. Months before the problems spiraled out of control, I had a discussion with a savvy AIG executive very knowledgeable in finance and accounting. He said those responsible did not know what they were doing or if they did, they were not doing it purposefully. He gave persuasive arguments of how they could have prevented the collapse of the firm and argued if Greenberg was still chief executive officer (CEO), it would be different. And he was not a long-time colleague of Greenberg, who thought he could do no wrong, but relatively new.

AIG had already unraveled a long way when Willumstad took office. A couple of months into his three-month tenure as CEO, he learned that Moody's would lower its rating of AIG in mid-September unless the company raised billions of dollars. This was because AIG was expected to be the countersignature and did not have the money to do so. This news sparked absolute panic inside AIG headquarters as senior executives met with potential investors who were invited in to look at the books. Overnight, their estimates of the financial needs of AIG ballooned from $20 billion to $80 billion or even more.

As Lehman Brothers began its spiral downward, which ended in bankruptcy, Willumstad could see he had limited time to turn the situation around, and this begin a flurry of activity with investment bankers perusing the books and trips back and forth to the Federal Reserve Bank. In no time, the bankers found their estimates of the financial needs of AIG blossoming to $100 billion or more, all because of the Financial Products Unit in London. About the only helpful response came from Eric Dinallo, New York insurance superintendent, who, with the authorization of Governor Patterson, let AIG borrow $20 billion from company funds that back the AIG operating insurance companies and move them to AIG itself, at the holding company level. At the time, this infusion seemed like a godsend, but as the shortfall AIG faced kept multiplying exponentially, it turned out to be a pittance of what was needed to survive.

So Willumstad and others involved worked night and day over the weekend of September 13–14 to come up with the funds. But they made no progress. Legendary investors like Henry Kravis turned them down as did others. On Monday, September 15, the worst happened— Moody's, Dun and Bradstreet, and other rating agencies lowered AIG's rating, handing it a devastating blow. Meanwhile, frequent calls to Federal Reserve Officials and the treasury secretary were not getting answered because of the concurrent crises at Lehman Brothers and Merrill Lynch that officials were dealing with.

Finally, on Tuesday afternoon, Treasury Secretary Paulson took charge, ultimately reaching the decision that an $85 billion loan was needed. The headlines this produced were even more shocking than those that got me started on this book initially. Instead of reading the 2005 bombshell: "Greenberg Forced Out of AIG" it was the even louder shocker: "AIG Preparing to Declare Bankruptcy, Saved by Treasury/Fed Action that Nationalizes the Company."

But why did Paulson let Lehman Brothers go under, which caused reverberations around the world, but save AIG? I sometimes think Paulson felt guilty. But the real argument, correctly put, is that AIG's role in insuring and countersigning financial companies all over the world makes it such an integral part of the world economy that it is, to coin a phrase that has become popular as the restructuring of AIG plays out, "too big to fail."

After he and Fed Chairman Ben Bernanke informed the president and briefed congressional leaders, they proceeded to rescue AIG. By Tuesday night, word had leaked out that the Fed would give AIG an $85 billion loan at an interest rate of about 12 percent and take a little less than 80 percent of the company. (There is quirky legislation that says the federal government cannot own 80 percent.)

Robert Willumstad who had been CEO slightly less than three months was told, apparently by Paulson, he was out, to be replaced by Edward M. Liddy, former Allstate CEO but also a member of the Goldman Sachs board. So with no search whatsoever, Paulson appointed a competent executive, but one with no international experience, to head AIG. Paulson knew Liddy when he was CEO of Goldman Sachs and Liddy was a director. The government has seemed to make a special case out of AIG. Though how the government arrived at slightly less than 80 percent ownership of AIG and at a usurious interest rate of at least 12% is beyond knowledge. One view is that not only did Paulson feel bad about letting Lehman fall, but he had to justify spending $85 billion in taxpayers' money to save an insurance company. So he did it with a high interest rate.

In any case, in September 2008 plan No. 1 was concluded, which in essence contained the following elements: an $85 billion loan to AIG and nationalization of the company taking just under 80 percent of the equity; 12 to 14 percent interest on the loan with up to $22 billion in interest possible and assets to be sold to pay the loan, which must be paid in only two years. But as Greenberg noted on more than one occasion, there will be several more plans to come until the government and AIG gets this fixed the way it should be.

After being bailed out by Washington, AIG executives engaged in some conspicuous consumption. Two former CEOs of the insurance giant testified before the House Oversight and Government Reform

Committee, and lawmakers took them to task for reckless compensation and an executive retreat at a California spa less than a week after
the government forked over the loan. Greenberg was ill and did not
come but submitted a statement.

The CEOs contested any wrongdoing, and according to their testimony, AIG failed because it was "caught in a vicious cycle" and hit
by "a global financial tsunami." Willumstad says: "I don't believe AIG
could have done anything differently." Greenberg, however, blamed
Willumstad and Sullivan.

The fact that the former head of AIG's Financial Products division, widely seen as the engine of the company's demise, continues to
receive $1 million a month appalled many in Washington. Willumstad
said it was a consulting fee necessary because they need his help to
straighten out the division. Legislators also criticized former CEO
Martin Sullivan, who engineered some $20 million in extra compensa-
tion as the company foundered. Sullivan attributed AIG's dire situation
to an accounting rule. "That's like blaming the thermometer for the
fever," a former SEC official said.

But there was no way to avoid the fierce criticism for AIG's lavish
expenditures at the resort on the West Coast. AIG is on its way to being
named poster child of the year for egregiously bad public relations.
Activities that contribute to the likelihood of winning this award: first,
the company throws a $440,000 days-long party on the West Coast at
about the time that two of the last three ousted CEOs of AIG are trying to explain to a congressional oversight committee that it certainly
wasn't their fault that the company got in trouble. Meanwhile, AIG was
planning a second party, also on the West Coast, but the outcry over
the first led to its cancellation. Then there was an uproar over the par-
tridge shoot in the English countryside that AIG hosted around the
same time.

Leading the list of those downsized at AIG should be the public
relations (PR) team. That department clearly deserves an award for
incompetence and mismanagement of core corporate communications.
They failed on two counts. First, given the timing, it was terribly dumb
to have these parties at this moment in time, since they provide those
lawmakers trying to protect the citizens' money a unique opportunity
to lambast the company they bailed out. (I suppose you can't use as

an excuse that it was understandable with a company in crisis mode. In their defense, it is not surprising that nobody remembered to cancel parties scheduled long ago.) Second, they failed to keep their new key business partner—the government—in the loop. Yet without these kinds of activities, AIG may not survive. Let me explain.

To show you the absurdity of having to respond to politicians who frankly are grandstanding at this point, Edward Liddy, AIG CEO, announced that the company would cancel 600 conferences and meetings because they "weren't essential to business." This was in response to the request of Attorney General Cuomo (an AG beginning to have the tinges of Eliot Spitzer about him, as shown in a press conference in front of Federal Hall where he announced: "The party is over. No more hunting trips. No more luxury resorts. They are not going to have the party and leave the hangover for taxpayers."). How could Cuomo or Liddy possibly know how many of these events were or were not essential to business?

Take the party that caused the original uproar—the $400,000 party at a California resort. It was probably planned at least a year ago. It was not a party for AIG employees but an annual party for highly successful insurance agents of AIG American General, an AIG company. All agents were self-employed. The party was held to reward them for success, keep their spirits high, and motivate them to do even better in the next year. Like it or not, that is the way business is done. And the same is true for most of the other events.

Customer and talent retention are even more important now that a weakened AIG is fighting to keep its business from going to competitors, and struggling to keep and motivate employees when the stock is worthless, bonuses are minimal, and costs must be kept at a bare minimum. Other ways need be found to keep them happy. Social events can work, even if it does appear to the outside eye like Nero fiddling while Rome burned. But if AIG loses large customers and top talent how will it make the money to ever repay the multibillion-dollar government loan?

And what doesn't make the headlines, or even the news, is that the events are not financed by taxpayers' money as has been so loudly accused. Those funds are coming from the coffers of the hundreds of successful and profitable businesses that operate under the AIG umbrella. Almost all of the government money is going to pay for the credit swaps that sunk the company—not for hunting parties. It is time to cease hectoring AIG and let the company get on with recovering and building a strong business.

Over the next six months, there would be correspondence, basically one-way correspondence, with Greenberg making suggestions to Liddy, generally with a carbon to the SEC. Liddy seldom acknowledged Greenberg's letters although he used his ideas. By the time of the March 2, 2009, earnings announcement, the correspondence had graduated to television and gotten nasty.

Before things turned malicious there was an interesting situation with Greenberg virtually tutoring Liddy. After Plan 1 was announced, Greenberg wrote Liddy, cc to the Securities and Exchange Commission (SEC), that the interest on the loan could amount to $22 billion and that AIG would never be able to pay this level of interest. He also argued that the government ownership should be reduced, and if AIG earnings were positive, you could attract sovereign wealth funds and begin to grow the company. Finally he argued that you should not sell assets in this economic climate and it certainly could not be done within two years.

Within a few weeks Liddy endorsed the idea that the interest rate was too high and that attracting investment was desirable.

Plan 2 extended the dollars available to AIG to $123 billion. This plan did not last long.

Greenberg was on a fair amount of television and gave a number of interviews, more often than not about AIG. He criticized the company, said he knew Liddy and he was not qualified because his insurance experience was limited to running Allstate, a domestic automobile insurer. Greenberg mentioned this at a luncheon I was at where he spoke, complaining he had serious doubts about Liddy's lack of international experience. "How can he manage the most international of insurers with operations in 130 countries?"

September's crash of AIG and the takeover by the government visibly beat down Greenberg for the first time in nearly four years of being on the receiving end of more than his share of bad news. The University Club lunch I mentioned, where I was sitting at the head table along with Greenberg and others, was sold out. There were at least 400 guests. Straightforward, straight-talking Greenberg who pulls no punches and does not need a note to tell his version of the AIG story, is still a big draw.

But Greenberg, while looking slim and energetic, for the first time since he left AIG, looked older: no longer an 83-year-old man who looks 60. But older. But while one might think it is the loss of money, several billion dollars, that aged him, it is not—it is the destruction of his life's work. He spent 40 years building AIG into the largest insurer in the world and a few other things as well. Watching his legacy fall must be hard to endure. And this is nothing compared to what would happen a few months later in March of the new year.

Plan 3 was by far the most reasonable of the restructuring plans. A cutback to a $60 billion loan, with interest payments of 5 percent instead of 14 percent, invest $40 billion in the company in exchange for preferred shares paying 10 percent. And the plan stipulated the setting up of two funds—Maiden Lane I and Maiden Lane II (Maiden Lane is the street where AIG was housed before moving to its headquarters at 70 Pine Street)—to house toxic assets up to $50 billion.

Greenberg's criticism of this plan was the high-interest payment to the preferred shareholder, twice what they were getting from other Troubled Assets Relief Program (TARP) investments. And he thought theFederal Reserve Bank should provide guarantees for all potential toxic assets as they do for CitiGroup, and wrote a *Wall Street Journal* op-ed to that regard.

Liddy again listens to Greenberg. Liddy said that when there is a new treasury secretary he would go to Washington and try to negotiate down the government ownership, a Greenberg theme. He also said he would try to lower the interest rates on the loan payment for the preferred shares the government owns.

Greenberg, meanwhile, predicted there will be another plan, Plan 4, as gradually the AIG problem gets brought to manageable proportions. And he thought Plan 4 would be even closer to what he wanted. In fact, he was quite optimistic about it.

Greenberg was correct, and there was indeed another restructuring plan, plan 4. But it is miles away from what Greenberg desired, and this upset him. For one thing, the Fed did not expand its coverage to the potential toxic waste on AIG's books like it did earlier for CitiGroup. Granted there are $200 billion plus at AIG compared to a much smaller number at Citi. Secondly, the government will lend up to $30 billion if AIG needs it. It is hard to believe Greenberg would oppose this. The other debt is being more or less forgiven, or rather paid with most of American International Assurance in Asia and the other life insurance company, American Life Insurance Company (ALICO), through IPOs.

Greenberg was furious at this. The last thing he wants is to break up AIG. He was equally angry at the notion of spinning off much of the worldwide property/casualty insurance operations to AIU Holdings. That was how the company got its real start and would be a dramatic breakup. About the only part of this plan Greenberg would enthusiastically endorse is the elimination of interest rates that were costing AIG about $5 billion a year.

This suggests it is not money he lost resulting from the AIG share collapse that is Greenberg's primary concern. Instead it is saving AIG, the company he spent a lifetime building. He does not share the concern of others who see the spinoff of companies, and separation from AIG as a chance for existing shareholders to regain some share value through the growth of the subsidiaries which AIG will still own.

But AIG has not succeeded in selling off businesses so far. Nine relatively small businesses have been sold off amounting to less than $2 billion dollars. The big sale was the Tokyo building across from the imperial palace which sold to Nippon Life for $1.2 billion (but according to Greenberg will have a tax of at least $500 million). Efforts to sell AIA, ALICO, Philippine American Life, and the ILFC have also been underway. But either the economy keeps the price down, potential buyers can't afford them, or buyers know the seller is weak and drives a hard bargain.

When you argue that plan 4 was the best possible plan, that there was no other choice, Greenberg has a different idea. I thought that given the size of the company's loss Greenberg would be willing to go along with plan 4. But no. He argued the company should be kept intact and take 15 to 20 years to pay back the government since over that period there should be a prosperous economy, AIG could be strengthened, and it would work itself out.

Obviously, the government would not accept this. Nor would Liddy. Liddy's view is that he was brought on-board by Secretary Paulson to sell off assets promptly and build a small, nimble company. He only discovered the hard way, after selling assets at below market value and having numerous buyers back out of other buys, that it could not be done. The most public lesson was the Hartford Steam Boiler Inspection Insurance Company, which Greenberg had bought in 2000 for $1.2 billion and Lilly sold for about half that. Greenberg blasted AIG for selling it so cheaply. But the reality was not only the recession, but Liddy's anxiousness to sell and the buyer, who sensed weakness in AIG. Meanwhile, Liddy was pushing the various investment bankers he had hired to close as many deals as he could.

Weeks before the earnings announcement in early March, AIG management had a sense of the gigantic loss they were looking at, although whether they knew they would have the distinction of the biggest corporate loss in history is unclear. So they had the good sense to enter into talks with the Fed and Treasury and to keep the rating agencies fully briefed as they went along. Liddy was convinced a breakup or partial breakup was necessary, especially to pay the debt and establish AIG as a successful operating company. He simply did not have the sentiment Greenberg has about his life's work.

The earnings statement and announcement of restructuring on March 2 commanded worldwide attention, much of it negative. Ben Bernanke, chairman of the Fed, expressed real anger at AIG, saying they took advantage of an unregulated area, that is, CDCs and derivatives. The Senate Banking Committee called a meeting on March 5 asking the regulators to explain how this happened and why they were bailing out AIG once again.

Federal Reserve Board Vice Chairman Donald Kohn is among several regulators scheduled to testify at the hearing to examine "what went wrong with government intervention, and implications for future regulation." Other regulators at the hearing were Scott Polakoff, acting director of the Office of Thrift Supervision, and Eric Dinallo, superintendent of the New York State Insurance Department, who were also slated to testify. At the federal level, the director of the Office of Thrift Supervision has supervision responsibility.

One of the biggest issues was the question of how AIG went through so much money so quickly. Then members of the Banking Committee starting demanding to know who the countersignatures were. Fed Vice Chairman Kohn argued that they not release the information since it would be unfair to them and to AIG in that they would not ask for such coverage again. Senators pushed hard and were told nothing. But within a couple of days, the information begin to leak.

A *Wall Street Journal* article on March 7 discussed beneficiaries of the government's bailout of American International Group including at least two dozen U.S. and foreign financial institutions that have been paid roughly $50 billion since the Federal Reserve first extended aid to the insurance giant.

Among those institutions are Goldman Sachs Group Inc. and Germany's Deutsche Bank AG, each of which received roughly $6 billion in payments between mid-September and December 2008, according to a confidential document and people familiar with the matter. Other banks that received large payouts from AIG late last year include Merrill Lynch, now part of Bank of America Corp., and French bank Société Générale SA.

More than a dozen firms with smaller exposures to AIG also received payouts, including Morgan Stanley, Royal Bank of Scotland Group PLC, and HSBC Holdings PLC, according to the confidential document.

The names of all of AIG's derivative counterparties and the money they have received from taxpayers still isn't known, but the *Wall Street Journal* has identified some of them and is publishing others for the first time.

The government's rescue of AIG helped prevent its counterparties from incurring immediate losses on mortgage-backed securities and other assets they had insured through AIG. The bailout provided AIG with cash to pay the banks collateral on the money-losing trades; it also bought out underlying mortgage-linked securities, many of which are currently worth less than half their original value.

Banks and other financial companies were trading partners of AIG's financial-products unit, which operated more like a Wall Street trading firm than a conservative insurer. This AIG unit sold credit-default swaps, which acted like insurance on complex securities backed by mortgages. When the securities plunged in value last year, AIG was forced to post billions of dollars in collateral to counterparties to back up its promises to insure them against losses.

Ironically, if Liddy is ready to close up AIG in a year or so, it will be difficult to do because there will still be billions of dollars of exposures with the banks. Since the word now is that saving AIG was really a way to save the international banking system, then AIG has to continue until the guarantees to the banks run; the only alternative would be to transfer this risk to an AIG company.

On Monday, March 2, the day of AIG's earnings and announcement of the reorganization of the company, it was revealed that Greenberg was suing AIG, the company he led for 38 years, saying AIG misled investors about its exposure to subprime mortgages. It is reported, almost surely correctly, that Greenberg lost millions as a result of the drop in AIG's share price. In the past four years there have been numerous lawsuits between AIG and Starr International but never one that was simply Greenberg suing AIG.

Greenberg said an AIG investor's meeting reported that AIG had no exposure or problem with subprime mortgages. So a short time later he cashed in his deferred compensation and then AIG crashed. But Greenberg also had to pay taxes on the value on AIG when he cashed out. AIG denied the charges but there is probably merit in them. This is why Martin Sullivan and Joseph Cassano are on fraught legal grounds now and could even draw jail time—for not telling investors all they know. But from a public relations point of view, Greenberg's complaints against the company he is proud of seem ungrateful.

During the week of March 2, Greenberg was lambasted by AIG and by the media. It was almost as if he had gone too far. Sympathetic friends either turned against him or kept quiet. He clearly needed some good press and a place to tell his side of the story, and he called a friendly journalist who fixed him up an interview with a Bloomberg reporter who is allegedly friendly.

Liddy, for him, took the rare jab at Greenberg. He said Greenberg was the one who oversaw AIG's foray into derivatives. That business "has literally brought us to our knees," he said on Bloomberg television. Greenberg retorts that when he was at AIG he held a weekly meeting to look at financial and other risks. So if he saw risks of concern he would hedge them. When Sullivan became CEO, he canceled the meetings.

A comment by Liddy that is absolutely on target is that the company is too complex and needs to be broken up. "AIG's conglomerate structure is too complicated, unwieldy and opaque," according to Liddy. As a former AIG executive who believes the organization of the company is brilliant, I have reluctantly reached that same opinion but probably for different reasons. Maurice "Hank" Greenberg, who was CEO for nearly 40 years, is the only one who really understands the company in all its complexity, much of which he created.

A breakup will allow AIG to finally find a successor to Greenberg because there will be several successors managing parts of a much less complex organization—one each for AIA, ALICO, the property and casualty business, and finally, someone to manage AIG, the holding company— if it continues to exist. Greenberg might get some solace from this—that AIG requires at least four executives to do what he used to do alone.

It is difficult to follow how much money AIG has taken from the federal government and yet, this kind of figure, little understood by the average Joe, infuriates Joe Citizen. In plan 1, AIG received $80 billion, plan 2 took that amount to $123 billion, plan 3, cut back to a $60 billion loan, and finally, plan 4, a loan up to $30 billion if needed. The press has repeatedly thrown around the figure of $150 to $180 billion. The number depends on what you add less the figures that were later cut back. An AIG executive explained to me in mid-May it owes $40 billion or $80 billion depending on what you decide to pay back.

Senators are irate and others are outraged as well that they cannot find out what foreign and domestic banks received payments from AIG, but estimates are that it was some $50 billion that passed through AIG. This has become a real political furor, especially because foreign financial institutions were recipients. And yet, given a world economy and AIG's role in it, it is what you should expect.

"One of the reasons we had to rescue AIG was the fact that it was going to bring down Europe," Pennsylvania Representative Paul Kanjorski told reporters after his subcommittee held a hearing on systemic risk.

But how does this work? First a loan of $80 billion, then $123 billion and then in short order to $60 billion. Obviously, these amounts were not all spent. Let's see if we can sort through it as of plan 4.

First, there is an Equity Stake of $40 billion, comprising the preferred shares purchased by Troubled Asset Relief Program (TARP). No dividend would be necessary and it would save the company $4 billion annually from what it was paying previously.

Next is the Addition Equity Stake of $30 billion to draw from TARP. There is no need to draw on this at present.

Line of credit: $60 billion, so far tapped at about $38 billion. AIG gives government a preferred stake in two international subsidiaries as well as securitized cash flow from domestic life operations to basically pay this debt.

Additional lending, provided by the Fed to create investment vehicles to buy, hold, and possibly dispose of bad securities held or insured by AIG. So far, AIG has used $43 billion of it.

In an interview with the *Financial Times*, Greenberg accused the U.S. government of impeding the insurer's rescue by imposing a high-interest loan. In regards to how government actions may influence a possible breakup, Greenberg said "You're not going to see an AIG— AIG will be gone, it will be broken up into many pieces. That's a way to liquidate a company, not save a company."

Greenberg also lambasted the president's proposed salary limitations. He believes that any plan to cap executive salaries will backfire, diminishing the level of talent that financial firms will attract. In President Obama's $787 billion stimulus package signed on February 17, 2009, there is a provision to limit bonuses for senior executives at banks that receive more than $500 million from the Treasury Department's Troubled Asset Relief Program. In a previous statement, the president proposed capping executive salaries of bailed-out banks at $500,000. Greenberg scoffed at this proposition, saying that this will engender a wave of startup companies (that will be free of government regulation).

He believes that government-regulated companies like AIG will face sad prospects. At a panel discussion, he said "What kind of people are you going to get for $500,000? Anyone with real talent will just go elsewhere."

Maurice (Hank) Greenberg will never be accused of being a shrinking violet. He consistently tells it as he sees it.

Conclusion

The book is finished but the AIG story continues, and the battles of Hank Greenberg will go on for a long time.

C.V. Starr was unquestionably one of the twentieth century's great entrepreneurs. He took a simple idea, went to a hospitable country, and started a venture that would ultimately expand to some 130 nations. He was one of the first American businessmen to place locals at top levels in his foreign operations. He built his business by attracting talented, extremely well-educated men, including refugees from Russia and an American scholar resident in China. Throughout his career, Starr would attract new talent to the business—and he cared little if they started knowing anything about insurance.

Starr, with many of his colleagues, played an important role in the U.S. intelligence activities in World War II. Greenberg also played a substantial role, more than can yet be reported. Starr had an active interest in art and especially architecture, underwrote a completely new production of *Madame Butterfly* (including selecting Japanese designers), and had an extraordinary sense of unique real estate opportunities. Besides the buildings he bought and built around the world, his personal estates—Morefar and Lookout, and the ski company, Mt. Mansfield—are a testament to his taste and judgment. He had a passionate interest in the welfare of young people. The latter led him to launch the Starr Foundation, which was one of America's largest foundations.

While Starr, like most business owners, had trouble giving up his hands-on control of the business, a transition was ultimately made to a dynamic, driven, brilliant, tough-minded, acerbic successor—Hank Greenberg. He took the business public, expanded it to numerous new countries, and acquired huge businesses so that by the time of his retirement it was the largest insurance company in history and one of the largest companies in the world in any industry. He played a tough, aggressive game with governments and regulators, often out of necessity to protect the interests of his company and employees around the world. Greenberg also played a highly visible role as a spokesman for the industry, served as a leader in the nonprofit and philanthropic worlds, and struck a visible figure in foreign policy circles.

Starr started his company in China, was forced to leave because of the Japanese invasion, returned, and then had to leave again because of the coming to power of the Chinese Communists. Greenberg reached out 30 years later to reestablish contact with the Chinese and eventually received the only license for a wholly foreign-owned insurance company, and invested in various ventures on the mainland. So AIG has returned to its roots and will play an increasing role in China's development.

In Chapter 11, I asked four fundamental questions. Why did Greenberg get in trouble and fiddle with such insignificant numbers in the earnings? Why did his group of hand-picked directors overthrow him? Why did Spitzer so zealously go after him? And how did the corporate culture of AIG contribute to his downfall?

Regarding the first question, Greenberg has not admitted doing anything wrong. So time and judicial proceedings should give an outcome. If he did do what he is accused of, which is fairly insignificant, one explanation is that he did not think he was doing anything wrong. The partner of a New York law firm, who has followed the Greenberg saga, said to me that he thought the accusations were penny-ante or, to coin a Greenberg phrase borrowed from tennis— "foot faults." Greenberg's success with overriding regulators around the world became a habit. He kept ahead of economic changes, insurance needs in society, political change. But his mistake was in not grasping the fundamental change in regulation that had been brought about by Sarbanes-Oxley. What had been acceptable a few years earlier was no longer acceptable. He also underestimated the determination of the most ambitions, ruthless attorney general in the nation.

His directors turned on him more than for any other reason because he said he might take the Fifth Amendment when he met with the attorney general. Sure, they were nervous about their own liabilities, and they were vexed by Brightpoint and PNC Financial Services. They might have overcome these reservations. But not taking the Fifth.

The reason Spitzer went so harshly after Greenberg is hard to gauge. He obviously believed Greenberg was wrong. He was incensed by the document caper (even though that seems to be David Boies's doing more than Greenberg's). When I asked him about Greenberg's power, he honestly believed Greenberg was the most powerful businessman in the world and perhaps saw that his fall would further his political ambitions.

Finally, the corporate culture Greenberg created clearly contributed to his downfall. Simply stated, it became essential to make your numbers, and even though in this case it was not increased earnings but increased reserves, it was still part of making sure AIG was well perceived on Wall Street. When I wrote the 2008 introduction to *Fallen Giant*, I said, "AIG will prosper, because it has an unusual worldwide franchise that could not be duplicated today." That is no longer true because of the intent of government and Edward Liddy to break up AIG and make it a small, nimble company although the launching of A.I.U. Holdings, with a possible partial public sell off gives hope. The name A.I.U. is close enough to AIG and is the historic name, so AIG is looking to change it. This will be the property and casualty arm of AIG, operating in 130 countries and the largest insurer in the world.

But barring finding a new leader who can match in the future what Greenberg did in the past, which means finding new products, new acquisitions, and squeezing more out of existing markets, it cannot grow as it has in the past. In some senses, it is a mature company. Yet one director said to me he thinks an innovation financial service company, which is what AIG is, has virtually unlimited growth possibilities.

How Greenberg fares in his pending legal matters will depend somewhat on who is conducting them. His civil suit did not begin before Spitzer was elected governor. That was to Greenberg's advantage but also his chagrin, since he wanted to take the then attorney general head-on and win. So Attorney General Andrew Cuomo is handling the case. Greenberg should fare better under Cuomo since he was a supporter of the governor (Cuomo's father), although it will not be lost on Cuomo or any attorney general that Spitzer's aggressive record helped him get elected governor. It is hard to believe that Greenberg will emerge from the case, even with the formidable legal team he has assembled, without having to pay a fine. And if it is a fine of some consequence, he no longer has the assets he had before, and it will defeat his purpose of being vindicated.

The chances are small that he will be prosecuted criminally. But since Chris Milton, who was handling the General Re issue for AIG, was convicted, then there is a chance.

If Greenberg wins the case with AIG over the SICO shares, then Attorney General Spitzer suggested that $6 billion of those shares is due the foundation. But the foundation is a dead issue, even more so with the decimation of AIG shares.

The sad and ironic conclusion is that even if Greenberg satisfactorily settles the civil suit, avoids criminal prosecution, wins the SICO–AIG case, and maintains his control of the Starr Foundation, he will never get back the one thing he most wants: his reputation. He will also never see the fruition of a great company he spent his life building. AIG may continue, but it will be a shadow of its former self.

Always the realist, Greenberg has finally accepted AIG will never be the same by announcing over the weekend of May 2 that he was selling all his AIG stocks to C.V. Starr and Company for a price expected to be at least $1.25 a share. While some argue this is because of the AIG-SICO lawsuit and it may be, although win or lose it does not impact his personal holdings. But if Greenberg were to lose the lawsuit, eventually SICO has to pay back what it sold for investments. This would provide funds to do so. While a spokesman said this was part of a plan to give his assets to charity in the future, he either needs the money or he has given up on AIG. Sadly, I believe it is the latter. Hank Greenberg has finally walked away from having an impact on moving AIG back to the company he built. The story is not over but his involvement with AIG is limited.

The Cast of Characters

Founding Fathers

C.V. Starr (1919–1968), founder

Mansfield Freeman (1924–1960), vice chairman, C.V. Starr & Co.

Artemis A.W. Joukowsky (1928–1960) senior vice president, C.V. Starr & Co.

K.K. Tse (1927–1997), chairman of AIU Hong Kong and honorary director, AIG

George Moszkowski (1920–1952), president, AIU Latin America

C.J. Smith (1920–1960), president, AIU West Coast

Brock Park, partner, Starr, Park and Freeman

Chief Executive Officers of AIG

C.V. Starr (1919–1968)

M.R. Greenberg (1968–2005)

Martin J. Sullivan (2005–2008)

Robert J. Willumstad (June 2008–September 2008)

Edward Liddy (September 2008–)

Founding Family Executives

Houghton (Buck) Freeman (1947–2003) president, AIU and AIG director
Artemis A.W. Joukowsky II (1957–1987) president, Socialist Countries Division
Stephen Y.N. Tse (1956–1996) vice president, Investments

China Connections

Frank Jay Raven, businessman
Zao Pan Ziu, compradore

New Leadership from Outside

William Youngman (1948–1968), president, C.V. Starr & Co.
Gordon B. Tweedy (1948–1970), chairman, C.V. Starr & Co.
Earl Carroll, president, Philamlife
Paul McNutt, U.S. ambassador to the Philippines and chairman, Philamlife
General Jesus Vargas, executive, Philamlife, later secretary general of SEATO
Cesar C. Zalamea, president, Philamlife
Edwin A.G. Manton (1933–1975), chairman, American International Underwriters (AIU) and AIG director
Ernest E. Stempel (1947–1996), chairman, AIRCO and AIG director
John J. Roberts (1945–1996), chairman, AIU and AIG director
Maurice R. Greenberg (1960–2005), chairman and president, AIG, chairman, C.V. Starr and SICO
Edward E. Matthews, vice chairman, investments and financial services (1973–2002)
John Ahlers, vice president and treasurer, C.V. Starr & Company

Other AIG Executives

Howard I. Smith, chief financial officer, AIG
Jeffrey Greenberg, executive vice president, domestic brokerage, AIG

Evan Greenberg, president and COO, AIG
R. Kendall Nottingham, chairman, American Life Insurance Company
Axel I. Freudmann, senior vice president, human resources
Louis Lefevre, president, American International Insurance Co., Nigeria
K.C. Shabani, president, American International Insurance Co. of Iran
Christian Milton, vice president, Reinsurance
L. Michael Murphy, counsel, SICO
Gladys Thomas, vice president, communications, AIG
John Wooster, special advisor, communications
Ronald K. Shelp, vice president, AIG
Helen Graham Park, decorator, AIG

Next Generation of Leadership

Martin J. Sullivan, president and CEO
Donald P. Kanak, vice chairman and COO

Board of Directors

Greenberg Directors

Maurice R. Greenberg, chairman/president and CEO
M. Bernard Aidinoff
Pei-yuan Chia
Marshall A. Cohen
William S. Cohen
Ellen V. Futter
Donald P. Kanak
Martin S. Feldstein
Carla A. Hills
Frank J. Hoenemeyer
Richard C. Holbrooke
Martin J. Sullivan
Edward S.W. Tse
Frank G. Wisner
Frank G. Zarb, chair, executive committee

Post-Greenberg Directors

Frank G. Zarb, chairman
Martin J. Sullivan, president and CEO
M. Bernard Aidinoff (left May 2006)
Pei-yuan Chia
Marshall A. Cohen
William S. Cohen (not standing May 2006)
Martin S. Feldstein
Ellen V. Futter
Stephen L. Hammerman
Carla A. Hills (not standing May 2006)
Richard C. Holbrooke
Fred J. Langhammer
George L. Miles, Jr.
Morris W. Offit
Michael H. Sutton
Edward S. W. Tse
Robert B. Willumstad

Publishing Business

Randall Gould, editor, Shanghai *Evening News and Post*
Ted Thackery, editor, various publications
Samuel Chang, editor, Chinese version of *News and Post*

Relatives of the Leadership

Mary Malcolm Starr, wife of C.V. Starr
Nelle Vander Starr, Starr's maiden aunt
Marion Breen, Starr's first cousin
Clare Tweedy McMorris, Gordon Tweedy's daughter
Mary Tweedy, Gordon Tweedy's wife
Robert P. Youngman, son of William Youngman
William S. Youngman III, son of William Youngman
Nasrin Shabani, wife of K.C. Shabani

Law Firms

(All represent AIG except where indicated)
Robert Morvillo, Morvillo Abramowitz, Grand Jason, & Silberberg (M.R. Greenberg)
Kenneth Bialkin, Skadden (M.R. Greenberg)
David Boies, Boies, Schiller & Flexner (M.R. Greenberg)
Bernard Aidinoff, Sullivan and Cromwell
Thomas L. Corcoran, Corcoran, Youngman & Rowe
Charles Brower, White and Case
Richard I. Beattie, Simpson, Thacher & Bartlett
Duncan Lee, Lee, McCarthy & Mulderig
Frank Mulderig, Lee, McCarthy & Mulderig
Henry Dudley
Stanley Lubman (and Kenneth P. Morse)
Richard Rivers, Akin Gump Strauss Hauer & Feld

Government Officials and Regulators

Eliot Spitzer, attorney general, then governor, New York
John Mills, insurance superintendent, New York
Arthur Levitt, former chairman, Securities and Exchange Commission
William J. "Wild Bill" Donovan, director, Office of Strategic Services
Mahmoud Ahmadinejad Khatami, president of Iran
Anastazio Somoza, president of Nicaragua
Donald Easum, U.S. ambassador to Nigeria
Cyrus Vance, secretary of state
President Jimmy Carter
Robert Strauss, U.S. trade representative
Matthew Nimetz, undersecretary of state

Starr Foundation

Mary Tweedy, president
T.C. Hsu, president
Florence Davis, president

Insurance Competitors

Warren Buffett, chairman, Berkshire Hathaway
Ronald Ferguson, president, General Reinsurance Co.
Elizabeth Monrad, CFO, Gen Re
Robert D. Graham, general counsel, Gen Re
Milburn Smith, president, Continental Casualty
Victor Hurd, chairman, Continental Insurance Companies

Council on Foreign Relations

Richard B. Haass, president
Leslie Gelb, president emeritus

Consultants

Michael Harrington, president, Irish Insurance Assn.
Howard Opinsky, Weber Shandwick for Greenberg

Timeline

AIG Timeline

1919 — Starr forms American Asiatic Underwriters (AAU) in Shanghai

1920-1930s — Starr expands AAU and Asia Life across Asia

1921 — Starr forms Asia Life Insurance Company in Shanghai

1926 — Starr opens AIU office in New York to do "home foreign" business

1930 — Starr buys *Shanghai Evening News*

1933 — Starr starts publishing Chinese-language version of *Shanghai Evening News*

1937 — Starr marries Mary Malcolm

1939 — Headquarters are moved to New York City

1940s — Starr, Park and Freeman is established, and Park tries to oust Starr; C. V. Starr & Co. is established; Companies are expanded throughout Latin America

1943-1946 — Companies collaborate with Wild Bill Donovan to help with war effort

1946 — Starr companies are reopened in China and Asia after Japanese defeated; Starr opens business to serve American soldiers in Germany; Starr opens business to serve American soldiers in Japan at General MacArthur's request

1948 — American International Assurance Company is launched; Starr establishes AIUO in Bermuda, which becomes SICO; also founded AIRCO

1949 — AIUA is established, and the process of making Bermuda an insurance center begins

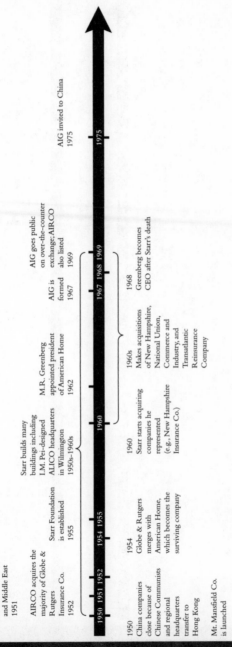

AIG Timeline

1950
China companies close because of Chinese Communists and regional headquarters transfer to Hong Kong

Mt. Mansfield Co. is launched

1951
Asia Life is renamed American Life (ALICO), with business aiming toward Asia, the Caribbean, Africa, and Middle East
1951

1952
AIRCO acquires the majority of Globe & Rutgers Insurance Co.
1952

1954
Globe & Rutgers merges with American Home, which becomes the surviving company
1954

1955
Starr Foundation is established
1955

1960
Starr builds many buildings including I.M. Pei-designed ALICO headquarters in Wilmington 1950s–1960s

1960
Starr starts acquiring companies he represented (e.g., New Hampshire Insurance Co.)

1962
M.R. Greenberg appointed president of American Home
1962

1960s
Makes acquisitions of New Hampshire, National Union, Commerce and Industry, and Transatlantic Reinsurance Company

1967
AIG is formed
1967

1968
Greenberg becomes CEO after Starr's death

1969
AIG goes public on over-the-counter exchange; AIRCO also listed
1969

1975
AIG invited to China
1975

AIG Timeline

1984
- AIG absorbs its parent, AIRCO, and lists on the New York Stock Exchange
- Trade in services amendments are passed by Congress 1984

1987–2000
- Franchises are built in Eastern Europe, Russia, India, China, and other locations

1990
- AIG buys International Lease Finance Corporation 1990

1992
- AIA is granted first foreign life insurance license by China 1992

1999
- AIG purchases SunAmerica 1999

2001
- AIG purchases American General 2001

2005
- March 13, AIG board asks Greenberg to resign as CEO
- Martin J. Sullivan is named as Greenberg's successor
- March 29, board picks Frank Zarb as chairman
- July, Greenberg sues AIG to get back art and other possessions 2005
- September 27, AIG sues SICO for possession of about $20 billion in AIG shares
- October 17, SICO countersues against AIG, defending ownership of AIG shares
- December 5, Spitzer charges Greenberg and fellow executors with defrauding Starr Foundation 35 years ago

2006
- January, Donald P. Kanak, vice chairman, resigns
- January, a series of lawsuits between AIG and C.V. Starr ensues over companies Starr writes insurance with; basically they decide to go separate ways
- February 9, AIG announces a $1.6 billion settlement with state and federal authorities 2006
- Civil suit between attorney general and Greenberg and Howard Smith anticipated
- Greenberg continues as chair of SICO, C.V. Starr & Co., and Starr Foundation

2007
- Government rescues AIG, grants $80 billion loan and takes about 80% ownership of company
- Government and AIG restructure company four times
- Former Chairman and three other General Reinsurance executives along with Chris Milton, formerly of AIG, now with C.V. Starr, convicted in Finite Insurance Case and receive prison sentences 2008-2009
- Fourth quarter earnings show $5.29 billion loss 2007

2008
- Governor Spitzer is forced to resign over participating in a prostitution ring
- First quarter earnings show $7.81 billion loss
- Martin Sullivan forced to resign as CEO. Succeeded by Chairman Robert Willumstad. Three months later he is ousted and Treasury Secretary Paulson appoints Edward Liddy as CEO.
- August, Attorney Cuomo and Greenberg try to reach a settlement with long pending suit but collapse of AIG ends negotiations. 2008

2009
- AIG granting of retention bonuses to employees of financial products unit becomes national issue and severely damages AIG brand
- CEO Liddy twice testifies before Congressional committees and has very unpleasant encounters
- AIG sells some twelve business units and announces plan to spin off IPOs of several of its companies
- In March, AIG announced largest loss in corporate history—$61.7 billion
- Edward Liddy announced he will leave as soon as a CEO replacement is found. Six new outsiders elected to AIG board and three do not stand for reelection 2009

References

Author's note on sources: This book covers the history of AIG and is principal players. I interviewed numerous credible sources including Elliot Spitzer, Artemis Joukowsky, Les Gelb, Ernest Stempel, Ken Nottingham, and many other AIG executives. Direct quotes seen in the text can often be attributed to an interview with the speaker conducted by the author.

For both the first and second edition, I've used outside sources to find comprehensive information. I've attempted to refer to these published sources by name where applicable in the context of the book's chapters. Among them, are: the *Wall Street Journal, Business Week, Fortune, Financial Times, Bloomberg, The New York Sun, and Forbes* (and the various periodicals' related web sites). The References section provides information on the specific articles used.

Chapter 1

Leonard, Devin and Peter Elkind, "All I Want in Life Is an Unfair Advantage." *Fortune,* August 15, 2005, p. 96.

"Hank Greenberg at War." *Business Week* online, March 27, 2006.

Chapter 2

A Short History of AIG, 1919 to the Present. American International Group, Inc.

"Contact," AIG employee publication. 1969.

Cornelius Vander Starr, 1892–1968. Prepared by Writing Services Co., New York.

Smith, Nancy. Mansfield Freeman Center for East Asian Studies, Part Three (Years in China).www.wesleyan.edu/east/mansfieldf/history/freeman3_china.html>. Nov. 15, 2005.

Tales of Old Shanghai. "Introduction." www.earnshaw.com/shanghai-ed-india/tales/t-intro.htm.

Chapter 3

A Short History of AIG, 1919 to the Present. American International Group, Inc.

Cornelius Vander Starr, 1892–1968. Prepared by Writing Services Co., New York.

Friedman, Thomas L. *The World Is Flat*. New York: Farrar, Straus and Giroux, 2005.

"Men of Shanghai." *Fortune*. January 1935. www.earnshaw.com/shanghai-ed-india/tales/library/fortune/t-fortune3.htm.

Chapter 4

Cornelius Vander Starr, 1892–1968. Prepared by Writing Services Co., New York.

Fritz, Mark. "The Secret (Insurance) Agent Men." *Los Angeles Times*. September 22, 2000. michagent.org/publications/magazine/nov00/history.htm.

Maochun, Yu. "The Role of Media in China in World War II."

The Institute of 20th Century Media. http://translate.google.com/translate?hl=en&sl=ja&u=http://www8.ocn.ne.jp/~m20th/activity/resume_1122_3.html&sa=X&oi=translate&resnum=1&ct=result&prev=/search%3Fq%3DYu%2BMaochun%2B,%2BThe%2BInstitute%2Bof%2B20th%2BCentury%2BMedia-%2BThe%2BRole%2Bof%2BMedia%2Bin%2BChina%2Bin%2BWW%2BII%26hl%3Den%26hs%3DoBh%26lr%3D%26client%3Dfirefox-a%26rls%3Dorg. January 8, 2006.

Chapter 5

Cornelius Vander Starr, 1892–1968. Prepared by Writing Services Co., New York.

Smith, Nancy. Mansfield Freeman Center for East Asian Studies, Part 4 (Years in China). www.wesleyan.edu/east/mansfieldf/history/freeman4_later.html.

Smith, Nancy. Part 5 (Houghton Freeman). wesleyan.edu/east/mansfieldf/history/freeman4_later.html.

Chapter 6

Cornelius Vander Starr, 1892–1968. Prepared by Writing Services Co., New York.

Chapter 7

Cornelius Vander Starr, 1892–1968. Prepared by Writing Services Co., New York.
Wall Street Journal. September 20, 2005, pp. 1, 8.

Chapter 8

New York Times. August 19, 1968, p. 54.

Teitelbaum, Richard. "AIG's Greenberg Felled as Probe of Practices Mounted." *Bloomberg News* Feature. March 15, 2005.

Youngman III, William S. Letter to Paul E. Steiger, March 22, 2005.

Chapter 9

Cornelius Vander Starr, 1892–1968. Prepared by Writing Services Co., New York.

"Getting Services on the Agenda by Working the Washington Crowd." *National Journal.* August 30, 1986.

Greenberg, Maurice R. "Softly, Softly." *Wall Street Journal.* October 20, 2005.

Kadlec, Daniel. "Down But Not Out." *Time* magazine. June 20, 2005. www.time .com/time/searchresults?query=%20ELIOT%20SPITZER,%20ATTORNEY %20GENERAL%20OF%20NEW%20YORK.

Leonard, Devin, and Peter Elkind. "All I Want in Life Is an Unfair Advantage." *Fortune.* August 15, 2005.

Chapter 12

Adams, Cindy. "Ex-AIG Executive on Friends, Family." *New York Post.*

CNN Money.com, May 20, 2005; reported from May 20, 2005 *Wall Street Journal.*

"Due Process—Even for Bigwigs." *Business Week* Online. April 25, 2005. www .businessweek.com/magazine/content/05_17/b3930176_mz029.htm.

Fisher, Daniel, Carrie Coolidge, and Neil Weinberg. "The Battle of the Titans over AIG," *Forbes* Online. www.forbes.com/business/forbes/2005/0509/082.htm. May 9, 2005–October 21, 2006.

Leonard, Devin, and Peter Elkind. "All I Want in Life Is an Unfair Advantage." *Fortune.* August 15, 2005.

Langley, Monica. "Collateral Damage Among Casualties of AIG Mess; Two Financiers Long Alliance." *Wall Street Journal.* May 20, 2005.

"Spitzer's Rules." *New York Sun* editorial. April 15, 2005.

Whitehead, John C. "Mr. Spitzer Has Gone Too Far." *Wall Street Journal*. April 22, 2005.

Whitehead, John C. "It's Now a War between Us," *Opinion Journal*; "Eliott Spitzer told me. 'I will be coming after you,'" *Wall Street Journal*. December 22, 2005.

Chapter 13

Adams, Cindy. "Ex-AIG Executive on Friends, Family." *New York Post*.

McGregor, Richard. "Ousted AIG Chief Welcomed by Chinese." *Financial Times* Online. March 17, 2006. http://us.ft.com/ftgateway/superpage. ft?news_id=fto031720061744061272&referrer_id=yahoofinance.

Morgenson, Gretchen. "Report Says Ex-AIG Chief Defrauded Foundation 35 Years Ago." *New York Times*. December 15, 2006.

"Report on Breaches of Fiduciary Duty by the Executors of the Estate of Cornelius Vander Starr." Office of the Attorney General. pp. 4-5

Starkman, Dean. "Greenberg Opens Attack on Spitzer, Allegations." *Washington Post*. December 16, 2005.

Starr International Company v. American International Group, U.S. District Court, Southern District of New York. February 17, 2005.

Chapter 14

Bandler, James. "Greenberg." *Fortune*. October 7, 2008. http://money.cnn.com/ 2008/09/26/magazines/fortune/bandler_greenberg.fortune/index4.htm.

Norris, Floyd. "AIG in Denial." *New York Times* Online. May 9, 2008. http://norris .blogs.nytimes.com/2008/05/09/aig-in-denial.

Stoll, Ira. "Greenberg Lashes Out at Spitzer, Defends His Role at Foundation, AIG." The New York Sun Online. December 16, 2005. www.nysun.com/ business/greenberg-lashes-out-at-spitzer-defends-his-role/24545.

Chapter 15

Bandler, James and Roddy Boyd. "Ex-AIG chief Greenberg takes the Fifth." *Fortune* Online. October 15, 2008. http://money.cnn.com/2008/10/15/news/ companies/greenbergfifth_boydband.fortune/index.htm.

Bray, Chad. "NY Ag, Greenberg Pact Derailed by AIG Near Collapse. *Market Watch*. November 24, 2008. www.marketwatch.com/news/story/story.aspx? guid=%7B9669765f-15d2-4bc7-9a0e-590aeca61371%7D.

Chayes, Matthew. "Claims that Greenberg Profited From Starr Foundation Dismissed." *The New York Sun*. March 6, 2007. www.nysun.com/new-york/ claims-that-greenberg-profited-from-starr/49846/.

Freifeld, Karen. "Greenberg Seeks to Delay Deposition in New York Fraud Suit." *Bloomberg.* June 7, 2008. http://www.bloomberg.com/apps/news?pid=20601087&sid=a0U4yEBuYY7E&refer=home.

Hill, Michael. "With AIG, Spitzer Is Sheriff of Wall Street Redux." *Associated Press.* March 19, 2009. http://abcnews.go.com/Business/wireStory?id=7125448.

Son, Hugh. "Greenberg Gets Wells Notice, May Face Civil Suit (Update4)." *Bloomberg.* May 21, 2008. www.bloomberg.com/apps/news?pid=20601087&sid=aqyXydIYE4sg&refer=home.

Stempel, Jonathan. "Judge: Evidence Showed Greenberg Phone Call in AIG/General Re Case." *Insurance Journal.* May 21, 2008. http://www.insurancejournal.com/news/national/2008/05/21/90208.htm.

Chapter 16

Glovin, David and Joel Rosenblatt. "Maurice Greenberg Sues AIG Over 'Inflated' Shares." *Bloomberg* Online. www.bloomberg.com/apps/news?pid=20601087&sid=aHDoc7YcjQZI&refer=home.

"Greenberg Attacks U.S. Over AIG." *Financial Times* Video Interview. March 8, 2009. www.ft.com/cms/s/0/e89d9ea2-0c10-11de-b87d-0000779fd2ac.html?.

Ng, Serena and Carrick Mollenkamp. "Top U.S., European Banks Got $50 Billion in AIG Aid." *Wall Street Journal.* March 7, 2009. http://online.wsj.com/article/SB123638394500958141.html.

Walsh, Mary Williams. "A Remake of A.I.G. Is the Goal of Rescue." *New York Times.* March 2, 2009. www.nytimes.com/2009/03/03/business/03insure.html.

Books by Ron Shelp

Beyond Industrialization: Ascendancy of the Global Service Economy
Services in Economic Development (co-author)

Contributor to:

A New International Commodity Regime
Managing Services
Service Led Growth
Services in Transition
Industrial Policy
Reference Manual on Doing Business in Latin America
Revitalizing the U.S. Economy
The Insurance Industry in Economic Development

About the Author

Ron Shelp has many years of experience in both the corporate and nonprofit sectors. He served as a domestic and international troubleshooter and also supervised world-wide government relations, corporate communications, and advertising/sales promotion at AIG. He also served on a number of AIG boards. Following his departure from AIG, Shelp worked at Celanese Corporation as a member of the management committee and for Burson-Marsteller. He later became co-founder, president, and CEO of an Internet company. Shelp's nonprofit experience includes serving as president and CEO of New York City Partnership, which was founded by David Rockefeller and simultaneously the New York Chamber of Commerce and Industry.

Visit www.fallengiantthebook.com for more information.

Index